ADVERTISING GRAPHICS

Third Edition

H. WILLIAM BOCKUS, JR.
Pasadena City College

Macmillan Publishing Co., Inc.
NEW YORK

Collier Macmillan Publishers
LONDON

Copyright © 1979, H. William Bockus, Jr.

Printed in the United States of America

Earlier editions copyright © 1969 and 1974 by H. William Bockus, Jr.

Macmillan Publishing Co., Inc.
866 Third Avenue, New York, New York 10022

Collier Macmillan Canada, Ltd.

Library of Congress Cataloging in Publication Data

Bockus, H. William.
  Advertising graphics.

  Includes index.
  1. Advertising layout and typography. I. Title.
HF5825.B6   1979   659.13'24   78-10219
ISBN 0-02-311490-8

Printing: 1 2 3 4 5 6 7 8   Year: 9 0 1 2 3 4 5

Come in ...

but first turn
and see the sky.

The wind
has changed.

PREFACE

This text is designed to be used by the advertising artist. It shows the tools, design elements and production processes that concern an advertising designer. Philosophies of art, economics and education are discussed and related to the advertising field. Several design problems are laid out in detail to assist the student in experiencing both layout and production techniques, and examples in the text provide a basis for building a portfolio that can be of great help in finding employment or entering an advanced school.

ACKNOWLEDGMENTS

To WALTER BENNETT, Assistant Professor at Pasadena City College and the Art Center College of Design, my deepest gratitude for the hours of technical advice, instruction and encouragement which made this book possible.

My sincere appreciation to Fred Hammond, Robert van der Veen, William Lindquist and the College Press staff for their valuable information and constructive criticism during the past year.

I am especially grateful to Russell Whitaker and Norman Abbey for their technical advice on photography and the experimental samples from students in the photographic classes. To John Caldwell my thanks for innumerable discussions and suggestions on a variety of problems, and to Shiro Ikegawa for his printmaking instruction and student examples in the printmaking section.

And finally my thanks to all the past students of the advertising design classes whose questions and ideas are incorporated in this text.

CONTENTS

SCHEDULE

PROJ. SEQ.		START DATE	SPECS AND NOTES	EST. HRS.	DEADLINE TIME	ACTUAL HRS.
A						
B						
J						
F						
G						
I						
K						
L						
M						
O						
P						
Q						
R						
T						
C						
D						
E						
H						
N						
V						
PROJ. SEQ.		START DATE	SPECS AND NOTES	EST. HRS.	DEADLINE TIME	ACTUAL HRS.

SUPPLIES

GENERAL

1 pad 14 x 17 white layout bond
1 pad 9 x 12 tracing paper
Pencils: 4H, 2H, HB, B, 2B
1 kneaded eraser
1 T-square, plastic 12 inch
3 sheets 30 x 40 neutral matboard
1 roll ¾-inch masking tape

PROJECT A (DRAWINGS)

1 HB pencil
1 pen holder
1 fine pen point
1 btl. India ink
1 Chinese water color brush
1 jar black tempera
1 flat water color brush?
1 pad 18 x 24 newsprint?
4 sheets rice paper?
1 flat ½ inch bristle brush?

PROJECT B (PENCIL RENDERING)

1 piece 10 x 15 hot press
  illustration board

PROJECT C & D (COLOR RENDERING)

1 set tube designers colors
  or equivalent plus white.
1 brush No. 4 sable
1 palette or dish

PROJECT E (STORY ILLUSTRATION)

1 sheet 20 x 30 dull chroma matboard
1 brush No. 4 or 6 sable
1 large palette
1 set watercolors or acrylics

PROJECT F & G (LETTERING INDICATION)

1 stick yellow ochre square pastel
1 stick olive green square pastel
1 small can spray fix
1 C-2 or C-3 Speedball penpoint
1 B-3 Speedball pen or equiv.
2 small jars tempera (complementary)
1 small jar white tempera

PROJECT H (AMBIGUITY)

1 sheet 8½ x 11 black paper
1 piece 6 x 6 illus. bd.
1 btl. glue or rubber cement

PROJECT I (TYPE CONSTRUCTION TEST)

1 piece 10 x 15 hotpress board
1 scissors
1 btl. mucilage or rubber cement
1 rapidograph pen or ballpoint pen
1 small jar black tempera
1 small pointed sable brush
1 circle guide or french curve?

PROJECT J (LAYOUT SKILLS)

1 knife with triangular blade
  or razor blade
1 sandpaper block
1 small packet of cotton
1 black crayon

PROJECT K (FIGURE INDICATION)

1 stick dark gray square pastel
1 stick medium gray square pastel
1 stick flesh color square pastel
1 charcoal or Wolff pencil?

PROJECT L & M (PRODUCT AD)

1 photograph of product (blk & wht)
1 small scrap illustration board
1 stick subdued chroma, middle value,
  square pastel
1 sheet cold type?
1 circle template?
1 ellipse template?
1 sheet drymount tissue?

PROJECT N (PACKAGE COMP)

1 scissors
3 sheets white construction paper
1 piece of Box Board or Bristol Bd.
2 pieces of illus. bd. 4" x 18"?
1 steel rule approx. 1 x 18 x 1/6?
1 hammer?

PROJECT R (MECHANICAL)

1 piece 10 x 15 hotpress illus. bd.
1 piece 10 x 15 frosted acetate
1 small jar rubber cement
1 roll ½ inch white tape
1 blue wax pencil
1 btl. acetate India ink
1 sheet red wax-backed artist aid
1 sheet cold type?
1 cylindrical nib pen?
1 ellipse or circle guide?
1 piece 50% cold-type dot screen?
4 registration marks?

DEADLINES:

In many phases of advertising there can be no extension of deadlines. The newspaper or magazine must go to press at a certain time. Therefore your work must be in at deadline time. Incomplete work will be evaluated by the instructor. Agencies must meet deadlines. Start your schedule now.

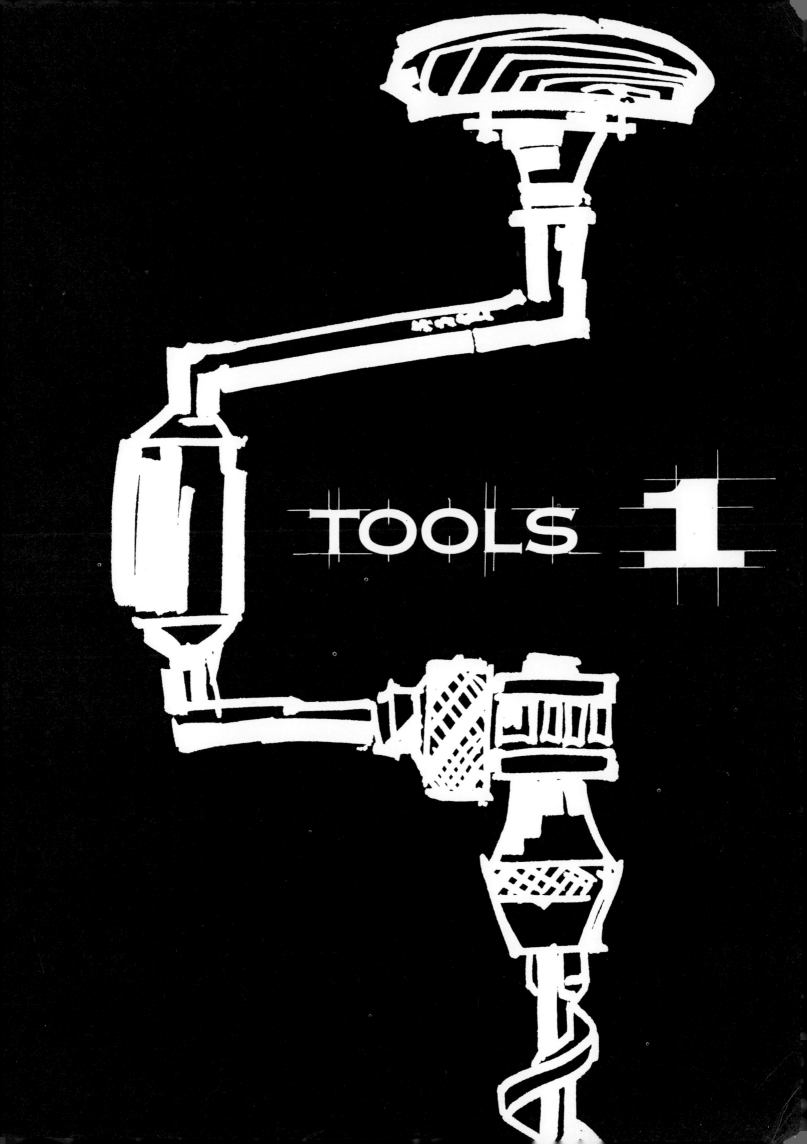

TOOLS 1

TOOLS

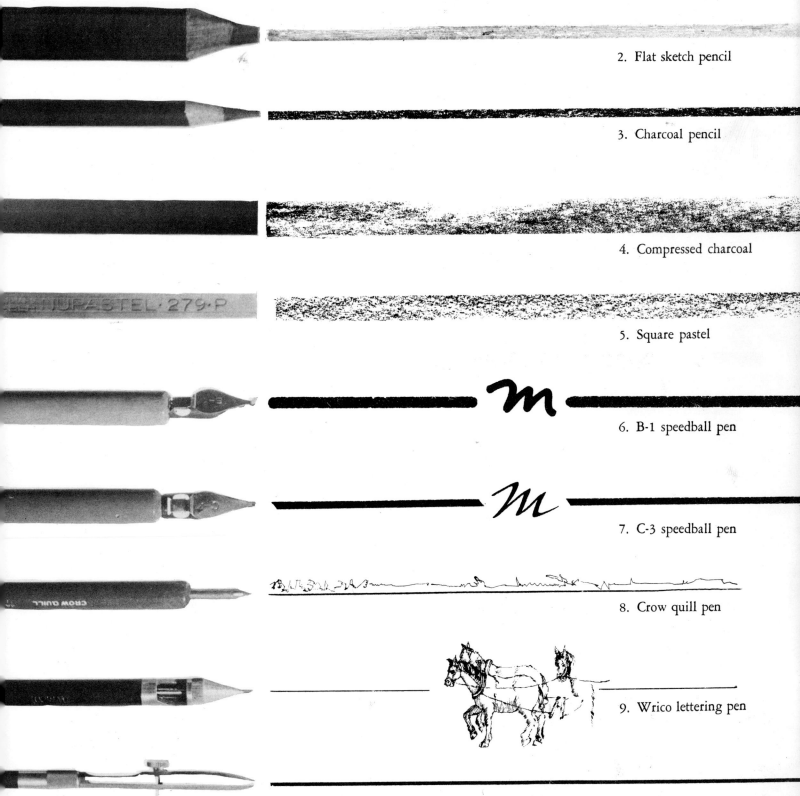

A chisel point HB is good for type in

1. Chisel point HB

2. Flat sketch pencil

3. Charcoal pencil

4. Compressed charcoal

5. Square pastel

6. B-1 speedball pen

7. C-3 speedball pen

8. Crow quill pen

9. Wrico lettering pen

10. Ruling pen

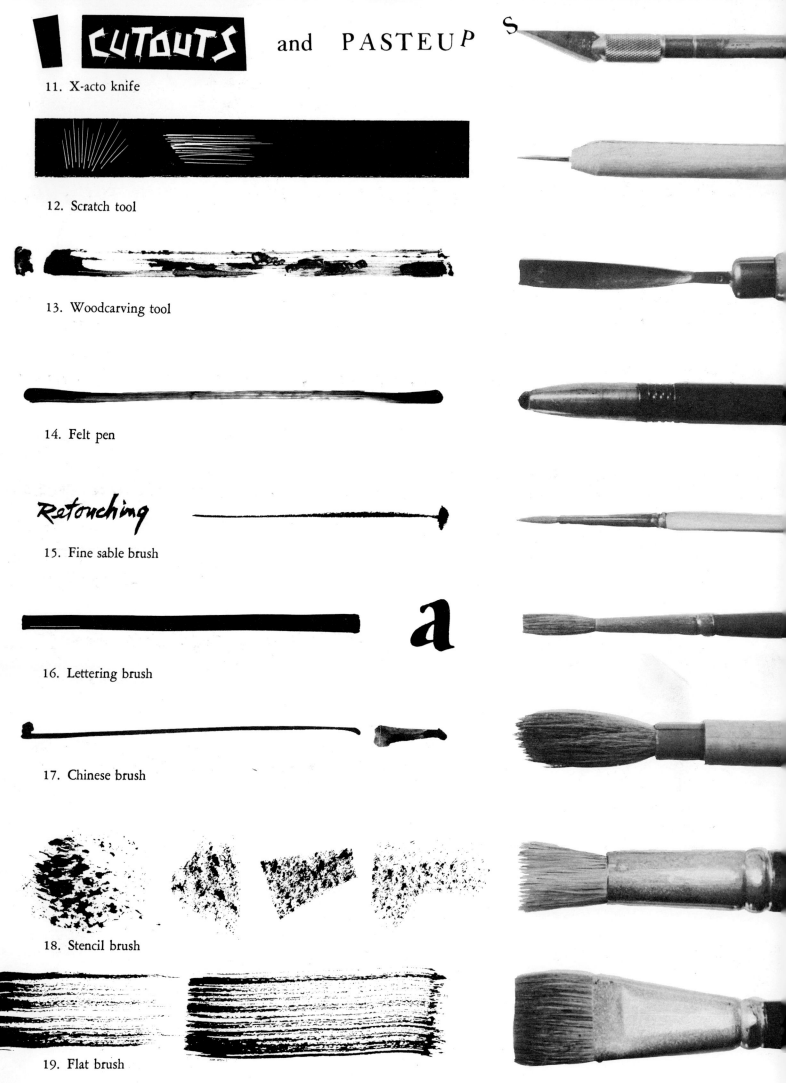

CUTOUTS and PASTEUPS

11. X-acto knife

12. Scratch tool

13. Woodcarving tool

14. Felt pen

Retouching

15. Fine sable brush

a

16. Lettering brush

17. Chinese brush

18. Stencil brush

19. Flat brush

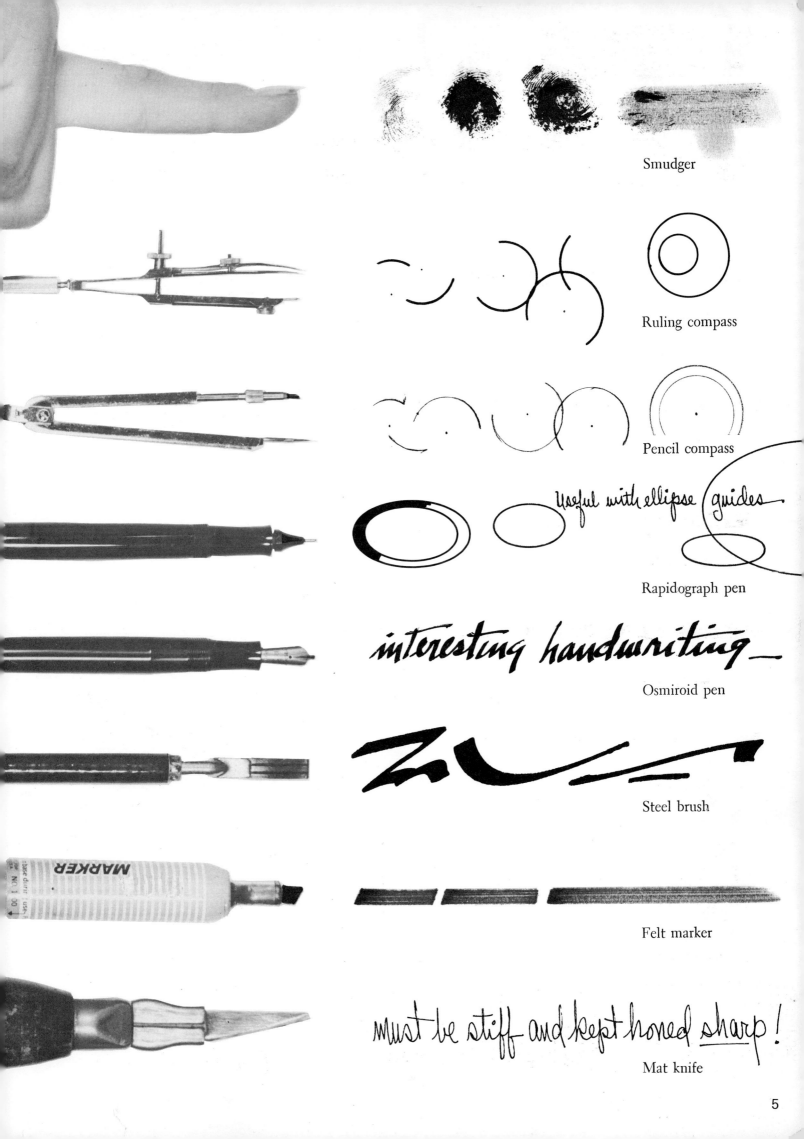

Smudger

Ruling compass

Pencil compass

Useful with ellipse guides

Rapidograph pen

interesting handwriting

Osmiroid pen

Steel brush

Felt marker

must be stiff and kept honed sharp!

Mat knife

5

DRAFTING INSTRUMENTS

1. Ruling Pen

Item 10 under "TOOLS" is a picture of a ruling pen. Open the prongs slightly with the set screw, and insert a few drops of India ink between the prongs by using the ink dropper in the top of the India ink bottle. The pen can then be run along any guiding edge. See illustration. By keeping the bowed part against the straight edge the ink line is kept from seeping back under the guide. If you have trouble starting the ink flowing, run the pen through a moistened spot on a piece of scratch paper.

Caution: Clean prongs well, inside and out. Keep prongs slightly apart when storing.

2. Ruling Pen Compass

Keep your hand AHEAD of the pen prongs when you scribe a circle and the pen will not chatter. See illustration. Start moving the pen BEFORE it touches the paper at the start. When the circle is joined lift the pen while it is still MOVING. This action prevents the blobs at the start and finish of a line. If you need a thick circle, scribe two concentric circles and fill the space between the circles with a brush and tempera paint. Circles can also be made accurately by using a CIRCLE TEMPLATE and a CYLINDRICAL NIB pen.

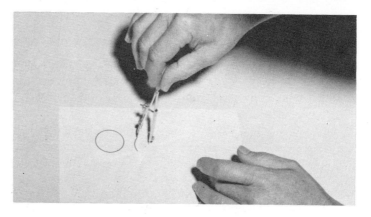

3. Cylindrical Nib Pens

Rapidograph, Wrico, and Leroy are some brand names for this type of India ink pen. The ink flows out of a small-diameter tube. The pen can change direction without changing the width of the line. These come in a variety of widths available from the very small diameter 0000 to 0,1,2,3,4, etc., which are the larger diameters. Number 1 is equivalent to the line drawn by an average "everday use" lead pencil. The smaller openings are difficult to keep flowing, so artists often use

FOUNTAIN India ink which seems to be thinner and does not tend to clog up the nibs. Others resort to mixtures of different inks or special thinners. These pens are particularly useful in scribing ellipses, circles or making small gothic letter forms. See illustration.

4. Templates and Guides

Ellipse guides, circle guides, french curves, spines, and lettering guides are all useful for special problems.
In general, they are grooved or die-cut plastic sheets which guide the pencil or ink nib to form a particular shape.

ELLIPSE GUIDES are stamped with an ANGLE figure such as 30 degrees or 60 degrees, etc. If you wish to use the guide to make a drawing of a circle as viewed from a particular angle, you can select that particular template. These are very helpful in drawing industrial perpectives. The ellipse AXIS MARKS on each side of the ellipse opening can be used as reference marks to keep the LONG AXIS of the ellipse at right angle to the CORE AXIS of the cylinder being drawn.

A FRENCH CURVE has a number of varying curves cut into the plastic template so if you need a short arc of a certain radius you can usually find a close approximation in the curlycews somewhere.

A SPINE is a flexible metal strip backed by a long, rather stiff, coil of wire. The spine can be bent by hand to any curve desired and will remain in that shape while you use it as a guide for your pencil or ink nib.

The LEROY LETTERING set is quite typical of lettering guides on the market. It consists of a flat, ruler-like piece of plastic with the alphabet letters grooved into the top surface. By following the grooves with a steel point attached to an ink stylus, the letters are formed on the paper. Spacing is done by eye. A different template is used for each different size alphabet. It is a very rapid way to make precise gothic letterforms for titles, captions, and callouts. With a little practice the operator can become fairly proficient with a set like this, and the results are usually less expensive for short departmental reports than typesetting.

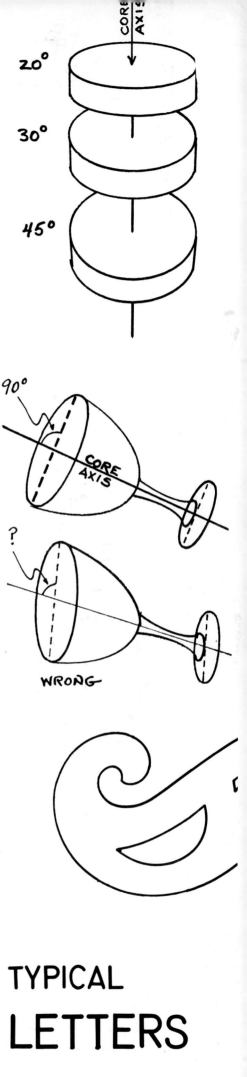

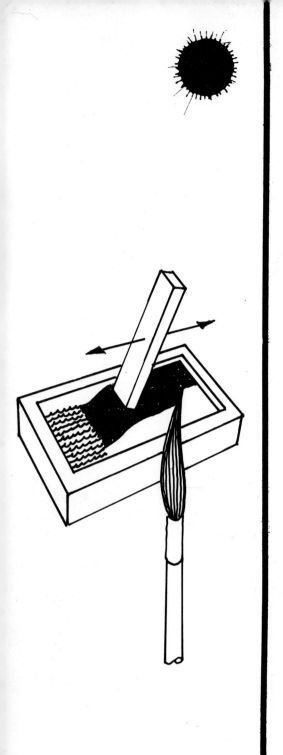

5. Inks

In ancient times India ink was made in stick form from lampblack, glue, and a few other ingredients, as liquids were hard to package and ship. In the modern factory, however, India ink is bottled and shipped all over the world as a liquid. There are three types that advertising designers use. The FOUNTAIN India ink which is the thinnest and flows most easily through the fountain pen or cylindrical nib pens; the REGULAR India ink which is most common, but tends to percipitate out when it gets old or the liquid gets low in the bottle, perhaps because of evaporation of the liquid media; and the ACETATE India ink which is designed to be used on acetate or other slippery surfaces without crawling. This seems to be somewhat denser than the other two types. India ink is essentially a CARBON ink and probably the most permanent of all the inks. It is almost impervious to acid or alkaline ink eradicators. It tends to permeate the fibres of the paper and thus resist abrasive erasing. Colored inks, on the other hand, are usually made from dyes, which are not considered as permanent.

SUMI is a stick ink used chiefly in the Orient for writing purposes. A small stone slab hollowed out to a shallow dish on one end is used to hold a few teaspoons of water. The stick is rubbed on the surface of the stone until the ink-water combination becomes the consistency desired. Some Sumi inks have a brown tinge and are a joy to use as washes on rice paper or other semi-absorbent watercolor papers. A large pointed Chinese painting brush or sable water color brush makes a good applicator.

6. Perspective Guide

When making product presentations or architectual structures, it is sometimes necessary to establish several VANISHING POINTS. One of these points may have to be located way off the drawing board, and to draw construction lines from this V.P. to the drawing is rather inconvenient. A T-square can be used with a cardboard arc as a guide. A long smooth arc with about a 3-foot radius is cut out of heavy cardboard and tacked to the side of the drawing board. (See illustration) Keep the center of the circle scribed by this arc coincident with the vanishing point. The T-square can then be swung against this guide to provide perspective lines. (The side of the straight edge on the T-square is not centered and thus does not point directly at the vanishing point, but for most purposes this slight error is not noticeable.)

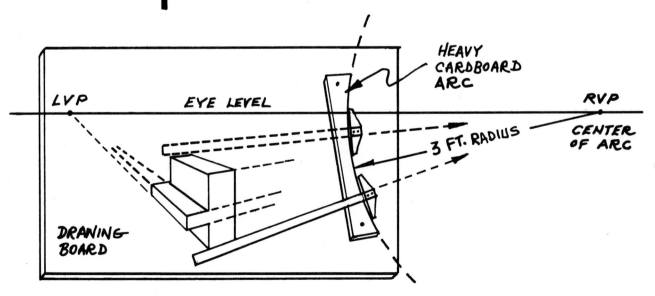

Drawing

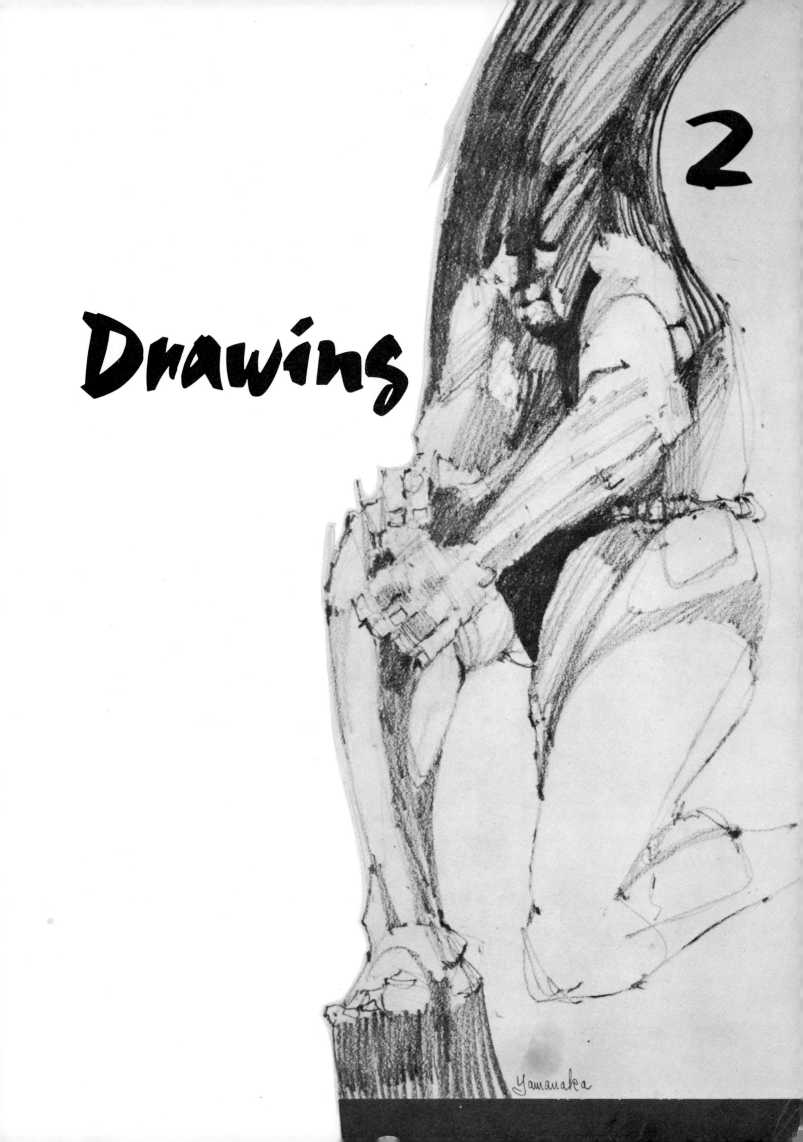

2

Yamanaka

1. CONTINUOUS LINE

Bring to class a small (maximum length 6 inches) complex twig or plant with one or more small leaves on it. Dried twisted leaves are often very interesting to draw also. Use an ink pen on white bond paper and draw the twig and leaves about 2 or 3 times larger than they are. Try several different views on one sheet.

Use a single continuous line only. Do not shade the drawing. Do not erase.

Draw very SLOWLY and observe carefully every bump ,vein, crack, and wrinkle. For example, instead of using a single line to show the veins in a leaf, draw a line on each side of the vein. You will gradually begin to appreciate the quality of the surface. When you SEE that the vein in the leaf has several sides, then your hand will DRAW that information, but NOT BEFORE.

Find one interesting fact about plants. Use an HB pencil and place your information in ⅛-inch high capital letters between 2 light (4H pencil) guidelines. Make the copy parallel to the bottom of the page and place it near enough to the plant drawing so it seems related. You have just finished your first illustration with copy.

2. CONTOUR DRAWING

Students can sit opposite each other for full face, or arrange themselves in a triangle for ¾ views of the head, or four in a group will allow for straight profile studies. Use a sharp HB pencil on white bond and make a CONTINUOUS line drawing of the head, neck, and collar.

Let your pencil move only when your eye is on the model. Draw very slowly. As you look at the model, pretend that your pencil is actually touching and moving over the surface of the head. Soft surfaces like cheeks may require a delicate soft touch on the pencil; bone may require a tougher harder line; gristle and cartilage as in the ear and tip of the nose call for a twisting, abrupt change in line width. Be sensitive to WHAT you are drawing as well as its SHAPE or PROPORTION.

Do not raise your pencil and do not keep "starting over." Finish the entire drawing each time you start. Grit your teeth and convince yourself that the total finished drawing is necessary BEFORE you are able to judge it. Keep the heads life size, as this allows for more detailed observation. Find an interesting fact about sinuses, orthodontia, skin disease, or old age and put this information in ⅛-inch high capital letters between light (4H pencil) guidelines. Keep the copy related to the head so that it seems to be part of the total composition.

After you have finished the head drawing try a page of "contoured" hands, full size, in different positions, but COMPOSED on a single sheet of bond. Find some interesting information about gloves, gauntlets, mittens, ski poles, or fencing and place this copy in ⅛-inch high capital letters between light (4H pencil) guidelines. Keep the COPY related to, possible overlapping, part of the drawing.

3. CHINESE BRUSH

Use a pointed chinese watercolor brush with SUMI or black tempera paint on the white bond, newsprint, or rice paper. Have a large jar of water handy and a palette or saucer. Dip the damp brush into the paint and twirl it on the saucer to bring it to a fine point. Hold the brush vertically and rest the heel of your hand on the paper. By using arm motions for the wide sweeps and wrist or finger motions for details you will be able to get a tremendous variation in line. This technique is most effective as a quick sketch approach with the emphasis on simplicity and restraint.

4. DRY BRUSH

If this rough DRY—BRUSH technique is chosen, fotografs of animals are often used as reference quite successfully. The use of fotografs will not hamper your expression unless you attempt to copy the foto very deliberately. Use a large ¾-inch wide bristle brush with black tempera paint. The coarse brush will force you to deal with the animal action or compositional masses of textures instead of tight insignificant details.

Try this technique on a heavy transparent tracing vellum over magazine pictures or **fotografs**. The technique is so "loose" that the limitations of tracing a photo are eliminated.

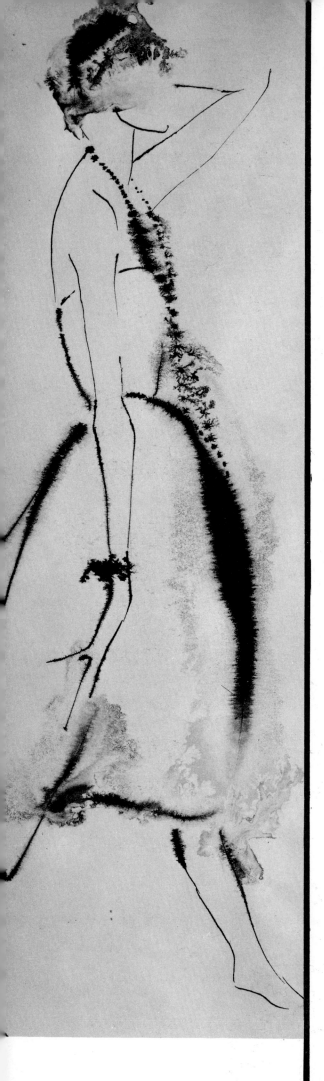

5. WATER AND INK

Dip a large water-color brush, flat or pointed, in water and wring it out easily with thumb and forefinger. Use the brush to dampen areas on the paper which best describe the subject. Observe these dampened areas from an angle until they appear to be almost dry. Then draw into the damp areas with a fine ink pen. The swirling and fuzzing of the ink line can lead to some interesting results. Use a free approach to the model and stop before you go too far. There is a great temptation to get so involved in watching the ink spread out into patterns that one forgets to view the entire composition. A few simple textures are often sufficient unto themselves.

Many of the ink or wash sketches you have attempted will not be successful from your point of view. But the principle involved is as follows: When you, as an artist, need a loose free drawing, you must see the advantages of doing a number of studies within a short period of time. Every now and then you will find that one of the studies succeeds and could be used for reproduction. The instructor can help you decide which ones of the group are successful. Therefore, do NOT throw your papers away before the instructor sees them. There are often choice wash passages or line quality that will help you learn. Actually, "learning to draw" is made up of a variety of factors. Several of these are listed below:

1. Being sensitive to or feeling strongly about a subject.
2. Knowing or having EMPATHY with an environment. Being able to recognize the characteristics of nature, such as inner structure, weight, or the subject's relationship with its surroundings.
3. Increasing one's ability to observe accurately and being sensitive to surfaces, proportions, and details.
4. The motor ability to drive your hand in the direction and attitude you desire, to achieve a certain result.

In the young artist's mind this fourth factor usually becomes the MOST important. That is, he tends to believe that drawing is a motor skill ONLY and can be learned in a manner very similar to bicycle riding or driving. It is difficult for the beginner to grasp the concept that: What he "desires" as an art form or result is dependent almost completely upon his past experiences and environment. To become a better "drawer" he must become more experienced, more sensitive, and become more involved in his environment. If these concepts can be recognized by the student and practiced constantly AT THE SAME TIME HE IS WORKING ON HIS MOTOR SKILLS, then he will become a more sensitive artist that much sooner.

Study pictures, books, nature, streets, children, colors, buildings, prints, rocks, advertisements, photographs, any of the thousands of things that make up the visual world. Developing your sense of touch will also help your sensitivity. Keep your fingers, your eyes, ears and thoughts aware of expressions of beauty and ugliness whether they are natural or man made. Then you will develop habits of observation, comparison and organization that will continue to help you grow.

"In Art the hand can never execute anything higher than the heart can inspire." Emerson.

Hand in the best pieces of your work at deadline time. When they are returned, mat a few in your portfolio.

RENDERING

This section shows a simple structural line drawing done on bond or tracing vellum and its transfer to illustration board. The light line drawing is gradually eliminated by shading the object with 3 or 4 tones of gray until it appears similar to a continuous tone fotograf.

A color wheel is printed with the trade names of various colors next to the swatch block. This matching exercise helps the student relate names of colors to hue, chroma, and value.

Exaggerating chroma and value in the color rendering of the small figure forces the student to not only match but also change chroma and value according to instruction..

White wax pencil on Canson paper and felt tip markers are presented briefly as architectural or product presents.

3

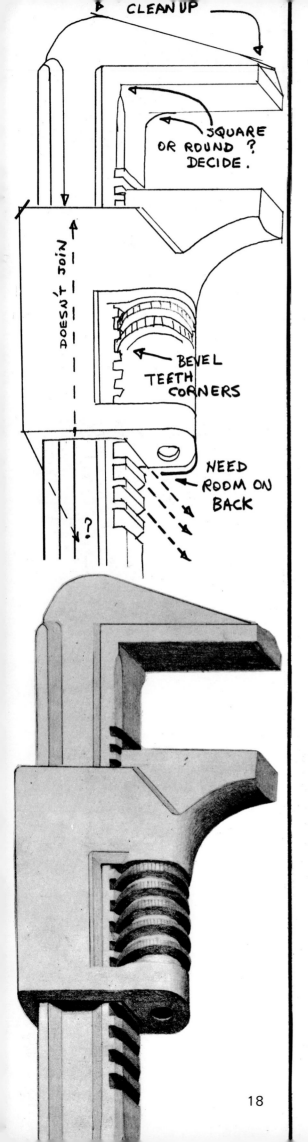

CLEAN UP

SQUARE OR ROUND? DECIDE.

DOESN'T JOIN

BEVEL TEETH CORNERS

NEED ROOM ON BACK

?

PENCIL RENDERING (Project B, 6 hrs.)

Step 1. Structural drawing in line only

Bring to class a pipe wrench or some other interesting tool and make a line drawing with a sharp 2H pencil in perspective on bond paper. Keep the length less than 12 inches so it can be matted on your 20 x 30 matboard without looking cramped.

Show 3 planes of the wrench or tool. Lay the tool at the upper left-hand corner of your drawing board. If it is a wrench you are using, open the jaws wide and point them to your right. Keep the handle parallel with the left side of the drawing board. This position will allow you to see the three planes, top, right side, and bottom surfaces of the jaws. In any case, always arrange the object in such a position that it is most interesting in silhouette or shows the important characteristics of the device.

If changes or corrections are necessary after the first sketch becomes messy, place the drawing under a clean sheet of tracing paper and trace the useable portions of the drawing in SINGLE LINE. This technique speeds up your work, because you do not have to draw the subject all over again. Hand in the line drawing unmatted at deadline time. No shading yet, please. It is easier to evaluate the structural drawing if the lines are not obscured by shading.

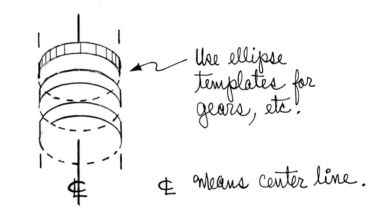

Use ellipse templates for gears, etc!

℄ means center line.

Step 2. Shading on the bond

After the line drawing receives an OK from the instructor, use a sharp 3H or 4H pencil and shade several different sections of the tool right on the bond. Use 3 or 4 definite grays to establish significant planes. Assume the light is coming from one side. Remember that surfaces exposed to light are not coal black. Save the extreme darks for undercuts or deep holes and crevices .If you use the dark values on exposed surfaces you have no range of value left to show the still darker places in the shadow or holes and crevices. Have the instructor check these sample shaded areas.

Step 3. Transferring the drawing to the illustration board

After the shading on the bond receives an OK from the instructor, rub the back of the drawing with a 2H pencil and cotton and transfer the drawing by tracing very lightly to HOT PRESS illustration board. Hot press is a smooth surfaced board which lends itself to smooth, even, value building with hard pencils. Caution: Do not press so hard when transferring the drawing that grooves are left in the illustration board. If you wish, a GRAPHITE TRANSFER sheet can be purchased from an art supply store. This can be used again and again for transfers similar to this.

Step 4. Shading on the board

Shade the drawing on the illustration board using the 3 or 4 definite grays. Assume a light gray for the top plane, a slightly darker gray for the side plane, a medium dark gray for the bottom planes, and crisp darks for holes and crevices. If you put too many different grays on a single plane, the surface tends to look irregular or bent and the tool eventually tends to lose form and becomes unuseable for reproduction. Also, a change of plane is merely a change of VALUE. Do NOT draw a hard wire-like line around the outside of each plane. The definition of a rendering is that the object **appears** similar to a fotograf, not a line drawing.

To avoid a coarse, grainy look, make certain the illustration board is wiped clean of dust particles and build the gray values very SLOWLY and evenly with strokes of the pencil as parallel as possible. A crosshatched surface is difficult to keep EVEN in value for a beginner. For a lighter touch, hold the pencil about 4 inches back from the point. Continue to use the POINT of the pencil, however, not the side of the lead. (You should be using 3H and 4H pencils.)

If you are copying an old tool, shade it to make it look new. Do NOT copy worn spots, chips, or rust marks. Sometimes ordinary COLD-PRESS illustration board is a good base for rendering surfaces such as cast black iron. It has more TOOTH than the hot-press board thus allows a coarser grain texture.

FORCING an edge is the technique of lightening or darkening the edge of a plane to make it have more CONTRAST with the adjoining plane. This makes the turn of the corner more obvious to the eye .

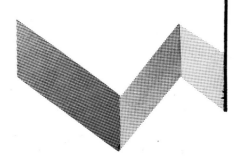

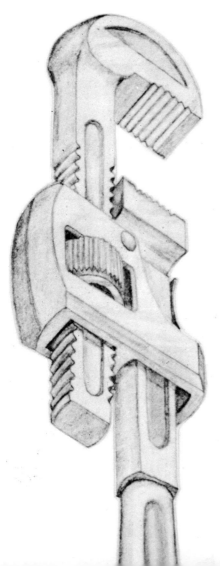

Step 5   Matting

Mat the rendering on one side of a 20 x 30 matboard as per instructions   in Section 4 and hand it in at deadline time.

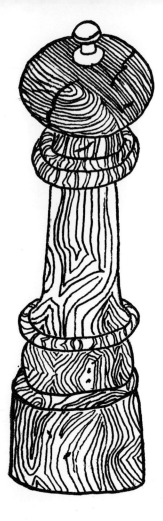

COLOR SCALES (Project C)

DESIGNERS COLORS are a high quality waterbase color similar to tempera. The pigment is finely ground so flat tones can be laid without streaking; the hues are more brilliant; the color BATCHES are keyed to rigid formulas and the pigment color thus remains consistent with the manufacturer's label. Although these opaque paints can be used as transparent washes, they are particularly useful in preparing comps of all kinds, opaque renderings, type and lettering indications as well as matching or touch-up work.

Fill in as many of the boxes in the wheel as you can by matching the box to the label on your paint tubes. Then fill in the empties by mixing adjacent colors together. This wheel is not an exact color notation system. It represents only the APPROXIMATE position of typical manufacturers' colors on the HUE circle and CHROMA diameters. The yellows are set somewhat closer to center than the purples and blues, because yellows have less tinting power than the stronger darker cold colors.

HUE is a scale of color around the wheel, so a change in hue would mean changing from yellow to orange, or from purple to green, etc. If you don't have designers colors, use your own paints. Start from the primary axes: Spectrum Red, Cadmium Yellow Light, and Ultramarine Blue (See arrow heads) and work around the wheel placing the other BRIGHTS, like orange and green, that you have and then mix the missing hues from adjacent colors. After the outside of of the wheel is completed, work the brights toward the dull center of the wheel along their chroma scales.

CHROMA is the intensity or purity of a particular hue. For example, Cadmium Yellow Light is more intense than yellow ochre. A color can be subdued or weakened by mixing it with the brown umbers, gray, or with the hues directly ACROSS the circle. (This opposite color is referred to as a COMPLEMENT.)

Beginners in painting tend only to use the INTENSE chromas outside the dotted circle (See wheel). The professional painter and color consultants use the entire palette. The SUBDUED chromas inside the dotted circle are the key to unusual color, harmony, and quiet relief to the eye. Nature uses color with restraint. Even bright flowers are small in scale and sunsets are limited in time span. Man has been conditioned for thousands of years in an environment of quiet subdued colors; and although the brights may gain his attention momentarily, they do not have the sustaining power of the DULL chromas. Use your brights with discretion and restraint.

VALUE is the luminosity scale (lightness or darkness) of any color. A color can be lightened by adding white (or a lighter color) and darkened by adding black (or a darker color).
Make a few value scales by adding white to different colors. See if you can keep the steps a regular progression to white. Note that the darker the color the greater its tinting power and the longer the scale can become.

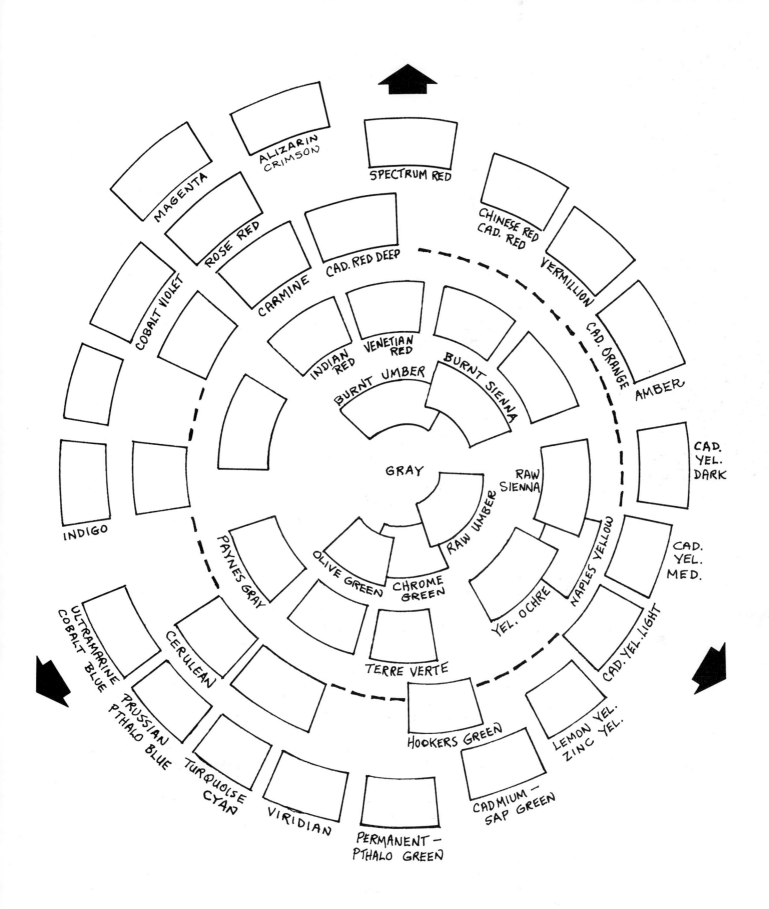

SPECTRUM RED

ALIZARIN CRIMSON

MAGENTA

ROSE RED

CHINESE RED
CAD. RED

VERMILLION

CAD. ORANGE

AMBER

COBALT VIOLET

CARMINE

CAD. RED DEEP

INDIAN RED

VENETIAN RED

BURNT UMBER

BURNT SIENNA

CAD. YEL. DARK

GRAY

RAW SIENNA

RAW UMBER

CAD. YEL. MED.

INDIGO

PAYNES GRAY

OLIVE GREEN

CHROME GREEN

YEL. OCHRE

NAPLES YELLOW

ULTRAMARINE
COBALT BLUE

CERULEAN

TERRE VERTE

CAD. YEL. LIGHT

PRUSSIAN
PTHALO BLUE

TURQUOISE
CYAN

VIRIDIAN

HOOKERS GREEN

LEMON YEL.
ZINC YEL.

PERMANENT —
PTHALO GREEN

CADMIUM —
SAP GREEN

VALUE

COLOR RENDERING (Project D, 18 hrs.)

Part 1. Selecting and mounting

Choose a full color photograph of a figure approximately six inches high from magazine scrap. Instead of choosing the first high-fashion, stick model in the magazine, search for a figure with character and an interesting silhouette. An old fisherman, a boy on a bicycle, or a mountain climber would tend to be less of a stereotype and might illustrate a greater variety of materials and textures. A figure in a bathing suit, for example, would not show your ability to render a variety of materials. Photographic magazines often have excellent reproductions in color.

After the figure has been checked by the instructor, tack a piece of DRYMOUNTING TISSUE to the back at several spots with the tip of a hot iron. (If a tacking iron is not available, an ordinary iron set at the "synthetics" heat will do. "Linen" heat is usually too hot.) Now cut the figure out carefully with a sharp razor, knife, or scissors; cutting thru the drymounting tissue at the same time.

Drymount the figure (See Section 8) to a piece of illustration board. If the drymounting tissue is not available, coat the back of the figure and the front of the illustration board with a thin coat of rubber cement and let dry. Position the figure on the illustration board; lay a clean sheet of bond over it and burnish the figure down tightly. Use a rubber cement PICKUP and pull up the excess rubber surrounding the figure.

Part 2. Transfer and Painting

Make a tracing with a sharp pencil of the mounted photograph and transfer it LIGHTLY to another piece of illustration board. Use a small pointed sable brush with your tempera or designers colors and copy the image in color as accurately as possible within the following limitations:

  a. Make the darks slightly darker than the photo.
  b. Mix the light values slightly lighter.
  c. Mix the chroma slightly more brilliant.

When an artist's work is photographed; made into a negative and printing plate; and finally printed; the finished piece has often lost some brilliance.

The darks tend to become slightly gray, and the white areas or HIGH-LIGHTS tend to become slightly darker. (See Section 14, Printed Halftones, for explanation.) Expert platemakers and printers can compensate for these problems and produce exact copies but, in general, this becomes more expensive. The trained artist, however, by understanding the reproduction process can **foresee** these problems and by compensating in his original art can insure that the FINAL printed piece will be what he desires at least cost.

This is to be an opaque rendering and not a wash presentation. 👉

This means that light values must be MIXED — color with white paint. Do not lay a thin color wash on the illustration board and make the light values by allowing the white surface to show through. This means not to go over and over each brush stroke. As you lay in a brush load of color, leave it alone. Put the next brush stroke close to it with a slight overlap. Avoid blending. Mix each brush stroke separately on the palette instead of stirring up a big batch of color and painting the area like a barn wall. On the other hand, do not attempt to copy the photo with a magnifying glass and a one-hair brush. **This is not the purpose of** the problem.

By following the above advice you will discover your rendering will have a brilliance and sparkle that is not possible when layer after layer is wetted down and pushed and scrubbed. Examine very closely some impressionist paintings by Monet, Manet, Van Gogh, or Cezanne. Although your brush stroke may be somewhat smaller, the principle remains. Let the eye blend the wavelengths of color from your painting instead of attempting to do it all with a wet soggy brush.

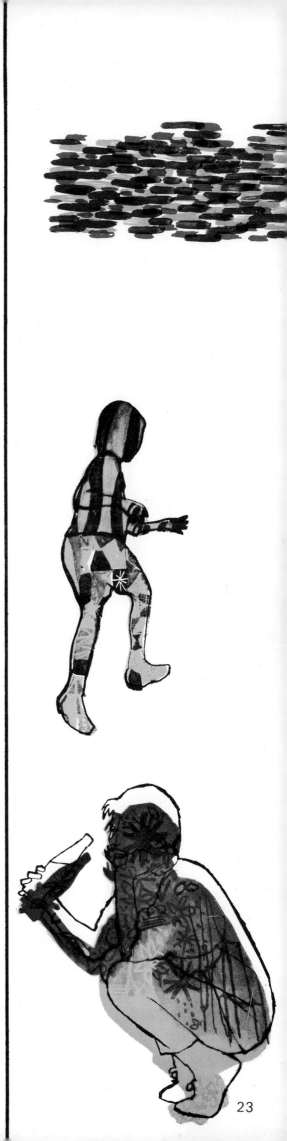

A start for skin tones can be made by mixing yellow ochre and white plus a bit of venetian red, cadmium red or burnt sienna. Complementary colors, like terre verte, or umbers may be used to reduce the chroma in shadow areas. DO NOT USE BLACK, EVEN IN MIXING. Shadows are areas of less light and subdued chroma. They are NOT ABSENCE of light. Black tends to make your color look sooty and dead, because it soaks up all the light. As you gain more experience you will be able to use black but for this problem leave it off the palette. Burnt umber and dark blue mixed together will give you as deep a dark as you need.

If your image is very complex you may wish to paint only part of it and finish the rest in a dark thin pencil line.

Part 3. Pattern and line

Make a tracing of the silhouette form or outline of the foto and transfer it to a third piece of illustration board. Within this outline paint a light value (HIGH KEY) pattern or design planned to destroy the form of the original. Use flat areas of color such as wide stripes, thick spirals, discs, flowers, etc. This time we will attempt to paint these areas in flat unstreaked color. And this time you CAN mix enough color to insure coverage, and you CAN paint these areas like a barn wall, FLAT. Remember to keep the design light in value so the ink line drawing on the overlay will be visible.

When the silhouette is painted, hinge a clear piece of acetate over the design. On the acetate draw in the original figure in detailed line by using ACETATE India ink and a flexible thin pen point. Use a CONTINUOUS line rather than trying to cross hatch or shade with the pen.

Mat the 3 units side by side about 1 inch apart in one corner of a 20x30 mat board and hand in at deadline time. (See Section 4). Later we can mat another item on another part of the mat board. If you place the units in the center of the mat board they tend to look OVERMATTED, which means there is too much frame.

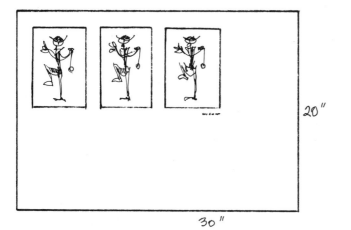

20"

30"

23

White wax pencils on a dark toned Canson paper make for interesting architectural renderings or product presentations. Use a straight edge or french curve as a guide. Press on the pencil at the start and as you WHIP the pencil along the guide , release the pressure and flick the point into the air. The resultant line is a needle-like, hard-edged high light which simulates metal reflections. A touch of Chinese white applied with a small pointed sable brush can add star lights. Use color sparingly.

Rely on the paper to say the most.

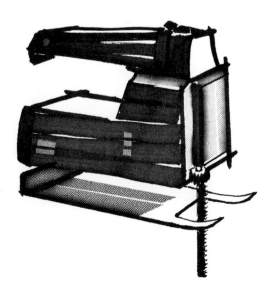

Felt-tip pens in several shades of GRAY and colors are great for quick roughs and product present-ations. The brace & bit on the division page of Section 1 is a wide felt-tip pen drawing shot in line on Ortho film & reversed.

STORY ILLUSTRATION (Project E, 24 hrs.)

There are various meanings of the word, illustration. A technical illustration or medical illustration is usually a precise rendering to show certain facts about appearance or relationships of man-made or biological objects. The story illustrator, however, has a separate problem of conveying a feeling tone to the viewer through action, relationships and possible symbolism, all integrated within his composition.

Almost all story illustrators use fotografs to work from. Models are hired to pose for a fotografer or the pics may be shot "on location" which merely means everyone involved goes to some scenic spot designated by the illustrator. The environment there then becomes the background for the fotos. A bridge , an old Victorian house, the desert, an empty stretch of hiway are all examples of possible scenes where the illustrator directs the shooting. The resultant 8 x 10 prints are then used by the illustrator in his studio for redrawing and tracing, or even cutting up and pasting into a selected composition. This last paste up is known as a collage, pronounced kō – lahzh'.

The beginning student, obviously, cannot afford this kind of action. Instead we will use scrap cutouts from newspapers or old magazines as our research material and pretend that the pictures we cut out are the actual shots taken on location with professional models. Caution here: when you look for material choose fotografs, not drawings, watercolors or oils. Copying another illustrator's technique does not give you as valid an experience as creating your OWN painting from a set of fotografs.

Also we must realize that ordinarily a professional illustrator is GIVEN a specific story to illustrate, and he proceeds from there within the limitations of the story. For this problem, however, we are going to find our research fotografs first and then invent a story or situation to fit our composition. If we chose a story first, it would be almost impossible to find the exact research material necessary by thumbing randomly through old magazines to portray our specific story situation.

Step 1. Size and Ground

Select a subdued chroma matboard, dark or light value depending on the mood of your material, 15 x 20. In the center of it draw a rectangular border enclosing a space 12 inches high by 18 inches wide. Use a white wax pencil to make the border and keep it very thin and light. We may want to shift it slightly later. The area we have just defined simulates a double page spread in a 9 x 12 magazine. Each page is 9 inches wide, and when the magazine is opened the two pages make a layout 18 inches wide and 12 high. The gutter, where the two pages meet at the center, obscures detail, so we don't want to put important images right in the gutter. To remind yourself of this, place a mark at the top center and bottom center of your matboard ground. (In place of the matboard ground you may wish to select another type of board such as illustration board, or other heavier stocks , but make certain they are heavy enough not to buckle as you paint on them.)

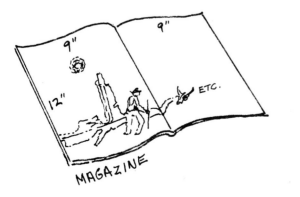

MAGAZINE

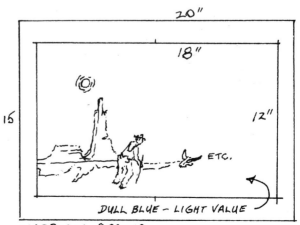

DULL BLUE – LIGHT VALUE

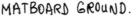

MATBOARD GROUND.

Step 2. Selection of Fotos

Collect 10 to 20 fotos from magazine scrap or newspapers and include figures in action as well as typical things one might find in story themes. Autos, motorcycles, race cars, horses, might be related to "the chase" or racing stories. Dark interiors, old mansions silhouetted against the skyline, a bent old hag, antique furniture, candelabras, a staring face might symbolize a mystery story atmosphere. Mountain climbers, a lacrosse player, several hockey players, mountain backdrop, grandstand of faces, might be arranged into a sporting story action plot. Use people rather than animals as the central figures. The times you will be asked to illustrate animal stories will be negligible contrasted with the times you will be asked to portray people in action. As you select research material try to pick fotos that have unusual silhouette shapes. The outline shapes of objects are important when you compose. If too many of your chosen fotos are people standing with their hands at their sides; if the forest, the house, and the car you chose are all sort of mushy oval shapes without any distinctive "bays or peninsulas", you will find it difficult to arrange your collage so that you have interesting negative areas.

Step 3. Visualization and Collage

Start by laying tracing paper over the pictures you have selected and make rather dark outline tracings of the objects or figure silhouettes. Think in terms of the foreground images being somewhat larger than the less important background images. Do not draw in all the details at this stage. Leave out mouths, door handles, shoes, hair, leaves, etc. Just get down the most interesting SILHOUETTE form that you can of the picture you are tracing. The details will come later.

Keep each outline drawing on a separate piece of tracing tissue so you can shuffle them around and rearrange their relationship with each other. Arms and legs can be redrawn in different positions to help the action or your composition. Parts of objects can be removed or added to. Get a little imaginative and create interesting shapes as you compose your collage. Some of the tracings may be too large or too small. Place them on the Lucy and enlarge or reduce them on other tissue until you are satisfied with the size and shape of each shape as it relates to your growing composition. (If a Lucy is not available use the gridding system.)

One limitation here: Leave 1/3, or no less than 1/4, of your background untouched. That is, the images will be a painted path, or interesting sihouette form in itself, with the flat matboard or illustration board color showing through to emphasize the negative areas of the composition. This does not mean just drawing everything smaller and plopping it in the center of the layout with 1/3 of the ground exposed around the edges. The composition should probably start at the left (as most eye movements travel from left to right when scanning a page) and move across the layout to the right-hand edge, forming rather complex "bays" and "peninsulas along the edges of the positive images. (See example.)

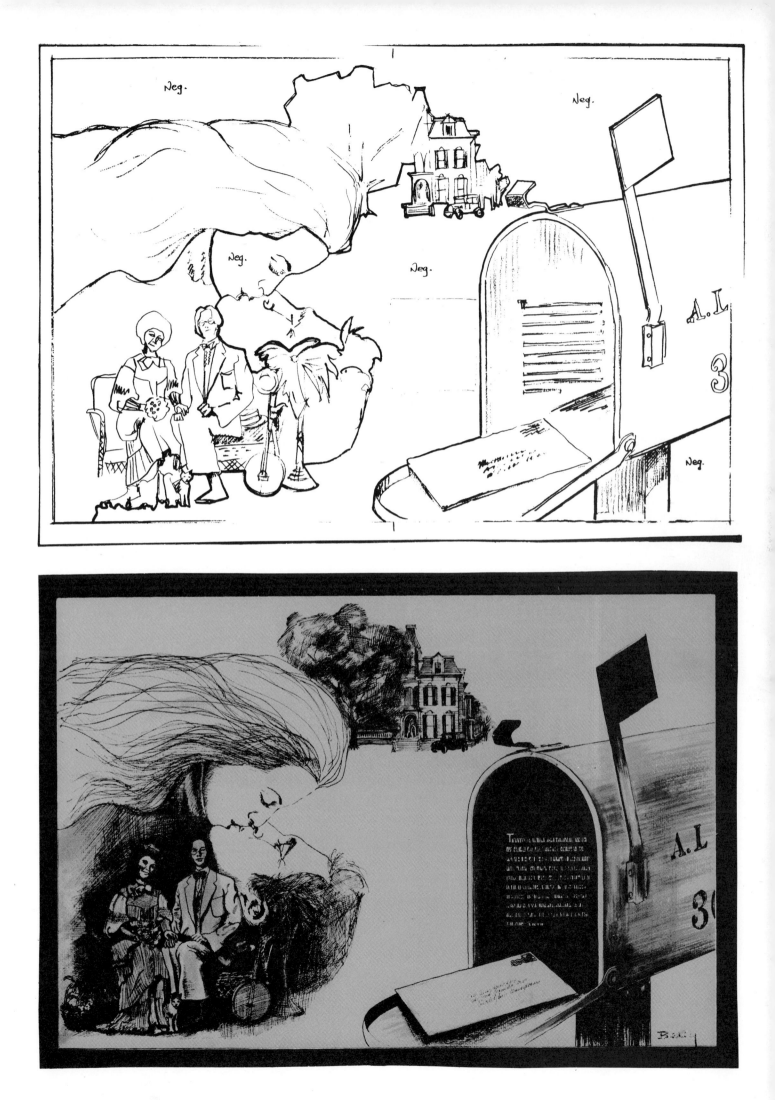

With the above suggestions in mind then, start placing your image outline tracings down within a 12 x 18 inch area on a sheet of bond and arrange them until you feel you have an interesting composition that follows a path from one side of the spread to the other. Leave about 1/3 of the background or negative area untouched and make sure there are no important details placed in the gutter area. Once you have decided what arrangement works, check it with the instructor and get his ok. The tissue images may be taped down to the bond sheet with bits of scotch mending tape to hold them in place. Then the entire sheet can be rolled up and held until the next class session without having to rearrange everything from scratch the next day.

Step 4. Transfer

Place a large piece of tracing paper over your line composition arrangement, tape it down at the corners and trace in all the outlines of the images with a 2H or 3H pencil. Do this very precisely, not sloppily. As you trace be sensitive to the outline shapes of both positive and negative areas, as they will often make or break your composition. This is probably the most important step in the entire unit. Too many students consider this step as merely "getting the stuff down somewhere in the general area so I can get on with the painting" and as a result end up with a mushy, sloppy, succession of insignificant shapes that eventually turn into an ill-defined "blah" illustration. Take your time and redraw a bit as you trace, holding every subtle outline shape that you can. One of the most important factors in great illustrations or paintings is often the configuration of the TOTAL image silhouette or outline shape.

Lift up your master transfer tissue now and transfer the images to your matboard or colored illustration board. If your ground is light in value use a graphite transfer sheet between the tissue and the matboard. If your ground is dark in value rub the back of your master tracing with white pastel. Trace down the images within the 12 x 18 area on your ground by using one of your 3H or 4H pencils because these usually give a thinner better definition to the traced lines than a dull soft pencil.

Step 5. Detailing

Place some clean tissue over your original fotos now and trace in the major details such as faces, collars, hands, window frames, tree branches, motorcycle handlebars,etc. Transfer these to your ground within the outline shapes already established. If you have changed the size you will have to make tracings from the Lucy or freehand in the enlargement or reduction directly on the matboard or illustration board. A white wax pencil is a handy tool when drawing directly on a dark ground. If you are detailing on a light ground be sure to use 3H or 4H pencils. The softer B pencils leave too much graphite which doesn't mix with the waterbase paints and causes the edges of your images to look rough and sloppy.

Step 6. Painting

Start painting directly on the matboard now using your rendering experience gained from project D. If your cut out fotos are too bright and gaudy you will want to modify or subdue the chroma as you paint. If some of your research material fotos are black and white you will have to make up your colors to fit your composition.

Notice the illusion of depth in the above illustration which is provided by having distinct foreground and middleground images with less distinct and smaller background images. Overlapping of images also helps create perspective of depth. Note the palette knife technique of buttering the paint on very heavily in the snow flurry caused by the skier in the center of the picture.

Leave the background areas untouched. As you paint you may see ways to enhance the composition by including a little more fence, say, or adding a bit more of that car coming into the picture from the left. If so, just paint your picture a bit higher or longer in the direction you need extra space. Then when you mat just shift the mat enough to take in the extra bit of composition. Now you see why we didn't grind in that original border too hard, and as long as the 12 x 18 layout isn't moved so far that the center gutter starts cutting into important images, you have some leeway to enhance your composition as you complete your painting.

Backgrounds are one of the things that "throw" beginning illustrators. The main reason for this is because the student doesn't prepare his research as carefully. He assumes a big field of grass is just a Hookers Green slab; the sky is just Ultramarine Blue; the road running to the distant horizon is nothing more than a brown triangle, etc. Confine your first efforts to painting from well researched specific fotos of tangible items. Later when you try large expanses of background take extreme care in observing or preparing your research for these "easy-looking" backgrounds. They are the "killers".

30

You may want to do the illustration in a very detailed rendering manner or you may wish to paint a little more loosely like the impressionists Manet, Monet, or Van Gogh. Some students have used a small flexible painting knife and laid the paint on rather heavily with an impasto technique that is quite effective. Others have painted the various positive images in with flat tones of color without any attempt to shade, "turn the form" or translate light logic. Then they draw over these flat forms with colored ink or use liner brushes with paint to describe details. (If you try this last method, spray a few coatings of workable fix over the flat paint tones. This isolates the underpainting and prevents it from dragging or picking up on the pen or brush as you work over the base.) Some areas may be left unpainted and finished in line only. Sometimes laying all the brush strokes in one direction gives a unique look. Spreading the paint on with varying widths of cardboard gives another rather chunky effect.

Mat the illustration with an appropriate matboard color. Identify with a small signature in an unobtrusive spot on the painting and hand it in at deadline time.

Flat color
and line.

Palette knife over rough surface.

Using different width cardboards to squeegee the
thick paint for "chunky" effect

MATTING

4

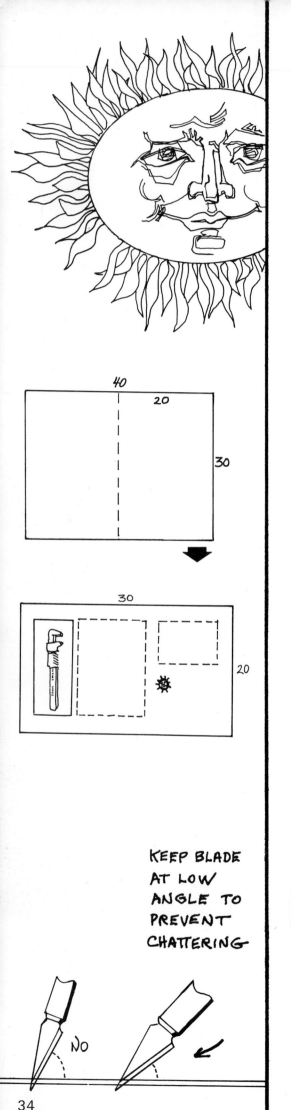

KEEP BLADE
AT LOW
ANGLE TO
PREVENT
CHATTERING

NO

Section 4   MATTING

Presentation is as important as the design itself, and matting is one of the first steps in preparing artwork for exhibit or critique.

Step 1.   Selection

Learn to use stone grays, sand, moss greens, saddle tans, and other neutral dark-colored matboards for your portfolio presentations. Do not use white or cream-colored boards. They get dirty quickly, and as much of a beginner's work is done on white surfaces like bond and illustration board, the light mats do not offer enough contrast. The majority of matboards measure 30 x 40. Cut one of these in half. This will give you two 20 x 30 mats. This is a good module size for a PORTFOLIO as it accepts a large drawing yet can still be carried under your arm. As you become experienced and have more finished production pieces, a smaller 10 x 15 portfolio is usually better. But until then you will have to depend upon some larger pieces to get "in."

Step 2.   Measurement

Lay the 20 x 30 matboard FACE UP. Leave about a 3-inch margin on the left side of the mat. Use a sharp 3H pencil and T-square to make light guide lines bounding an opening large enough to accept the tool rendering on the left side of the mat. Leave the same amount of space above and below the opening.

Step 3.   Cutting

Use a sharp, freshly honed, stiff mat knife with a good sized handle. A small blade tends to bend and waver if you try to cut heavy board with it. Cut along the guide lines from the FRONT side. This pushes the frivels and rough edges out to the back side. On the first cut keep your forearm on the mat with the knife edge held almost parallel with the surface of the board and merely cut through the top layer on the

first pass. It is not necessary to put extreme pressure on the knife.

It will cut easily if it is sharp, and your efforts should be spent to keep the blade following the guide line exactly. (If you think you absolutely have to use a steel edge, have **someone** else help you hold it tightly to keep it from slipping, AND keep the steel edge on the outside of the line so if your knife slips it will cut into the center waste not into the mat.) On the next pass increase the knife pressure. On the third and fourth pass you will cut all the way through. Do not knock out the center. Cut the corners neatly and carefully until the center piece FALLS out. A bit of fine sandpaper will remove any rough edges left on the back side of the cut. Do NOT sand the front edges.

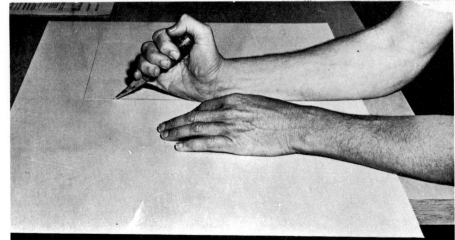

Another method is to use a single-edged razor blade or razor holder. Let the mat extend over the edge of the table face up. Insert the razor thru the mat and pull it the length of the line. A bevel can be put on the cut by angling the cutter outward.

Step 4. Matting from the back

Leave the mat board face up on the table. Place the tool rendering under the mat opening leaving about an inch underlap all the way around. After you position the rendering in the center of the opening, pull the whole unit out to the edge of the table, reach under and affix a small piece of masking tape to each of two corners of the rendering to bind them to the under surface of the matboard. Turn the whole project over and finish placing masking tape around the edge of the rendering. The back of the matboard should look as neat as the front. Trim the ends of the masking tape with a razor blade. Don't leave torn edges and wrinkles. Many an amateur artist has been hired on the craftsmanship of the back of his mounts! Practice excellence and craftsmanship in everything that requires precision. Live good design, and soon you cannot create a poor one.

Step 5. Mounting on the front (Optional)

Occasionally artwork with flaps, masks, bleeds, or three dimensional material needs to be attached to the front of the matboard. A quick way to do this is to cut a rectangular hole in the matboard about one inch smaller all the way around than the card to be mounted. Place the card over the hole, position it level, and tape with masking tape from the back of the rectangular opening. This method will be used to mount the MECHANICAL for the PRODUCT AD COMP, because the black plate is covered with an acetate flap (called a color separation) which needs to hang free.

Step 6. Relationship of items on matboard

Use the area just to the right of the tool rendering to mat the problem, LAYOUT SKILLS. Leave about an inch margin around the border of layout skills. This prevents the border from getting lost and gives AIR around the item. In general, it is better to keep the spacing between the various items on the matboard NARROWER than the width of the margins allowed at the outside edge of the mat. Don't OVERMAT. That is, putting a 10 x 15 item in the middle of a 20 x 30 matboard looks ostentatious. The mat becomes more important than the framed item. Sometimes a small 3-inch by 5-inch drawing, print, bit of calligraphy, or constructed typography will add a "touch" of color or relief to an otherwise monotonous presentation. Your prospective employer, school counselor, or scholarship committee usually looks only ONCE at your portfolio. Anything you can do to present your philosophy of design, your creative thinking, your craftsmanship and engineering will help those people that much more to know WHO YOU ARE.

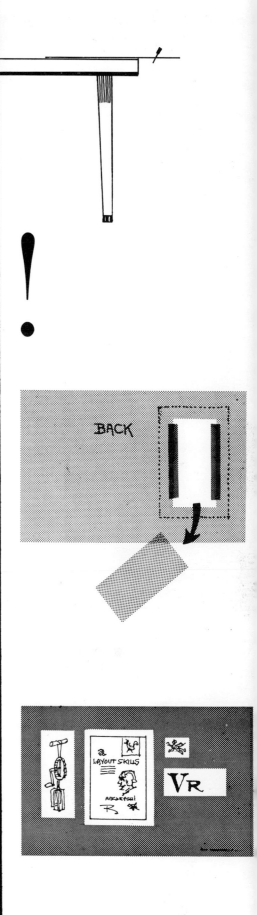

Protecting Artwork

The presentation piece can be wrapped with thin (1 mil) acetate. Pull the acetate taut over the front and tape the edges down tightly on the back. The piece can then be matted or mounted in the regular fashion. If desired, the entire matboard may be wrapped.

There are loose-leaf notebooks with glassine envelope pages that allow the advanced artist to insert a variety of units. These are convienient to carry and have the advantage of showing both front and back of the art work.

Map companies have wax-backed, frosted acetates that can be pressed down over maps or other chartlike presentations which get fingered, taped, or marked on. The frosted appearance disappears when the covering is adhered tightly to the surface. It cannot be used on pebble board or coral-finish papers, because the bumps prevent the acetate from adhering tightly to the surface, and the image will appear ghostlike.

For more detailed information on presentation techniques refer to Chapter eight of Bill Bockus's "Designer's Notebook," 1977, Macmillan Publishing Co., Inc., 866 Third Ave., NY 10022. This basic text is for product designers and covers design drawings, drafting practices, sales presentations with boards, slides, and flip charts plus model making, exhibit structures, and illumination.

INDICATION

The layout artist must be able to indicate or simulate typography, lettering, and the human figure quickly and clearly.

Type is usually indicated by using chisel-point pencils of varying width.

Exact CONSTRUCTED lettering or the free calligraphy will very likely be purchased from a professional letterer. The techniques that follow in this section are not meant to produce this kind of finished lettering. — Rather they are meant to be used as quick layout INDICATIONS on the visual rough to show what style will be DESIRED in the final reproduction. However, these short-hand techniques have some de lightful characteristics and can often be exploited further.

Figure indication will be taken up in Section 7, Layout Skills.

"The pretty can never be beautiful; the ugly often can."   Gauguin

"Ugliness may be OK if it's dynamic."   Construction foreman

"Ugliness is in the eye of many beholders. Beauty is a sometime thing."   Student

".... the magnificent leprosy of the sphinx's head."   Cocteau

"No man is an island."   Donne

"Everyman is an island."   Student

"Ask not what the community can do for you. Ask what you can do for yourself."   Student

"Do unto others as they would have you do unto them."   Golden rule, revised

"Greater love hath no man than to give his life for a friend." "Except he who gives his reputation ?"

"I'm not trying to make a social statement; I just want to shout for joy !"   Enking

"Censorship is a double edged sword."

"What you can't get - to hell with it. Don't worry what the other fellow has." Louis Armstrong

"That's his good luck - not your bad luck."   The Bocchi

A fanatic is one who redoubles his efforts when he has lost sight of his objective.

Work done with an anxiety about results is far inferior to work done without
        such anxiety." Gita

" The face, the voice, the music that have true beauty belong to people too full of
        life to be afraid of making mistakes. When you sing it safe, play it safe, paint it
        safe, write it safe, you paint and write and sing the life out of it."   Baudelaire

Character is how a man acts during adversity, not how he acts when things are going fine.

Training teaches you what others have learned.

Education teaches you what to do with curiosity.

"Art is the finest way of doing anything." Doug Stone

"Times Square ... what a wonderful place if only you couldn't read !" Chesterton

"Each progressive spirit is opposed by a thousand men appointed to guard the past." Maeterlinck

"We should always examine the optimums and forget about feasibility; it will
        compromise us soon enough."   James Rouse

"What is the use of a house if you haven't got a tolerable planet to put it on ?"   Thoreau

"Peace" obtained by relinquishing principles is a living hell.

Hard work relates to artistic creativeness. The individual mobilizes , solves more,
        produces more responses, and is apt to find a more unique and better answer.

"Don't be afraid to use what talents you possess; the woods would be very silent
        if no birds sang except those who sang best."   Queen Anne's Record Observer (Md)

"I don't turn my back on my mediocre experiences. They are part and parcel of
        my creativity."   Bradbury

A photograph may be either a picture of something or an esthetic object by itself.

Is "snapping" a picture the equivalent of "found" sculpture ?

"Architecture is frozen music."   Schelling

Esthetic experiences may be relatively "pure" such as singing or painting; or the
        esthetics may be interwoven within the architecture or industrial design.

The creative individual tends to respond to his environment by indulging in symbolic
        behavior as well as survival behavior.

"The responsibility of the educated man is that he make articulate to himself and to
        others what he is willing to bet his life on." Edward Eddy, Jr.

"Freedom means responsibility."   Goldmann

Complete freedom of thought is often misconstrued to mean complete freedom of behavior.

LETTERING INDICATION ROUGH (Project F - 3 hrs.)

Choose a short paragraph or several sentences concerning a principle you think is important to remember at this time in history. Check it with the instructor. Be prepared to defend your choice as a philosophical truth. That is, do you firmly believe it? OR COULD you write a better version ? The instructor will try to find weaknesses in it or even argue against it. Is it WORTH lettering or printing? The page preceding this has a few ideas or revised quotations which may provoke an idea from you that is WORTH printing. The layout will consist of your paragraph, one line from the paragraph and the author's last name arranged in three horizontal rectangles (two of which are toned) on a bond sheet.

FINISHED MATTED COMP

● 1. PARAGRAPH

The spaces for guide lines and sizes of pens and brushes listed below should be considered as approximations only. After practicing, use any spacing that you think will adapt itself to your stroke. Always use a T-square and a hard pencil when making guide lines. After trying the a, b, and c variations below, choose one method and letter the entire paragraph over a pastel rectangle at the top of a clean sheet of bond.

guide on line
DONE W/ C-2 PEN

Choose a pastel stick that is not too brilliant in HUE. Russet browns, yellow ochres, olives would be better for a background than brilliant oranges, reds, or yellow greens. Powder some of the stick on a piece of scratch paper by rubbing it on sandpaper or scraping it with a knife. Cut out a rectangular hole in a piece of bond for a stencil as large as necessary to hold your paragraph. Now position the stencil at the top of the sheet of clean bond, dip a piece of cotton into the powdered pastel and rub it carefully over the area to be toned. Remove the stencil. Turn the bond pad over in a short arc with a rapid motion and strike it a sharp rap from the back. This will get rid of the excess pastel. If you try to blow it off, it will make streaks radiating out from the rectangle. Give the area two light coats of WORKABLE FIX. Hold the spray can far enough back so it doesn't blow the chalk over the page. It is now ready to accept ink without fuzzing.

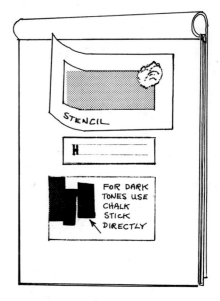

START OF ROUGH

STENCIL

H

FOR DARK TONES USE CHALK STICK DIRECTLY

(a) Pen Script

Use the C-2 or C-3 Speedball pen or equivalent and on the bond pad try your everyday handwriting on a SINGLE, light, 3H guideline. This method often produces a free beautiful SCRIPT. It is not necessary to change your whole approach to writing merely because a Roman italic letterform is called for. If the stroke appears too thick in proportion to the letter, write LARGER or use a smaller pen point. In general, keep the letters CLOSE TOGETHER and not too slanted. People read words not letters. The two main causes of "poor" illegible handwriting are that the letters are spaced too far apart, and the letters are slanted so far to the right they become distorted and prevent the reader's eye from seeing the words. By writing more vertically and keeping their letters closed up, most people can improve their handwriting in two hours of practice. Try it.

Slanted handwriting has been taught for centuries. But in the past few decades people have become so used to reading typography that their optical habits have changed. It is becoming much easier for the modern generation to read vertical letters than slanted ones.

Vertical

slanted
DONE W/ C-5 PEN

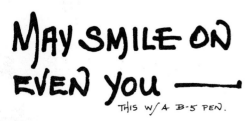

R

Cursive

adagio

Rogelio Mejía

ABC

THESE W/ A B-3 PEN.

FORTUN

FORTUNE

FORTUNE

MAY SMILE ON

EVEN YOU —

THIS W/ A B-5 PEN.

(b) Cursive

Now try lettering the quotation in a CURSIVE style. This means you use your own handwriting again but do not join the letters. Do not slant the letters too much as they become difficult to read. If you wish, add a guide line for the top of the ascenders and the bottom of the descenders. However, sometimes the irregularity of your own handwriting has a rhythmical flow that may be just as beautiful as the precision of guided lettering. If you find the ascenders and descenders look shaky and have too many different slants, keep them shorter. In this cursive style it is important to glance back occasionally at the previous letters to check the slant and the letter spacing. Shift the paper now and then to prevent your hand from getting too far to the right of your eyes, or you may find the letters slanting more to the right. Try varying the BODY CIRCLES of the lower case letters by making them into slight VERTICAL ELLIPSES. Keep the letters almost touching.

(c) Brush

An interesting variation is to use the number 4 sable brush or a Chinese watercolor brush with black tempera paint. (India ink tends to destroy the fine hairs on the tip of a good brush.) Hold the brush at an angle or VERTICAL with the paper. Keep it well loaded with paint at a medium consistency. (If the paint is too thick it will "dry brush". If it is too watery, it will make the letters look weak and thin.) Twirling or paletting the loaded brush on a piece of cardboard will point the brush and keep the loading consistent. At first you will have a tendency to be too deliberate or "labor" the stroke. Try lettering a little more rapidly. Let the side of the brush aid the tip in producing the letter. This method can be very similar to handwriting or the cursive style practiced above. Keep it CASUAL and free.

NOTE:
Never go back over the above types of freehand lettering and attempt to correct strokes. The corrections are usually worse than the errors. The whole philosophy of the above type of lettering or writing is to retain the free flow of "color" of the line. Constructed corrections kill the very feeling they are attempting to hold.

2. SINGLE LINE IN GOTHIC CAPS

Place this line a little below the quotation.
(One line in printing means from one side of the column to the other. It does not necessarily mean a sentence.)

Use a B-3 Speedball pen or equivalent on hot press illustration board on a smooth white bristol. Use light guide lines one half inch apart, and this time you may be as tight and deliberate as necessary to keep the letters perfectly straight, vertical and touching the guide lines exactly on top and bottom. This type of lettering is useful in producing small show cards, name plates, and the many "quickie" signs that are in demand from every art department. Try EXTENDING **F** or CONDENSING **F** the letters. Add SERIFS **F** for variation. It is feasible to correct this type of lettering. This may be done with black tempera and a good sable brush. Smudges may be "WHITED" out by using white tempera and the sable brush. However, when whiting out, paint only over the exact smudge or bulge and do NOT let the white paint smear over onto the white paper. The white paint over the paper appears much whiter than the same paint over the black smudge or bulge and thus makes the whole correction area look messy and unprofessional. Keep corrections PRECISE.
For a fresher look, letter the line very rapidly allowing some strokes to go above or below the guidelines and nesting letters to provide better unity or 'color'.

Lettering done casually with the side of the brush can be quite interesting. Use light 4H guide lines for line level. The letters may run over or under the guide lines, but your eye should glance back at the weight and spacing of previous strokes as you letter to keep the total line from being condensed or extended.

Mejia

PLEASE DON'T EAT THE DAISIES. YOU'LL FIND THE ARTICHOKES TASTIER

MIXING CAPS AND LOWER CASE LETTERS IS NOT THE CRIME IT WAS 50 YEARS AGO. ONLY A MISDEMEANOR

● 3. SIGNATURE

Place the author's last name at the bottom of the bond layout in a light, subdued color over a dark subdued color rectangle. Use a dark pastel stick and rub the side of the stick directly on the bond. Use masking tape or the edge of a sheet of paper to keep the edges straight and sharp. Remove excess chalk and fix the area with WORKABLE fix. Remember the fix will make the chalk several shades darker.

Mix some tempera paint together to get a subdued CHROMA. Complementary colors may be mixed together, or browns or grays may be added to a color to lessen its brilliance. Then lighten the mixture's VALUE by adding some white to it. Use a 1/4 or 1/2-inch wide stencil or bristle brush and scrawl a free calligraphic signature across the dark color block. Before using the mixed color you can practice with black tempera on a sheet of bond until you get the free, unlabored feeling of a signature. Readability is not a requirement. If you are rushed, use a light subdued chalk to SIMULATE the tempera signature.

● 4. COMPOSITION

Remember that a good VISUAL is always a close approximation   of the final job. If you have in mind a certain arrangement of the three blocks, then arrange them that way on the bond. To simulate the mat opening around the single line of gothic caps, draw a pencil line rectangle around it. Sometimes a dark pencil line around the other two color blocks helps give the illusion of the mat window.

Here is a spot where one small item such as a single small letter, a 3-inch by 3-inch pen drawing of an old fashioned bicycle, a brush calligraphic letter, a pasteup sun cut from gold foil, or some small illustration related to your quotation would enhance the presentation. It would provide a small interesting relief to the larger, more formal blocks of lettering. Show it in your layout. If you have doubts about your color selection on the rough, include a few extra swatches to show the instructor what you are planning for the final COMP. A VERBAL description of two color relationships is practically worthless, but a color SWATCH is a definite design answer, and the more likely you are to receive constructive criticism from the instructor. Letter your identification on the back and hand in the visual on the whole 14 x 17 bond sheet. Do NOT crop it down to a smaller size. The margins act as a frame and are used for correction notes and other suggestions from the art director or account executive.

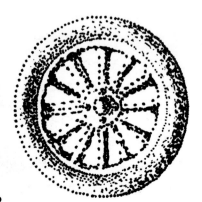

LETTERING INDICATION COMP (Project G - 3 hrs.)

After the instructor's criticism of your lettering visual, prepare the COMPREHENSIVE. The comprehensive (Comp) is the presentation to the client and is made as much like the final ad as possible. Chalk, pencil, and tempera take the place of printers' ink, but in the hands of a skilled artist the final comp can be effective and inexpensive.

● 1. PARAGRAPH

Letter the quotation on a light-value STOCK (another name for paper) of subdued CHROMA (the brilliance or intensity of a color). Box covers, backs of packing inserts, etc., often provide interesting subdued tones for this part. Use light guide lines, and it is NOT necessary to erase them. Rubbing over the India Ink letters tends to scrub the black away and leave the letters looking washed out. Furthermore, the guide lines often add a crispness to the edge of the letters that is desirable.

Allow plenty of margin around the paragraph to prevent it from looking cramped when it is matted in your portfolio. You might wish to relate the color of the subdued stock to the paint you are mixing for the signature. Sometimes a BROWN INDIA INK on a toned paper is very interesting.

● 2. SINGLE LINE IN GOTHIC CAPS

Letter the single line of Gothic caps in BLACK with a B-3 point on hot-press illustration board or heavy white paper to keep it from wrinkling. KEEP THOSE 3H GUIDE LINES LIGHT AND 1/2 INCH APART.

● 3. SIGNATURE

Put the light colored signature on a DARK-VALUE stock of subdued CHROMA. This will give it contrast. You should have several pieces of the dark stock, because the first signature scrawl may not be successful. You will discover there are very few dark papers on the market. If you can not buy the color paper you wish, make it by covering a heavy stock with dark pastel and fixing it.

● 4. COMPOSITION

Mat the three or four items on the right-hand side of one of your 20 x 30 mats. Leave the left-hand side blank. Put identification on back and hand in at deadline time. Make certain masking tape is trimmed neatly.

(See example top of page 39 or 44.)

USE STIFF BRISTLE-BRUSH IN A FREE SWINGING APPROACH.

DO NOT LABOR THE LETTERS. SIGNATURE SCRAWLS NEED CHARACTER — NOT LEGIBILITY.

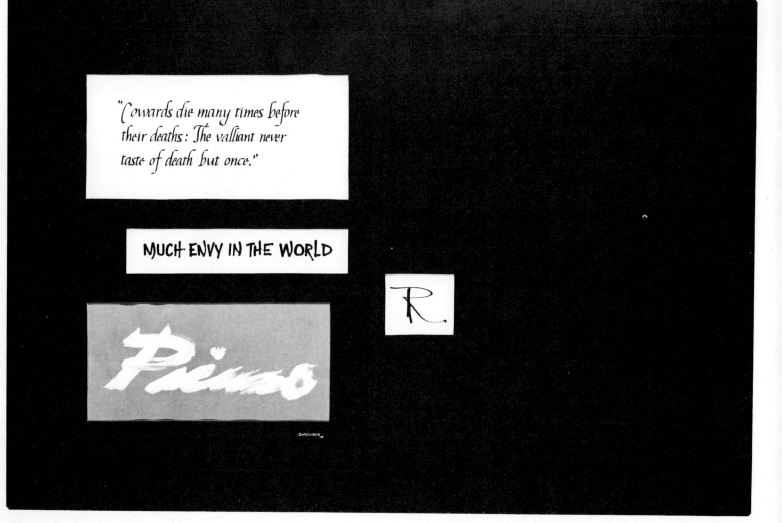

Two or three other items of design or typography could be placed later on this side of the mat board.

a chisel point HB is a good point for type indication

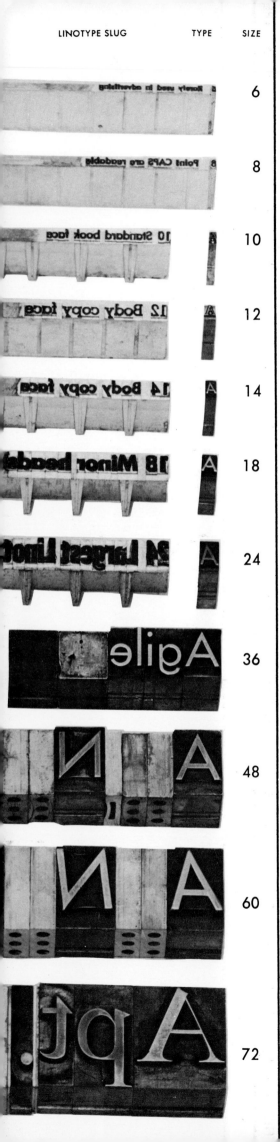

SIZE
6
8
10
12
14
18
24
36
48
60
72

TYPE A metal block 0.9186 of an inch high with the top face shaped to print a character.

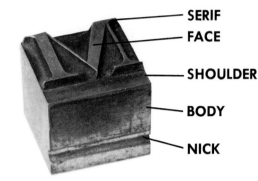

SERIF	Short cross stroke
FACE	Style or cut of a letter. The printing surface.
SHOULDER	Space for the descenders such as g j p q & y.
BODY	The solid metal block which supports the face.
NICK	A mark identifying the bottom side of the face.

SIZE

Type size is measured in points. Each point is 1/72 of an inch. A printer's LINE GAGE (see below) is used for measurement instead of the ordinary ruler. It is difficult to label each one of the 72 divisions so they are partitioned into groups of 12 points each known as PICAS. The numbers on the left side of the gage represent picas and must be translated into points (picas X 12) when designating type SIZE.

Note below that although the type size (overall body) measured by the gage is (in this sample) 72 points, the actual letter face is less than that. Ordinarily the type size is selected from a TYPE SPECIMEN SHEET (See section 10) which has the type size listed beside the letters. However, the artist can also estimate a type size by applying one of the APPROXIMATIONS below:

CAPITALS Measure the height of a capital letter in points and add the shoulder space. (The shoulder is roughly ½ the height of the capital letter.)

LOWER CASE Measure from the top of an ascender to the bottom of a descender vertically in points.

The center scale on the gage is used mainly in newspaper work to measure Agate (5½ point) lines.

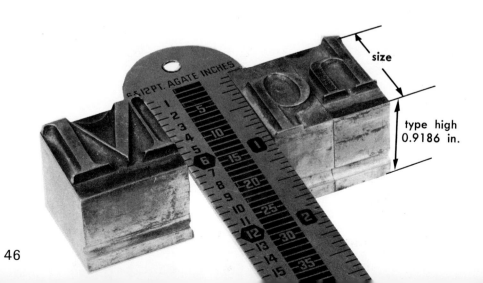

size

type high 0.9186 in.

TYPE FACE CHARACTERISTICS

Kind — Abbreviation

Kind	Abbreviation
CAPITALS	*Caps*
SMALL CAPITALS	*S.C.*
lower case	*lc*
italic	*ital*
Caps and lower case	*Clc*

Weight

LIGHTFACE CAPS	lightface lower case
MEDIUM CAPS	medium lower case
BOLD FACE	**boldface lower case**

Width

EXTENDED

Regular

condensed

J

Design Variations

h **h**

R R **R** r r r r r r R R

A a **a** a a **a**

5 **5** **5**

hi hi

ITALIC MEANS SLANTED TO THE RIGHT

SIZE	COPY
6	6 Rarely used in advertising
8	8 Point CAPS are readable
10	10 Standard book face
12	12 Body copy face — NOTE SMALLER FACE ON 14 BODY
14	14 Body copy face
18	**18 Minor heads**
24	**24 Largest Linotype**
36	Agile
48	A N — NOTE EM SPACING
60	A N — NOTE EN SPACING
72	Apt.

47

TYPE

LINOTYPE AND INTERTYPE are automatic type casting machines. As a key is struck on the keyboard it releases a mold or MATRIX into a slot until the line is completed. Hot metal is squirted into the line of matrices, cooled, and ejected as a line of type. These machines cast type up to 24 points high. See Section 10 for more information.

LUDLOW type is produced as follows: Individual molds of letters called MATRICES are set by hand in a special STICK or clamp. The stick is then inserted into the Ludlow caster. The hot metal is forced into the matrices, cooled, and ejected as a line of type. This method is used mainly for the larger type used for headlines and display work which cannot be set on the linotype.

MONOTYPE is produced by a casting machine which casts individual letters in hot metal from individual matrices.

WOOD TYPE are large letters used for poster work and are measured in LINES. A line is equal to a pica. An 18-line letter would be 18 picas or 3 inches high.

RULE LINES and borders are often used in printing business forms, invoices, charts and graphs. If so, the width should be specified in point, such as a 2-point or 4-point rule line. In some cases, where these lines become complex and difficult to set by letterpress type-high rules, they can be drawn on the pasteup and copied photographically. Also they can be scribed directly through the negative emulsion by the stripper using a narrow, sharp, chisel-edged knife against a steel straightedge. The lines made by this method are often cleaner and straighter than pen lines drawn on illustration board.

COLD TYPE

Most handset type and linotype slugs are made by forcing molten metal into molds or matrices. The type is then inked and proofed to give the artist his copy for pasteup. There are other methods of making reproducible copy and, in general, these methods are called COLD TYPE because they do not involve molten metal.

One common method is to print multiple alphabets of both CAPS and lower case letters on sheets of thin, transparent, acetate which have an ADHESIVE-WAX backing. A fine hairline is printed under each row of letters to help the artist line up the copy. Each individual letter is cut away from the backing sheet with a section of the hairline and tacked lightly in place by BURNISHING a corner down on the pasteup. A light thin BLUE GUIDELINE may be drawn on the pasteup, and when the letters are arranged, the hairline under each letter is placed to coincide with the blue guideline. This keeps the letters level. Spacing the letters from left to right is done by eye, and usually words look best when the individual letters are almost TOUCHING. The letter ''i'' ordinarily needs more space than the other letters to prevent it from looking squashed. When the line of cold type is arranged to suit the artist's eye, he places a piece of clean bond over the row of letters and burnishes them down by rubbing hard. The black hairline is then cut carefully, stripped up, and thrown away. As the guideline underneath is in BLUE, it will not photograph, so its removal is not necessary.

There are a number of companies that manufacture these alphabets and each company issues a catalog of its type faces and sizes. Besides type there are also sheets of electronic symbols, arrows, lines, borders, textures, ellipses, and screens which assist the artist in many ways. Indexes correlate sheet numbers to standard hot-type faces.

These artist aids have many different brand names in industry. However, certain terms, which are sometimes contractions of brand names, have become fairly common. Art type, zip, artist aid, ruby red, are all references to this particular line of wax-backed aids.

These wax-backed sheets are also printed in a great variety of colors which can be used for visuals, comps, and also production work. Thinners and applicators are available which will soften the color emulsion and allow rough edges to be sponged in. Stylus pens are used to scribe fine lines through the color surface for other effects. In some cases the finished-art comp becomes the color-separated mechanical **1** ready for the process camera. This method of preparation is an obvious saving in time, if the job lends itself to the media. Some manu-**2** facturers lease special filters which are placed over the lens of a regular process camera. These filters allow only the light from the specially prepared pencil, liquid wash, or pastel to pass through. Thus the printer and the artist have control over backgrounds or other areas that they don't want to print without making time consuming DROPOUT MASKS or OPAQUING OUT on the negatives.

TRANSFER TYPE is another kind of cold type. The alphabet is printed on the reverse side of a transparent sheet and is transferred from this carrying sheet to the surface of the comp or mechanical by rubbing or burnishing the letter directly to the surface. In this case there is no surrounding acetate left to cause glare.

PAPER TYPE printed alphabets are also available in pads or "sticks" with adhesive backs.

PHOTO PROCESS is another method of producing cold-type heads. These machines produce letters, words, or sentences from negative alphabet masters. The letter is usually "dialed" on the machine by the operator and appears as a black photographic image on a smooth white strip of opaque paper or transparent film. The entire strip can then be pasted directly on the pasteup or used as a positive film. Different type sizes require different master negatives to be inserted into the machine. There are also adjustable lenses which will CONDENSE, EXPAND, SLANT, ENLARGE, or make other photographic distortions of letters and words.

Most of the above cold type is used for heads. For the small faces used in body copy there are TYPE WRITERS with inter change-able fonts. The body copy is typed on a smooth white stock which can be pasted directly on the mechanical. Vari Typer is one trade name for such a machine.

In certain cases layouts and mechanicals can be made with cold type much faster and cheaper than relying on regular type or on written specifications to the printer. This is particularly so when the type is overlapped, nested, set piggyback, interlocked, bounced, staggered, or tumbled. (See page 56 for examples.)

1 BOURGES SHEETS
2 FLUORCOLOR FILTERS

INTERCHANGEABLE FONT

TELETYPE TYPESETTING (TTS)

The latest linotype keyboards can be designed with SOLENOIDS (small electromagnets) under each key on the keyboard. Then as a perforated tape is run between a light source and a PHOTOELECTRIC CELL, the code holes in the paper tape cause the corresponding letter on the keyboard to be pulled down. The linotype machine thus clatters merrily along like a robot but still needs an attendant to watch for jams or errors. However, the machine can run faster for longer periods of time and is especially useful for setting large amounts of copy like books and technical manuals. Operator fatigue is reduced considerably.

The perforated tape is made by a special typewriter (called a PERFORATOR) which punches holes across a strip of paper. The paper tape is 7/8 inch wide with a series of tiny sprocket holes running down the center. There are 6 code hole positions which allow 720 combinations. Each letter has one code, but the upshift code will call for a capital letter and the downshift code will call for lower case letters, etc. The other code combinations are used to call for numbers, punctuation marks, spacers, line return, etc.

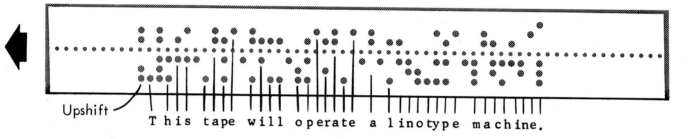

Upshift

T h i s tape will o p e r a t e a l i n o t y p e m a c h i n e.

As the perforator punches the tape on the side of the machine it also types the copy in a normal manner on a sheet of paper in the carriage. Thus spelling, leading, column width estimates, etc., can be checked. Minor errors can be corrected on the tape by filling in holes or punching a new one to change the code, or in the case of major errors a new section of tape can be punched and spliced in to the original.

PHOTO TYPESETTING

One of the latest applications of this perforated tape is feeding it into a computer which in turn activates a photographic printer which prints out the copy on photographic paper. The size, face, leading, etc., can be set on the computer which activates a set of lenses, a stroboscopic light, an alphabet negative, and a moveable prism. A negative with all the characters on it is wrapped around a drum which revolves at a high rate of speed around a strobe light. On command from the computer the strobe light flicks a ray of light thru the transparent letter on the negative at the exact instant it arrives opposite the lens. Electronic circuits can give commands in millionths of seconds, and light travels at 186,000 miles per second. Thus the letters on the whirling negative drum seemingly stand still when the strobe light flicks on and off.

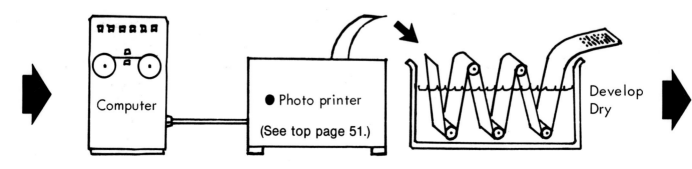

Computer

● Photo printer

(See top page 51.)

Develop
Dry

The light image of the letter is then focused by the lens and passed on to the prism. The image reflects off the prism at a 90° angle and hits the strip of photographic paper. As the next letter comes thru, the prism moves one letterspace to the right and the latent image of the next letter is printed and so on. When the tape is finished, the strip of photographic paper is torn off the feed roller, developed, dried and is ready for pasteup in about 5 minutes. Different negatives can be installed on the drum for different faces.

● PHOTO PRINTER

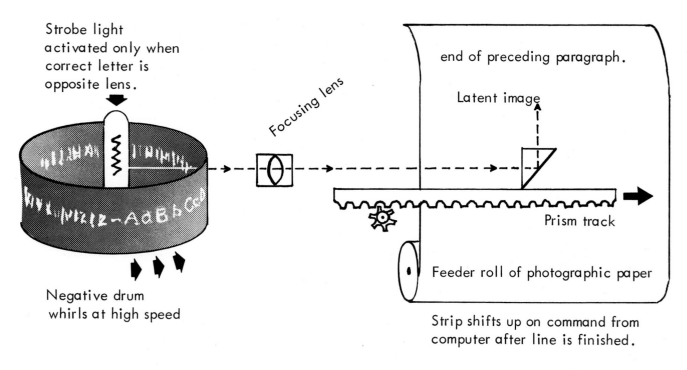

Strobe light activated only when correct letter is opposite lens.

Focusing lens

end of preceding paragraph.

Latent image

Prism track

Negative drum whirls at high speed

Feeder roll of photographic paper

Strip shifts up on command from computer after line is finished.

SCHEMATICS

A negative drum containing portions of lines, electronic symbols, or engineering symbols, plus the necessary alphabet font can be used to print drafting layouts, schematic diagrams, printed circuits, or engineering and business flow charts. These can be printed out on transparent vellum which can then be enlarged or reproduced in various ways for plant or public consumption.

The original sketches or drawings are MARKED UP with numbers, letters, and computer symbols by trained personnel. These notations are then typed on a perforator by a typist who may not even understand what she is typing. The tape, however, will be able to tell the computer exactly how many vertical or horizontal lines to print and where, where to position symbols, numbers, or call outs.... and "Voila'" , out comes a complex schematic drawing 2 feet wide and ten feet long.

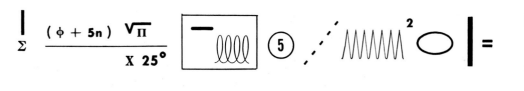

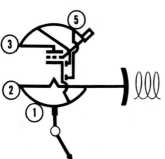

PERSPECTIVES

Perspective drawings can be programmed also. More exotic equipment is required, but, in a sense, the principles are the same. For example, in designing a cockpit for a carrier borne jet fighter, the designers wanted to know how much view the pilot would have from a certain size windshield as he made his approach pattern to the carrier deck. The computer was given the dimensions of the carrier profile, the typical attitude of the plane in reference to the horizon, the size of the proposed cockpit windshield, the location of the pilot's dominant eye, etc. The computer was then "instructed" to make a series of drawings of the carrier deck as seen thru the glass of the cockpit from 1/2 mile out, 1/4 mile out, 220 yards, 110 yards, 50 yards, and on landing. From the results they were able to evaluate a variety of windshield sizes and shapes and come to a much faster design decision as to the optimum solution without making and testing the time consuming mockups.

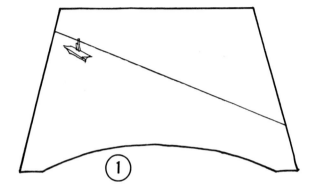

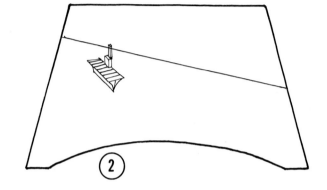

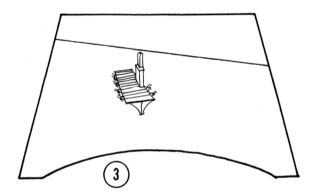

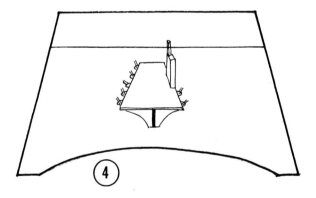

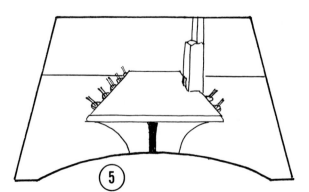

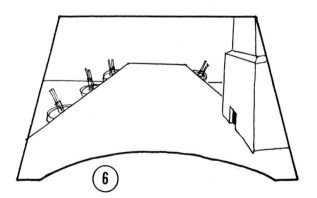

TYPE CLASSIFICATIONS

Regardless of the method of printing, the major type face designs follow a somewhat CONTINUOUS progression from the delicate wedge-serifed Old Roman to the sans serif or Gothic letter which was developed later.

Wedge stems
and serifs

Straight stems
and hairlines

Square
serifs

Block stems
(no taper)

Within this range , artists use certain terms to identify the major areas of type design. These four general classifications are listed below in a typical sample face:

1 ROMAN OLD STYLE
wedge serifs

2 MODERN ROMAN
fine hair lines

3 GOTHIC no serifs

4 CONTEMPORARY
GOTHIC SQUARE serifs

[SANS SERIF MEANS WITHOUT SERIFS]

Several other general classifications are used to identify various categories. Some of these are:

5 TEXT imitates mediaeval writing

6 OLD FASHIONED oversize serifs

7 Script Modern Handwriting

8 CURSIVE unjoined script

9 BRUSH

by: H. MASSIE

53

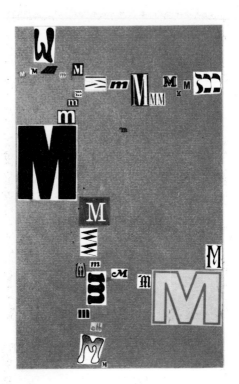

E

6"

G

a

Select one letter. For example, the letter G. Cut out of scrap magazines all the letter G's you can find, caps or lower case. When you have thirty or forty different letters, arrange them on a 7 x 9 piece of illustration board, but adhere to a vertical and horizontal AXIAL arrangement. Make the composition asymmetrical and leave the NEGATIVE (background) areas different sizes. Let some of the letters touch or BLEED off the edge. In general, keep the letters from tilting but at the same time don't center them all on the axes. Avoid a TUMBLED look in this problem.

After the instructor checks your composition, glue the letters down neatly. It is not necessary that each letter silhouette be cut out. Just leave the letter on its paper rectangle. But be certain that each rectangle is trimmed neatly with square **corners.** These tiny DETAILS often make the difference between a good ad and a mediocre one.

AMBIGUITY (Project H - 3 hrs.)

AMBIGUITY is the characteristic of being understood in two or more possible senses. Artists often use this type of arrangement to force the viewer's eye into different paths or to do a double take. Advertising also uses it to attract attention.

Select an interesting TYPE letterform. Enlarge it to eight inches in height precisely and proportionately. (Check those NEGATIVE PROPORTIONS AS WELL AS THE REST OF THE LETTER.)
After the instructor checks your enlarged letter in relation to the original, cover the back with white chalk, trace it on a piece of black paper , and cut it out exactly.

Now make two paper L's and compose part of the letter within the rectangle formed by the L's so that the largest dimension is no greater than 6 inches. You must retain the letter identification, but you must also hold back its readability by making use of AMBIGUOUS negative and positive shapes. That is, the L's must be arranged so that the eye has a certain amount of difficulty determining whether the white space or the black space was meant to be read. You will find with practice you can compose the shapes so that as the design is studied, first one shape and then the other jumps into dominance. Sometimes the negative cutout left in the black paper can be used also.

When you have a solution, draw a line over the letter where it is intercepted by the inside edge of the L's. Cut the letter along these lines and mount it on a square or rectangular piece of illustration board. (If you have followed instructions , the piece of illustration board will be no greater than 6 inches in its longest dimension.) Do a neat job. If the glue or drymounting tissue sticks out over the edges, start over.

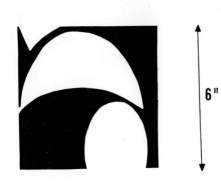

6"

Before taking the following test it might be well to have done the previous problem on AXIAL ARRANGEMENT.

TYPE CONSTRUCTION TEST (Project I - 3 hours)

Rough layouts on bond, tracings and cut outs may be prepared ahead of time. However, all work on the illustration board must be done within the designated 2 or 3 hours of class time. Please hand in the illustration board at the end of period. If you use color, keep it SUBDUED in chroma and limited to 2 or 3 letters.

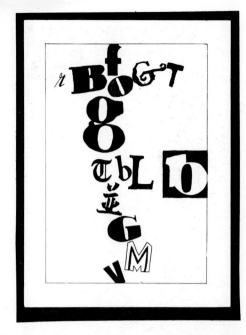

On a piece of 10 X 15 hot-press illustration board, lay out a rectangle 8 X 13, leaving a one-inch margin outside a ruled pencil line. Inside the rectangle place the following typography along one major vertical axis and one or two minor horizontal axes. A minimum of 6 letters must be painted on the board directly. The other letters may be pasteups, but must be cut with a sharp knife or scissors. You may PIGGYBACK or NEST letters but do not overlap. You may use rubber cement.

Unless otherwise specified, letters must be at least 1/2 inch high and not more than 3 inches high. Keep majority of letters vertical. A slight tipping now and then is allowable but avoid TUMBLING the whole layout. If a cylindrical nib pen is not available, a ball point pen may be used with the usual ellipse or circle templates and a straight edge to give crisp clean edges to the type faces. The letterface outlines can then be filled in with a small pointed sable brush and black tempera.

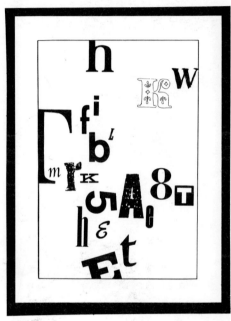

1 Roman Cap, black, 3 inch
1 Gothic Cap, sans serif
1 Gothic Cap, square serif

2 Gothic lc, gray
1 Hollow letter, decorated, 2-inch
1 Letter, half black, half color
1 Paper cutout, flat color
1 Paper cutout, heavy texture

1 Roman lc, black
1 Extended letter
1 Condensed letter
1 Italic
1 Reversed in 1-inch square
1 Printed (Cut type from eraser, potato, or cardbd.)
1 Numeral

EVALUATION

1. Are the axes significant?
2. Is there variety in type faces and sizes?
3. Is there variety in negative area size?
4. Is it clean and precise?

overLap

neSTeD

PIGGY BACK

INTELROCK

bOUnce

STAGGER

emotion

𝔉or 𝔆hristmas

CASTLE

TITANIC

toaster

alligator

SCREEAM

Pasadena City College

A N N U A L

sprinG ArT exHibit

MAY 19 TO JUNE 17

AWARDS PRESENTATION

3:30 200 C

MEJIA

ALPHABETS

An advertising person should have enough background history in language to understand the possible development of writing, lettering, and typography in the future. A quick look at some of the limitations of typography might lead later to some interesting experiments or research.

For example, our language is visually meaningless. The alphabet is composed of rigid code characters based on PHONETICS (sound) which have no visual meaning. It is rather unique in that it has superseded completely, the previous pictographic, hieroglyphic or idea calligraphy which were essentially VISUAL in concept.

Our typography is effective for business use, efficient in the sciences, does a reasonable job (as we seldom attempt to visualize any other method) for the fiction writer but leaves something to be desired by poets or writers in all fields who tend to be as sensitive to visual esthetics as they are to the idea of the story or the phonetical rhythms.

The transition from a calligraphy that was visually meaningful to an auditory alphabet has been so complete that rarely does the modern student of typography even realize that the typography he uses has no visual meaning. The word no longer makes visual sense or connection with the original idea. The word itself no longer expresses the character of what the author is trying to say. It is a group of meaningless letters which relate to meaningless sounds. The word TREE could as readily mean bee, or horse, or ice cream. On the other hand a primitive calligraphic word for WIND could be written to immediately portray the essential feeling as to whether it was a mild zephyr, a brisk breeze or a gust.

The word tree in calligraphy conveys the structure of the tree by its visual form. Thus the symbol might evoke grace, ruggedness, lightness or heaviness in the character of its structure, particularly in oriental poetry. Reading poetry in the oriental sense is a matter of becoming involved VISUALLY as well as audibly.

It might be interesting to write a short poem or paragraph as a word REBUS. Let the key words be represented, not by pictures, but perhaps by modifications of your handwriting or printing approach, so that the meaning of the whole was reinforced by subtle visual variations or accents in the WAY you developed the paragraph.

Can you envision a linotype machine which carried matrices of different "character"" which typographers or artists could call for to denote different meanings through different structure of the words ? The day will undoubtedly come when the machine will translate the operator's SPOKEN word into reproduction proofs. Suppose you were the inventor. Could you design the electronic system so that the voiceprint or the WAY the word was spoken would be translated into the printed repro ? Can sarcasm, irony, the difference between a masculine and feminine voice be evident visually in typography ? Don't say "No" too soon. Maybe the answer is to teach children to read voiceprints from oscillograph tapes instead of the alphabet ?

● ONE VOICEPRINT OF THE WORD "YOU" ▶

or

57

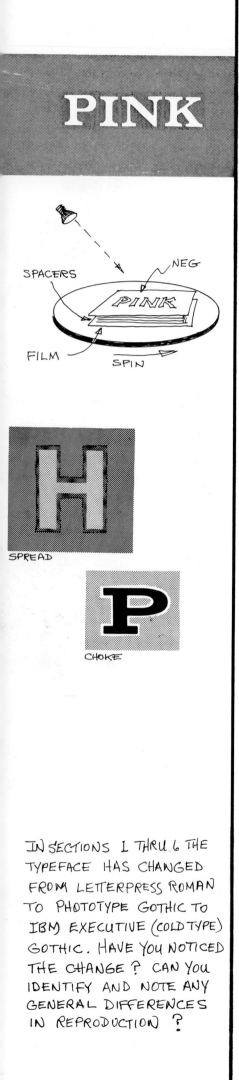

PINK

SPACERS   NEG

FILM   SPIN

SPREAD

CHOKE

IN SECTIONS 1 THRU 6 THE
TYPEFACE HAS CHANGED
FROM LETTERPRESS ROMAN
TO PHOTOTYPE GOTHIC TO
IBM EXECUTIVE (COLD TYPE)
GOTHIC. HAVE YOU NOTICED
THE CHANGE? CAN YOU
IDENTIFY AND NOTE ANY
GENERAL DIFFERENCES
IN REPRODUCTION?

MODIFICATION

When printing heads or body copy in color in a dark background, it
is customary to drop out the type in the background. Then when the
second color (head or copy) is printed, it registers over the dropped
out image and prints directly on the white paper giving a more brilliant color. A pink head, for example, printed over a black background would read very muddy and mottled. However there is a
problem in registration when printing this type of job, as the slightest misregister leaves unwanted leaks between the head and the background. Therefore the printer usually modifies the copy or heads by
SPREADING them. He makes them slightly larger so when he prints
the second color the heads or copy overlap the dropout image by two
or three dots or a 1/32 of an inch and leave no leaks.

One simple way to produce a spread is to place the regular neg over
a piece of litho film in a contact printer with several clear sheets of
acetate between the neg and the film. These are called spacers. A
light is then placed at an angle from the contact frame, and the frame
is whirled on a turntable arrangement while the film is being exposed.
Obviously the light fans out under the spacers enough to make the
image of the type slightly larger on the film under the clear spacers
and this gives you a larger image. If you have used duplicating film
you have a negative ready to go. If you have used regular film you
will have a positive and must make a contact negative before you burn
the plate.

Sometimes the job requires the typography to be smaller than the
dropout area in the background. This is known as a CHOKE.

Remember a SPREAD is a planned LAP
         a CHOKE is a planned LEAK

The student should realize the difference between TYPOGRAPHY and
LETTERING. He should not try to use a lettering book to choose
samples of type faces; nor should he attempt to follow a type specimen
sheet when he is doing freehand lettering. Type is a cast piece of metal
that is inked and stamped on paper with unchanging precision.
Lettering is a unique letter face or word formed by hand in which the
irregularities or characteristics of the artist's "FIST" give it a special
grace. Some typefaces imitate lettering, but they do not yet imitate
the irregularities or individual characteristics of handwriting.

Savor the individuality in lettering and respect it.
Savor the type designer's attention to precision and respect IT.

The lead in pencils is made by mixing refined graphite with pulver-
ized clay which acts as a binder. By using different amounts of
graphite and clay the degree of hardness can be varied. After being
shaped into thin cylinders, the leads are baked and laid into parallel
grooves in a slat of wood. A similar grooved slat is coated with glue
and pressed over the first. The pencils are then cut apart, sanded, var-
nished and stamped with the degree of hardness. A range of hardness
used by artists runs from 4H (very hard), 3H, 2H, H, to F to HB
(medium), to B, 2B, 3B (very soft).

LAYOUT
skills

This section includes the individual layout techniques such as:
tracing techniques, typography lifts, transfers, copy indication, foto
reductions, idea sketches or practice sheets, figure indication, and type
construction.

The advertising designer must learn to use simple inexpensive materials
(pencil, ink, chalk and tempera) to simulate more expensive media.
He must be able to make his layouts quickly. He should understand
also a few basic compositions such as : band, axial, grid, group and
path so his early layouts do not become too random or spotty. These
layout structures can then support the elements used in the ad.

It contains a composite layout problem involving the above elements
with the student selecting his own subjects, making his own composition plans, and producing his final layout.

THE SKILL TO INDICATE SMALL
TYPE OR BODY COPY CAN BE
LEARNED QUICKLY WITH THE

Square pastels or felt markers make excellent tools for indicating the
human figure. The indication strives to show the ACTION,
POSITION, and relative VALUE of the figure in the advertisement.
It should not be concerned with details. The fotogra f of the figure
which is reproduced in the ad later will supply plenty of details. The
emphasis in the visual should be on COMPOSITION.

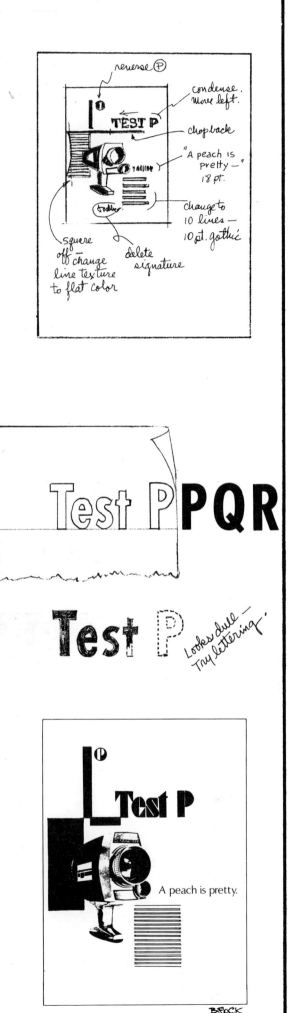

TRACING TECHNIQUES

Much of the work in advertising is concerned with the development of the original idea thru to the finished printed piece. Of necessity, this almost always requires beginning sketches, modification by tracing, redrawing, changes, notes in the margin, and retracings until the idea is jelled. Artists are very aware that tracings from original drawings or photographs never have the feeling or quality of the original. However, in this case, the student must realize that tracings in advertising work are used for many different functions than just attempting to COPY. Tracings taken from the beginning idea sketches often BETTER the drawing, because the trained artist REDRAWS as he uses the tissue overlay. He does NOT slavishly follow every original line. Quick tracings are used to define a shape, or position it quickly in another location.

Altho your bond pad is somewhat transparent, a VELLUM (tooth) finish tracing paper does the job much better. One common use for this tracing technique is to put major and minor headlines in the layouts so the large typography can be judged with the other artwork.

MAJOR and MINOR HEADS

A straight line is drawn on the tracing paper. The tracing paper is laid over the TYPE SPECIMAN sheet (See back of Section 10) with the line positioned at the base of the chosen alphabet. The first letter is traced in OUTLINE. The paper is then shifted until the second desired letter is just to the right and ALMOST TOUCHING THE FIRST LETTER. Continue this procedure until the word is completed. Leave a whole letterspace between and start the next word until the headline is completely traced in outline form. It is not necessary to black in the letters until later. This tracing is called a LIFT.

Now darken the back of this headline with a 2H pencil and rub it with a bit of cotton. This puts a graphite coating on the back of the tracing lift. The tracing can now be positioned OVER the layout and TRANSFERRED by going over the outlines of the letters with a sharp H pencil. Graphite transfer paper can be purchased from an art store if you would rather use that.

If the bond paper is thin enough, the type speciman sheet can be positioned UNDER the bond and the outline of the letters traced directly on the layout.

After the letters are transferred to the layout they are outlined again carefully with an H or 2H pencil to clean and strengthen the edges. Then the letters are filled by using an HB or softer pencil. A 2B probably gives a blacker value to the letters than harder pencils, but it also tends to be coarser and rubs off easier. These softer pencils simulate the BLACKNESS of the printer's ink . The harder pencils give you a cleaner line for EDGING.

The coming Project J – LAYOUT SKILLS, will acquaint you with the variety of things that can be done with pencils and tracing paper. At this point turn to Project J and read thru the entire JOB SHEET at least once BEFORE you start. There are 12 items to be drawn in the 8 X 11 rectangle. Know what they are BEFORE you start the composition of your layout.

LAYOUT SKILLS (Project J)

The following exercises are planned to give the student skills that are
needed in preparing layouts and camera-ready art of all kinds.
All items, in this problem, must appear in PENCIL within the
8 X 11 rectangle on the bond paper even tho some of the original work
will be done in ink or crayon on other paper. Save all original art and
preparatory sketches until the layout is graded.

On a piece of bond paper on your layout pad, lay out an 8 X 11-inch
vertical rectangle with a sharp HB pencil. Use a T-square to insure
90 degree angles at all corners. Bounding lines must be DARK so
they read as a definite border.

Within this rectangle place the following items . If you wish to make
a few smaller compositional sketches before you start, check them with ▶
the instructor.

1. A Roman capital letter 2 -3/16 inch high - black
2. A Gothic lower case letter 1-1/32 inch high - gray
3. One script word traced from a magazine
4. The words "Layout Skills" traced from a type speciman sheet
5. A Gothic caps alphabet (Use a B pencil with a DULL point)
6. A Roman lower case alphabet (Use a chisel point B or HB)
7. A six line block of copy indication 18 picas wide
8. A three inch square of light gray bleeding off edge
9. A drawing of an animal filling the 3-inch square
10. One calligraphic letter no higher than 2 inches - black
11. A kindergarten drawing of a figure no higher than 3 inches
12. A black and white fotograf reduced

Use IMPLIED LINE relationship between the items as you place
them on the layout. That is, relate edges, corners, or centers to other
items. The NEGATIVE (background) areas may be varied in
SIZE and SHAPE to provide more interest. In some cases, when
the items are grouped together, the negative areas between the items
may not be significant because they are so small. Then the silhouette
shape of the total group of positive images becomes most significant.
In general, you must start learning to observe carefully EVERY shape
within your layout whether it is negative, positive or grouped. Individual items, positive shapes, negative shapes (the space between the
items) the total shape of any group of items. This overall awareness
of the TOTAL IMAGE is what makes for organization, interest, and
design in the final layout. Next to your capacity for creating an idea
this TOTAL IMAGE awareness is probably the most important trait
you must develop. With it, you become an artist. Without it, you remain anybody.

1. A ROMAN CAPITAL LETTER, 2-3/16 INCH HIGH

Choose a Roman Old-style letter from a type speciman sheet (See
back of Section 10.) or a magazine and ENLARGE it to the specifications above. By enlarging it you will have to note its proportions
and thus become better acquainted with type faces. Remember the
thin parts of the type face have to be increased in width as well as the
more obvious parts of the letter. Another help is to check the proportions of the NEGATIVE spaces between the staff and stems of the
letter.

TYPOGRAPHERS REFER TO THESE NEGATIVE AREAS AS THE "COUNTER".

For some typical layout structures in thumb-nail form see page 62.

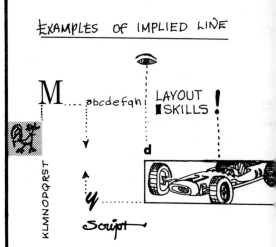

ROMANS THICK AND THIN

gothics SAME WIDTH

EXAMPLES OF IMPLIED LINE

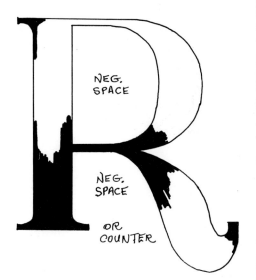

M ....abcdefghi LAYOUT SKILLS !
d
y
Script
KLMNOPQRST

R

NEG. SPACE

NEG. SPACE

OR COUNTER

THUMBNAILS

A good designer is known by the white space he leaves.

AXIAL

GROUP

BAND

GRID

RUSSELL AND BILES.

Serbin

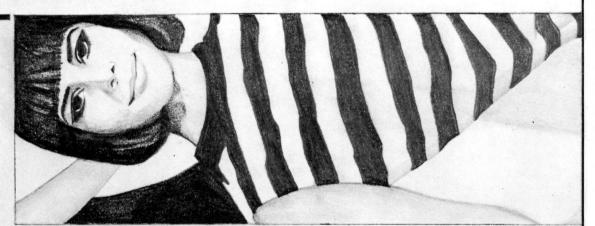

ABCDEFGHIJKLMNO

abcdefghijklmn

LAYOUT

TR Fashions k

LAYOUT SKILLS

abcdefghijklmnopqrstuvw

ABCDE
FGHIJ

MINTZER

Construct the outline on tracing paper. You may use straight edges
compass, ellipse or circle templates, or french curve. In fact, use ANY
tool or aid in these jobs that YOU THINK will do the job faster and
better. After you feel you have a well proportioned, graceful piece of
typography, — transfer it to your layout. Define the edges with a
2H pencil and fill it in BLACK with an HB , B, or 2B.

2. A GOTHIC LOWER CASE LETTER. 1-1/32 INCH HIGH

Choose a Gothic lower case letter from a type speciman sheet or a
magazine and enlarge it to the specifications above. Transfer it into
position on the layout and this time fill it in with an H or 2H pencil.
Build the value up into a medium GRAY. If you do this slowly it will
not looked streaked. (The softer B pencils are usually too coarse and
black to give a soft gray value.) Do NOT DEFINE the edge of this
letter with a line , as you are simulating a typeface printed in a gray
value and there should be no line around it.

3. ONE SCRIPT WORD FROM A MAGAZINE

Choose a script word from magazine scrap. Trace, transfer, and fill
black or gray. Your choice of VALUE will depend on how much
emphasis you want this word to have in the total layout. Another thing
you will notice is how difficult it is to find script words in most publications. The majority of type is set from traditional Roman or Gothic.

4. THE WORDS, LAYOUT SKILLS

Draw a single straight line on your sheet of tracing paper and LIFT the
the words, Layout Skills, from a type specimen sheet. Keep that line at
the BASE of the alphabet as you add letters to the line. Keep the letters that you trace ALMOST TOUCHING and you will solve most
of your spacing problems. One exception is the letter , i, which needs
a little extra room on each side to keep it from getting a squashed look.
Some type specimen sheets contain only part of a sample alphabet, so
you will have to make up missing letters in your tracings from parts of
the others. An R can be made by using parts of a B, a V can be
made from an upside down A, an O from two sides of a C, an E from
an F, an L from an H, etc. To help your observation of type proportion, look for the following:

The crossbar on a capital A is usually slightly lower than center.
The middle crossbar on a capital B is usually slightly higher than
center.
The middle crossbar on a capital R is slightly lower than center.
The crossbar on the top of the capital T is short.

The point of the middle V in a capital M comes all the way down to
the base line.
The point of the middle Λ in a capital W or lower case w comes all
the way to the top of the letter.

The capital M is usually as wide as it is high.
The capital N is narrower than the capital M .
The bottom of a lower case t hooks to the right.
Ascenders and descenders on lower case letters are usually shorter than
the diameter of the body circles.
The thin strokes on the Roman letters A,K,V,W,X,Y, all slant up
to the right

After you have the complete lift, Layout Skills, position it carefully
with IMPLIED LINE relationship to the other items on the layout,
transfer, and fill in black. Don't forget to keep the letters clean by defining the edges first with a hard pencil.

30% gray

80%
gray

Script

See page 60.

layo

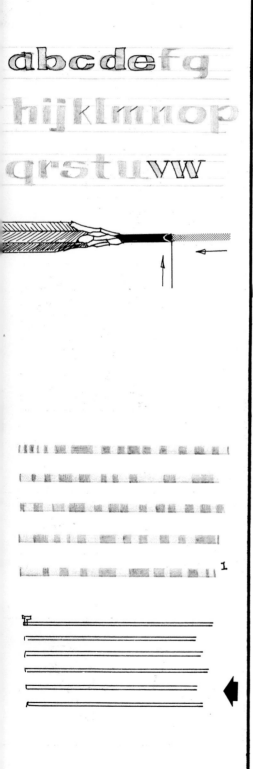

ABCDEFGHIJ KLMNOPQRS

abcdefg
hijklmnop
qrstuvw

1. Mh Mhh luuilhut luuuui w uluu Mlluui.

5. A GOTHIC CAPS ALPHABET, Freehand

Make two LIGHT guidelines 1/4 inch apart. Use a B pencil with a dull point and print FREEHAND a whole alphabet of Gothic Caps. You may break the alphabet if you wish to turn a corner or otherwise change direction of the alphabet to conform to your layout design. But do not STACK the letters like a Cafe sign. Words were meant to be read from left to right, not up and down. It is a good idea to look at a Gothic alphabet before you put the final on your layout and compare your letters with some of the typical proportions.

C
A
F
E

6. A ROMAN LOWER CASE ALPHABET

Use a sharp 3H pencil and T-square on all guide lines. Make two guide lines 3/16 inch apart. Place another guideline 1/16 inch above and one guideline 1/16 inch below the first two. The middle two guidelines are for the body circles, and the top and bottom lines are for the top of the ascenders and bottom of the descenders.

Now cut back the wood on an HB or B for about 1/2 inch. Sand the tip to a two-sided wedge similar to the blade of a hatchet. This gives you a tip that leaves a wide line when you pull it toward you and a thin line when drawn left or right. Print a lower case alphabet within the guide lines holding the pencil firmly and not twisting it. As the tip moves, it will translate vertical strokes into wide lines and horizontal strokes into thin lines. This CHISEL POINT is a very handy tool and allows you to make minor heads in your roughs that have the look of a Roman face.

7. A SIX LINE BLOCK OF COPY INDICATION, 18 PICAS WIDE

Lay the chisel point against the T-square. Slide the tip back and forth with irregular movements, varying the pressure. This will leave a series of light and dark wide lines which simulates a line of copy. Do not raise the pencil from the paper, as this tends to make a series of regular dashes somewhat like morse code which becomes too strong and busy when the whole paragraph is finished. Turn the chisel point over now and then to keep it from wearing away on one side.

Leave a wider space between the lines than the width of one line or DRAG. As in any paragraph of type, there must be enough space above and below the body circles for ascenders and descenders. If you run the drag indication lines too close together, they appear as a solid gray mass on the layout and do NOT give the illusion of type-set copy.

FLUSH the lines LEFT with no INDENT at paragraph start. Make the COLUMN WIDTH approximately 18 PICAS. If the lines are not quite flush on the left, lay the edge of a piece of paper along the left side and erase the ends that stick out beyond the paper. This gives a neat, crisp appearance to the left edge of the paragraph. The right edge may remain RAGGED RIGHT.

There are other methods of indicating typography. .NONSENSE indication, TVTCO — CITH TI HXT TEH is usually used to indicate larger heads which have not been specifically decided upon.

Vertical SCRIBBLE uuu uuu uu uuuuu uuu may be used to indicate the smaller type sizes such as 6 or 8 point.

8. A 3-INCH SQUARE OF LIGHT GRAY, Bleeding off.

It is often useful in preliminary sketches or roughs to indicate a gray or color area with a pencil tone. Oftentimes these color areas are printed to the edge of the ad without margin. Anything printed at the edge of an ad is known as a BLEED

Cut a precise 3-inch square hole in a piece of bond. Position this at the exact EDGE of your layout. Powder some graphite from an H pencil on a scrap of paper and rub a bit of cotton into it. Now rub the cotton on the layout thru the square in the stencil. Rub from the stencil edge toward the center to prevent the graphite from working under the edge and fuzzing the borders. Keep the rubbed tone a VERY LIGHT GRAY so the line drawing of the animal will show up on it.

9. A DRAWING OF AN ANIMAL FILLING THE TONED SQUARE

On a separate sheet of paper draw a series of boxes, 3 inches square. Use a fine pen point and draw your animal in each box using a thin CONTINUOUS LINE. Do not lift the pen from the paper as you draw, and make certain the animal FILLS the box. (If the art director had wanted an animal two inches high only, he would have asked for one that size !)

Do not make the animal in OUTLINE only. Draw through the form by looping in scales, feathers, or whatever he is made of. In other words, the animals are not merely an outline or silhouette; there are wings, arms, rib cages, or muscles that need EXPLAINING in the center of the drawing. So think a bit about these forms or textures and fill the animal up also.

When you have an ink animal that you think fills the specifications, slip it under your layout, position it beneath the light gray square, and transfer the drawing to your layout with a sharp B pencil. The line should be quite dark to simulate the ink. Save your original ink drawing. All original art should be saved until the entire production job, including reruns, is completed. Original art belongs to the agency and is not yours to throw away without permission !!

10. ONE CALLIGRAPHIC LETTER, No higher than two inches

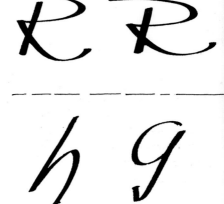

CALLIGRAPHIC refers to any freely drawn or written letter as opposed to a tight constructed form of letter.

On a separate piece of paper draw several light, 2H LIMIT lines, about 2 inches apart, horizontally across the paper. Note that they are called LIMIT lines and not guide lines. They are there to limit the height of the letter but should NOT touch or be used in any way to guide on. Calligraphy must be free in this case, as your handwriting is, and not labored or deliberated over.

Use a square tip, C-3 or C-2 Speedball pen point (or equivalent) with India ink and practice a series of freely written letters both capitals and lower case. Do not PRINT them. Write them, rather rapidly, as you would the letters in your signature. The square tip will give you an interesting varied line from thick to thin. Try holding the pen at different angles. Do not attempt to place the base or top of your letters on any line. Write them freely between the limit lines which are there

WXYZ
E E

TOO LARGE !
OVER LIMIT LINE

COMPOSING L's

TAPE HINGE

MASK

PHOTO

only to keep you from exceeding the 2-inch maximum as defined in the specifications. After you have tried a page of various letters select one that you like. Position it under your layout and transfer it. Fill it in black with a sharp B pencil to simulate the look of ink. Save the original art as before.

A final caution here: Do not attempt to imitate a medieval letterform like Old English Text or Italic Cursive as shown in lettering books. These old letterforms require many hours of work under professional guidance with specific pens. Your objective here is merely to form graceful Roman-Style faces in your own handwriting, so that you can use your natural talents to INDICATE what may be required LATER from a professional letterer or typographer.

11. A KINDERGARTEN DRAWING of a FIGURE, Maximum 3 inches

On a separate piece of paper draw two limit linesspaced to 3 inches. Use a black crayon and draw a girl or boy full figure between the lines, so it appears as if a kindergarten child had done it. Try a number of drawings before you choose the "best" one. If you discover your drawing looks too sophisticated or "old", put the crayon in your left hand and draw with your eyes closed. Position the one you select under your layout, transfer, and fill the lines in with a soft pencil to simulate the black crayon. This time it will NOT be necessary to define the edges with a hard pencil first, because to simulate the crayon coarseness you WANT the edges to remain fuzzy.

Why this item ? There are many instances in advertising when a child's drawing is necessary for illustrating anything from a philosophical viewpoint to a box of crayons. The artist does not have time to run to the nearest elementary school, give directions as to size and shape, and tear back to the agency. Artists have to learn to produce a variety of forms. Each time he is asked to draw some thing, it makes him that much more aware of the "thing" the next time he sees it. After trying this doll you may look with new eyes at your kid sister's drawings. You may even become a collector of children's drawings.

12. A BLACK & WHITE FOTOGRAF REDUCED

Composing and masking

Select a LARGE snapshot, or black and white fotograf from a magazine. Make sure it has whites, grays and blacks.(In this exercise it is important that you learn how to imitate the various grays in a picture, and if you select a weak grayish foto your layout will look flat and you will not have had the experience of copying grays.)

Cut out two paper "L's" about 6 inches on a side and use these to frame various compositions. (Ordinarily an artist selects only a part of the fotograf to use in an ad, as the commercial fotografer gives him an extra amount of background in most prints.) When you have selected a composition that pleases you, clip the L's in position. Cut out a rectangular opening in a piece of bond so the composition is framed within the opening exactly as it is in the L's. Attach this MASK (It masks out the unwanted areas.) as a flap to the top of the fotograf with masking tape. Remove the L's. Do not cut the foto or mark on it. It may be used again for a different ad and remasked without the additional expense of developing another print.

Professionals often use CROP MARKS instead of a mask to indicate the desired composition. These are 8 marks drawn on the white margins of the foto. One set of four defines the top and bottom, The other set defines the left and right side. These are quite satisfactory if the desired composition is square with the borders of the foto. If an angle composition is desired or an irregular shape is necessary, then the exact areas are often drawn on a tissue flap hinged to the foto. Whether the artist uses crop marks, tissue overlay or masks, any rectangular fotograf is referred to as a SQUARE HALFTONE. This differentiates it from fotos which have the background taken away leaving the subject item by itself. These others are known as SILHOUETTE HALFTONES or dropouts and will be discussed later in another problem.

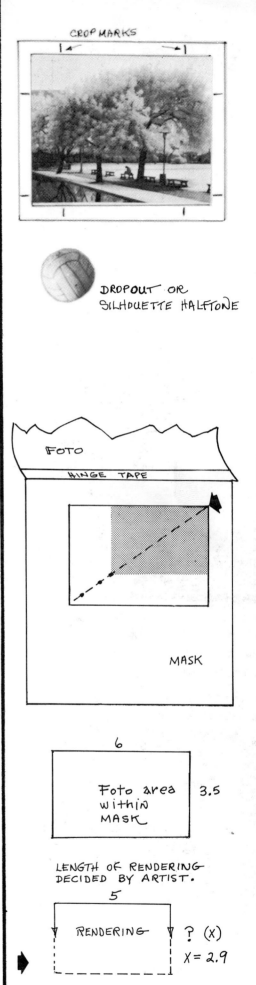

CROP MARKS

DROPOUT OR SILHOUETTE HALFTONE

FOTO

HINGE TAPE

MASK

Scaling

It is difficult to reduce the drawing on your layout in proportion to the foto unless you use a few simple techniques to SCALE down the RECTANGLE first.

SCALING can be done by Geometry or Arithmetic, or by mechanical methods with special instruments.

Geometry Method

Place the upper right-hand corner of the opening in the MASK over the upper right-hand corner of the foto position on your layout. Draw a light diagonal line from this corner thru the lower left-hand corner of the mask. You may locate the lower left-hand corner of the rendering at ANY point on this diagonal line. Shaded area in diagram represents a typical reduced size for the rendering.

Arithmetic Method

1. Measure the width and length of the opening in the MASK. Say it's 3.5 by 6 inches. The next step is to arbitrarily determine ONE dimension of the rendering, preferably the length. Suppose you decide on five inches as a length that would best suit your layout space. Now make up the following equation:

Foto Length	is to	Foto Width	AS	Rendering Length	is to	Rendering Width
6	:	3.5	::	5	:	X (Unknown)

Now multiply the two inside numbers together and divide this answer by the known outside number, 6.

3.5 times 5 = 17.5 ÷ 6 = 2.9 inches, which is X, the unknown, or the width of your rendering.

6

Foto area within MASK

3.5

LENGTH OF RENDERING DECIDED BY ARTIST.

5

RENDERING ? (X)

X = 2.9

Therefore, if you make your rendering 5 inches long and 2.9 inches wide, it will be in proportion to the 6 by 3.5 foto, and you will be able to render the picture smaller without having to distort it to make it fit.

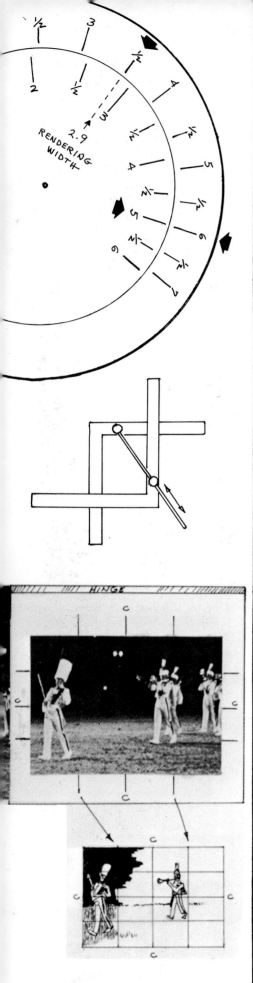

Remember again that the reason most fotos are reduced in production is to keep the final printed picture as sharp and clear as the original foto. Therefore the artist must be able to scale down the fotos so they will appear on the comp just as they appear on the final printed advertisement or brochure.

2. Another arithmetic method is to use the SCALING CALCULATOR (See page 12-2x) Set the rendering length you have decided upon (5) opposite the known foto length. The reading opposite the known (3.5) foto WIDTH will be the correct proportionate rendering WIDTH. You have now learned how to operate a slide rule. Not so difficult, eh ?

Mechanical Method

One mechanical scaler on the market is known as the Scaleograph. It is made of 2 plastic L's joined by a diagonal steel rod that runs thru a swivel locknut on each L. To operate, the two L's are positioned to coincide with the edges of the MASK opening or whatever composition you choose. The locknuts are then tightened to clamp the nuts to the L's and prevent them from swiveling. Thus the angle of the diagonal or the PROPORTION is "locked in". One L can still be slid in or out on the steel rod diagonal. The artist can now slide the rectangle encompassed by the L's to any proportionate size, smaller OR larger than the original mask opening, and simply draw in the rectangle on the layout

Rendering the Fotograf

It sometimes helps in reducing and drawing the fotograf onto the layout to use horizontal and vertical CENTER LINES on the foto mask and on the rendering area. (Do NOT draw on the fotograf.) Or if the foto is rather complex you may want to draw other center lines thru the quarter sections until you have a GRID drawn on both the edge of the fotograf mask and the rendering position. By using center lines within center lines, the proportions of each divided section remains in proportion to the whole. Now you can draw each section of the fotograf in the corresponding section of the rendering.

The rendering should have the same VALUE weight as the fotograf. That is, the darks must be as dark and the grays exactly the same value gray as those in the fotograf. A fotograf often needs CONTRAST (lights and darks) to be effective. If you choose a foto that is weak, washed out or FLAT, or if you indicate the foto by making the rendering pale, the layout will be that much weaker.

Remember to build the grays slowly and carefully with the hard pencils or the drawing will have a coarse GRAINY texture which is usually unwanted if you are simulating a foto with subtle variations in grays and soft shadows. The deep darks and blacks can be laid in faster. You may want to use some of the B pencils to give the darks that extra snap. Save the masked fotograf.

Mat the Layout Skills visual next to the tool rendering. See Section 4, MATTING. Turn in the entire matboard presentation at deadline time. Keep the back neat. Trim that tape !

FIGURE INDICATION (Project K – 3 hrs.)

Select a light gray and a dark gray pastel chalk. Preferably the square stick type, as it can give you sharp edges or thin lines by merely using the corner or edge of the stick. A soft black graphite pencil, a Wolff pencil, or a black pastel pencil are useful for detailing after the MASSES are laid in.

Choose a full figure illustration or fotograf from a magazine, tear it out and slip it under a sheet of tracing paper or thin bond. Work on a PAD surface to get the most gradations out of your chalks. A hard undersurface will make the figure look streaked, and you will have difficulty making subtle gradations of value.

Break off about an inch of one of the DARK GRAY sticks. Use the SIDE of this piece and swatch in the main DARKS of the clothing. Remember, you are only INDICATING the figure's dress, or posture, or action on the layout. Do not copy a rigid outline with the corner of the chalk. You should not attempt to shade with numerous "hen-scratching lines". Stop burying your nose in the paper and squinting at the hemstitching or shoelaces on the figure thru myopic eyes. Relax and see the overall indication.

By pressing harder on one end of the stick you can make variations in VALUE within a swatch. You should complete the figure within ONE MINUTE. Speed is essential in all layout work. The artist that can make four sharp visuals in one day is entitled to TWICE the salary of the artist that can only make two. Try to indicate a man's coat with FIVE strokes of the chalk. Now try it in THREE. Women's skirts can often be indicated in TWO strokes with a few squiggles placed in for pleats, darts or significant wrinkles. If the figure looks too flat, give the arms a light side and a dark side, and the body a light side and a dark side. VALUE change shows FORM.

When you have a reasonable facsimile of the DARK MASSES, break off an inch or so of the LIGHT GRAY pastel and swatch in the face, hands, handkerchief, purse, or any area that you think is a different VALUE or TEXTURE than the clothing. Skin, shoe leather, jewelry, are all examples of items that usually need different treatment than clothing. It is not necessary to treat every texture separately. Ordinarily the two values of gray pastel will do the job.

If the clothing is white or lighter in value than the skin tones or sandals, etc., merely reverse the chalks. Use the light gray to lay in the masses of clothing or bathing suit and use the darker gray to simulate the skin tones. If the figure has a pure white shirt, it is quite effective to leave the white paper for the shirt value and fill in the BACKGROUND with a darker gray. But don't make this background area too large or it will interfere with the silhouette image of the figure.

At the very last, use one of the graphite, Wolff, or dark pastel pencils and add a few SKETCHY details. Rapidly drawn string of small circles will give the effect of a necklace. Darks under the handle of a suitcase, a black bow tie on a tuxedo, a flat slash of dark across a wrist to indicate a wrist watch, drawing a few fingers on a hand, flicking an irregular line around a light gray scarf blowing in the wind, are examples of DELINEATION that help the readability. Keep the detailing CASUAL and SKETCHY.... not labored and exacting. Otherwise you destroy the entire ACTION of the figure which is much more essential than the details.

The purpose of figure indication is to LOCATE and show the relative VALUE of the figure in the composition. The fotograf will supply the details later. Simulate rapidly; don't trace and copy laboriously.

Leave the features in the face OUT. If you feel the head looks too blank, use the CAST SHADOW type of indicating form but do not start detailing every eyelash, each hole in the nose, and each lip. It almost always destroys the entire image. As a student you will undoubtedly learn how to draw heads in figure drawing classes or in Illustration for Advertising. And at the same time you will come to know what to emphasize in your drawings, paintings, or prints. It may be action, it may be texture, it may be a myriad of details, it may be color or facial expression. That will be up to you or the objective of the assignment. BUT in this case, the face is NOT the point of emphasis. These indicated figures are used only to indicate rather rapidly where a figure is to appear, or what the overall silhouette or action looks like in relation to the other positive or negative shapes in the TOTAL IMAGE of the layout. Don't overdo it !

CAST SHADOW indication is achieved by making a dark swatch under the significant protruding feature. For example, the bone or orbital ridge behind the eyebrow casts a shadow over the eyes. A wide gray box-like swatch in the location will give the impression of the sunken eye sockets without having the pupils, irises, and eyelids staring out of the face. A narrow swatch under the nose, under the lower lip, under the jaw line, are all possibilities. But don't overdo it ! Usually one or two of these will give the quick illusion of features without calling excessive attention to them. This same technique can be used to give overhang depth to cuffs, collars, elbows, or a jacket overhanging trousers, etc.

After you have practiced for an hour or so, arrange several of the more interesting figures into a group on a sheet of bond. If you wish, indicate a bit of body copy with drag indication, add one or two headline lifts and you have the start of a fashion ad rough. Place the figures and type with care. Relate them and be aware of the NEGATIVE areas between the items or the ad will be a chaotic jumble and you will be disappointed with the result. Design ALL areas, EVERYTIME you draw !

DAY CO

ROUGH
STUFF
AND
LEVIS

FASHION FIGURE - AMBIGUOUS composition (Optional)

(Review page 54 for understanding of ambiguity.)

1. From a scrap fashion magazine select a single fashion figure in an interesting pose. Place a sheet of tracing vellum over it and make a line drawing from the foto. Now cut out two large composing L's and arrange the drawing within the rectangle formed by the L's so that the negative and positive spaces fight for maximum attention. Draw the border around your selected composition by running a pencil around the inside edge of the L's. Transfer this AMBIGUOUS composition to bond paper.

2. You may add 2 or 3 type letters or a single type word to the layout but RELATE them to the figure and keep them ambiguous also. Letting the edge of a letter coincide with the edge of a garment would be one method of destroying its readability. Another poss - bility is to darken half of the letter face, etc.

3. Lay another sheet of tracing paper over the bond layout and start laying in solid BLACKS and 50% flat grays with your pencils. In the line drawing you used a SPATIAL arrangement to make the ad somewhat ambiguous so far. Now use the pattern of 3 VALUES (black, gray and white) to make the ad even more ambiguous. Perhaps an arm could be black from shoulder to elbow and gray from elbow to finger tips. Perhaps one side of the face or garment could be the same value as the adjacent background value, etc. Feel your way thru the ad by relating and spacing the 3 definite values thruout the **composition**. The type can be treated in the same fashion. It is not necessary to black in every letter.

4. When you are satisfied you have an ambiguous feeling (similar to a double-take) and that it requires more than a passing glance to understand the figure, check this tissue value study with the instructor. After his OK, lay in the values on the BOND and complete the layout by adding a narrow black border. While you work keep a piece a clean paper under the heel of your hand to prevent smearing.

Movies today often start with the titles and credits backgrounded with ambiguous shapes and values or colors that gradually or abruptly change into more READABLE or realistic forms. The public's viewing habits have been conditioned to this "music of form" by years of flat shape animated cartoons with accompanying distortion and abrupt scene changes. Many advertisements and divider pages in brochures are also using a similar double take or way out psychedelic approach. Abstraction and nonobjective art are becoming a real part of our communication system, and you as an artist might as well be sensitive to it, understand it's use, or the public will pass YOU !

PARTIAL TRACING FROM A MAY CO AD PASADENA STAR NEWS

AMBIGUOUS COMPOSITIONS

Made in three values (black, white & gray)
from fashion advertisement tracings

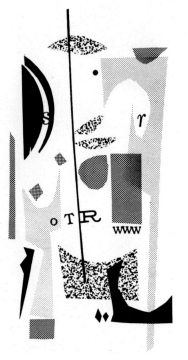

NONOBJECTIVE design units

In basic courses students often think, and the courageous sometime even ask, "Why are we doing this nonobjective design problem ?" "It doesn't seem to have any practical application!"

Many instructors answer questions like this BEFORE the problem is begun. Sometimes a problem dealing with nonobjective units can teach esthetic principles more quickly.

At the same time the student will gradually come to realize there can be creative or viewing satisfaction that is inherent in non-objective work itself. Nothing in the above paragraphs should imply to the beginner that the study of nonobjective shapes or abstraction is ONLY a step toward something of a realistic or "practical" nature. To the contrary... the advanced artist will often find enjoyment in creating or viewing within ALL areas; realistic, abstract, or non-objective. And eventually he will probably find himself arguing philosophically that a nonobjective form is the true esthetic realism. At least the nonobjective form has the honesty of not pretending to be like something else ?

end

VISUALS ⑧

NORDICA

This section contains a composite layout problem involving the items usually found in advertisements: Main head, minor head, fotograf, body copy, trademark, and artwork. Five typical layouts (band, axial, grid, group, and path) are shown which enable the student to better understand negative (white space) & positive (imagery) relationships. The techniques practiced in Section 7 are used now to create his own roughs (Project L) and final comp (Project M). Type specimen sheets at the end of Section 10 may be used for tracing major heads ..

DISTRIBUTED BY BRIAN ARCHERINC

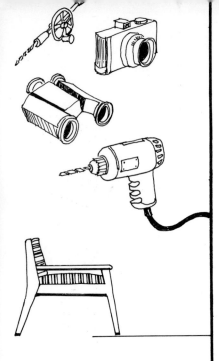

PRODUCT AD

Select a product

Find a black & white photograph, approximately 3 inches high or larger, of a well designed contemporary chair or any other industrial product. For this first problem, do not use a food item or insurance policy or subject that has an amorphous, uninteresting shape.

Let us assume that a client, Brian Archer, has asked you to design an ad for him and has handed you a fotograf of the product he wants advertised. For this book example we have chosen a chair, because it has several different interesting views, and the combinations of metal, wood, or cloth give us interesting textures to demonstrate. However, you may choose any industrial product you think is interesting to you.

Drymount the foto

First of all let us DRYMOUNT the rectangular foto on a rectangular piece of illustration board, leaving at least an inch margin all the way around for later notations. (Do NOT cut around the edge of the product.)

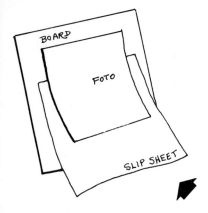

Drymounting tissue is a thin sheet of heat-sensitive glue. Lay the foto face down on a CLEAN surface. Place a sheet of drymount tissue over the back. With the tip of a hot iron TACK the four corners and several other spots of the tissue to the foto back. Pick up the foto and with a scissors trim off the excess drymount tissue all around the edge.

Now position the foto, face up, in the center of the piece of illustration board; lay a clean sheet of bond paper over the face of the fotograf to prevent scorching; and iron the foto flat. Use a regular iron set at the "synthetics" setting and press down hard on the foto for about 8 to 12 seconds. "Linen" setting is often too hot and tends to warp the foto and mountboard.

There are standard drymounting presses on the market, but one is not always available in the classroom.

If no drymounting tissue or iron is available, coat the back of the fotograf and the surface of the illustration board with a thin, SMOOTH, coat of RUBBER CEMENT. Wait until both coats are dry. Position the foto directly over the illustration board, register two corners carefully and press the foto onto the board. When the two surfaces of dry rubber cement meet, they grab immediately and it is almost impossible to get them apart. Artists often employ a clean sheet of bond paper laid lightly between the foto and the illustration board base until the two corners are registered. This prevents the foto from adhering to the base until it is in correct position. Once the corners are registered, the bond sheet is gradually slipped out while the foto is being pressed down on the illustration board. This technique is known as SLIP SHEETING and is extremely useful when mounting large pictures or other pieces of artwork.

Once the foto is down on the board, place a clean sheet of paper over the top of the foto and wipe outwards from the center with your hand to press the foto down tight. This helps eliminate small bubbles or wrinkles that may have been left.

There is a ONE-SIDED rubber cement on the market now with which it is only necessary to coat one side of a mounting unit to get a good bond. This is not old enuf to have been tested yet, but should certainly be considered as a possible time saver.

Flap the foto

It is recognized practice at this time to make a tissue or bond paper FLAP, exactly the size of the illustration board mount, to cover and protect the foto surface. Hinge the flap with masking tape at the top of the mount. CROP MARKS or SIZING can be indicated on this flap also without marking directly on the foto.

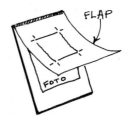

Many industrial fotografers charge $100 per day to clients, or $20 per print. It is very annoying to your client to be asked for another foto print because the first one had ink spilled on it or became wrinkled. The great majority of manufacturers and distributors have a tough time making a profit at the end of the year. They operate within our free enterprise system, which is the best system yet devised to make optimum use of people's spirit, time, and materials. BUT the catalyst for this system is COMPETITION. Your client is competing against his competitors in the field every day in the areas of service and price. And if he is not efficient he FAILS. If you treat your client's production pieces, samples, and brochures with care and show him that you are concerned with his COSTS, then he soons begins to believe that he can expect the highest quality art at the least expense from your office instead of your competitor. And he will probably be right ! Because, if his judgement of costs were wrong too often, he would not be in business. A more efficient competitor would have taken his place !

You have now chosen your product and mounted the foto. We are ready to begin the layout. First, however, we must know the limitations imposed on the job.

A country's wealth is determined by the productivity of its educated individuals ...... not by the gold lying in its vaults.

IBID

PRODUCTION LIMITATIONS

Let us assume that the ad we are going to prepare will be run in TWO COLORS. In advertising, black is counted as a color, because any time paper is run thru a printing press a certain amount of MAKE-READY time is necessary, whether the ink for that job is going to be purple, pink, yellow, or black. With a two color limitation then, we can run Mr. Archer's ad in black and green; rust and pink; green and blue; or any other combination, as long as we don't raise cost by running it thru the press more than twice.

As Art Director on your first ad, I am going to insist that one of the colors on this ad be BLACK. You may choose the other. Do not choose too dark a color, or the specified black line drawing will not show up very well when it is printed over the dark color. (See specs) Choose a HUE of medium value and subdued chroma like yellow ochre. This color that you do choose will be known as the SOLID. Any change of value elsewhere in the ad will have to be lighter than the solid.

These lighter values are known as SCREENS, because they are printed as a screen pattern on the paper which allows the white paper to show thru the tiny pattern of ink dots. (See Section 11 for more information on screens.)

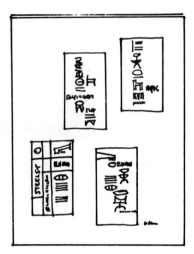

See thumbnails on
page 82 & 83.

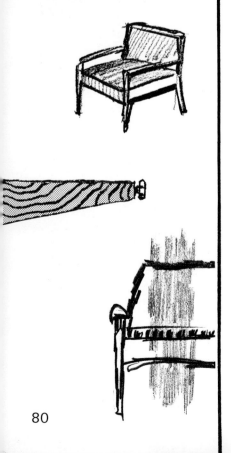

PRODUCT AD ROUGHS (Project L, 4 hours)

Before we make a comp for the client, let us prepare 4 pencil THUMBNAILS. These are small composition plans. The color areas may be indicated by using a bit of cotton rubbed in graphite dust from your pencil. Allow 1 hr. for each.

Lay out 4 thumbnails, 3 1/2 X 6 inches vertical, on a sheet of 14 X 17 bond. Use T-square and exact thin dark borders plus every technique you learned in the previous section to make four different.precise, fresh layouts. Indicate Roman or Gothic alphabets in your headlines with your wide chisel points or with quick constructions. Use crisp DARKS in the product foto indication. Use compass or ellipse guides when necessary in the trademark. Keep the body copy drag indication crisp, LEVEL, and well spaced. Keep the pencil drawings and headline indications BLACK to simulate ink.

Remember to do all the thumbnails in pencil only. No ink or chalk.

SPECIFICATIONS

The design components to be used in these thumbnails are the same as those specified in the final comp (Project M) but scale them down approximately one half by EYEBALLING. In other words, estimate it by eye. Don't spend a lot of time measuring and reducing every item exactly. This is not necessary. The items in these small thumbnails will obviously not be as accurately done as in the later full size visual, but they can be fresh, neat and CLEAN with interesting good sized areas of WHITE SPACE left here and there. In other words, don't let yourself jam all the items together merely because you are working in a small area. Scale items down accordingly as you locate them or you will have a solid mass of pencil lines with no white space left to rest the eye.

At this point STOP. Turn to Project M, **page 87**, and read the entire job sheet. This will help you understand the entire job. Then turn back to this page and continue making up the thumbnails. A few sample layouts are printed here to give you an idea of a variety of structures which can be used to hang your imagery on without jamming everything together. Again, be AWARE of the white space you use in your thumbnails. These negative areas are just as important in design as the positive images you draw in !

Specifications

1. Small picture of the product rendered. Indicate this quickly with darks, grays and lights to simulate fotograf.

2. A line drawing of a detail or part of the product. This to be drawn over a light color area coinciding exactly with the edges of the drawing. This is known as REGISTERED color. The "color" in thumbnails can be indicated by a light tone of graphite ~~usually~~ rubbed on with a bit of cotton thru a stencil if necessary. This light value allows you to judge its shape and value in relation to the composition without immediately resorting to hues.

3. A large line drawing of an ELEVATION of the product. This may bleed off the edge if you wish. Keep the line rugged and interesting. Do NOT use a fine hard mechanical line in this unit. Place this "gutsy" drawing over a ROUGH-EDGED swatch of color. Again this color area may be indicated with a light graphite tone to save time in the thumbnails.

4. Major headline: EVANS Check the type specimen sheets at back of Section 10 and use your type face choice about 1/2 size for the thumbnails.

5. Minor head: Distributed by Brian Archer, Incorporated. Use a chisel point or dull pointed pencil here to indicate this line in Roman or Gothic, whichever you think you will be using in the final.

6. Some body copy. Use level, chisel point drag indication.

7. The model name. Choose or make up a model name and indicate.

8. Circular or elliptical trademark. Use templates for border and Cold-type lifts for monograms inside unit.

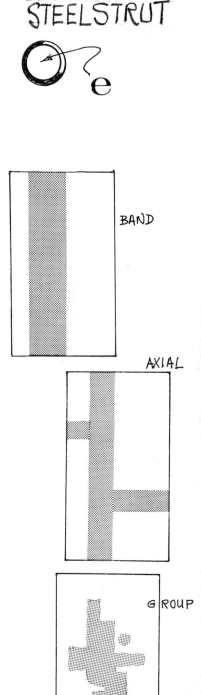

Do three 3 1/2 x 6 layouts as specified below, plus one of your own:
(See examples and description of several typical layouts on next page.)

1. A "BAND" composition (Keep components closed up and packed together. Try to alternate dark & light components. Keep edges flush.)

Note small and large negative "white space" around medium width band.

2. An "AXIAL" composition (Keep background areas varied in size and shape. Keep components closely knit. Don't use diagonals.)

Possibly use one major axis and several minor axes.

3. A "GROUP" composition (Keep the outline silhouette interesting. Keep components almost touching around a mutual center. Huddle 'em.)

4. Your own composition in the fourth rectangle.

Remember a good designer is known by the way he uses WHITE SPACE.

Hand in the four thumbnails at deadline time. The instructor will check them with you and discuss any possible changes. After you and he make a decision and select one, use it as a compositional guide for the 7" x 12" Product Ad Comp. No MAJOR changes in composition should be made without the Art Director's ok.

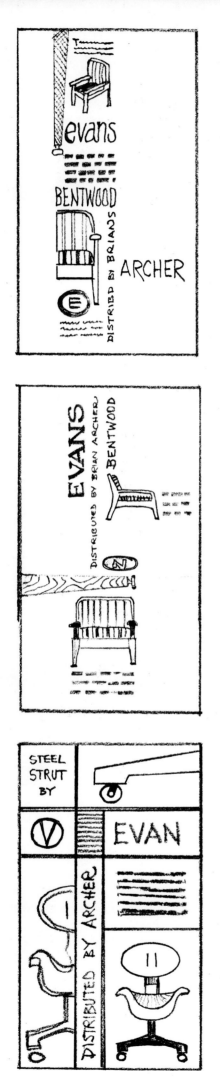

FIVE TYPICAL LAYOUTS

There are, of course, an infinite variety of layouts but these five help the beginner understand SIGNIFICANT patterns or structures and the use of white space or negative areas.

(Avoid strong diagonals in your early work)

BAND

Elements are packed together in a band which may be vertical or horizontal. Keep components tightly packed or slightly overlapped to prevent a spotty, random look. Try not to get all dark values at one end, etc.

An occasional word or item may be placed outside the band area! Note the small, medium, and large negative spaces. Don't make the band so wide it obliterates the whole ad.

AXIAL

Bands are arranged in vertical and horizontal combinations. Keep negative (white space) areas different sizes for more interest.

Note that positive images are different sizes — small, medium and large! There are no diagonals. Borders are clean but strong. Liken an axial layout to a tree, one strong thrust and several weaker or narrower branches.

GRID

Components are placed in separate boxes or rectangular areas which fill the complete ad space. Make your grid lines about 1/16 inch thick. Keep your boxes different sizes and shapes for interest. Avoid diagonals.

Leave air around body copy. Bleeds can be accomplished by edging images against sides of rectangles. Some small rectangles could become areas of color or flat value. If the inside lines are thick keep the border line fairly heavy also — at least be aware of the relationship.

GROUP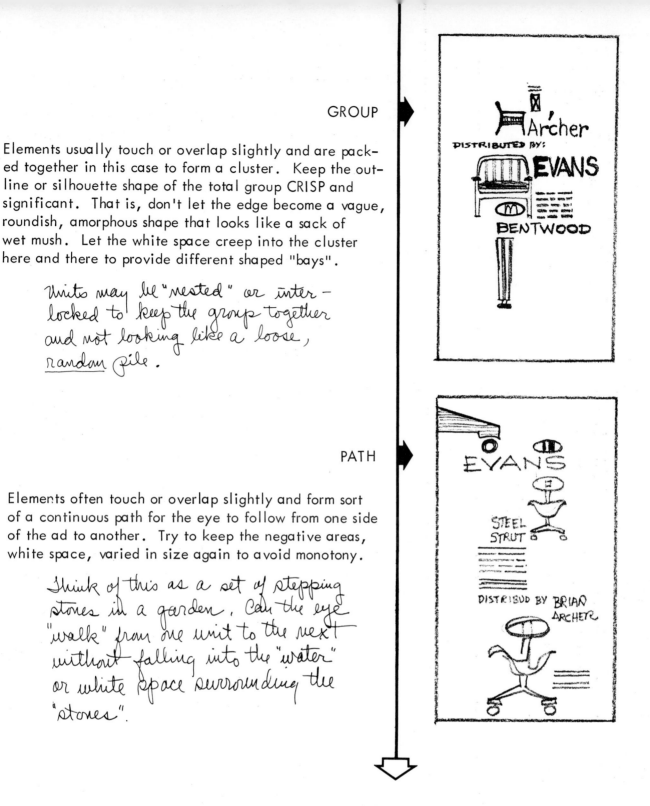

Elements usually touch or overlap slightly and are packed together in this case to form a cluster. Keep the outline or silhouette shape of the total group CRISP and
significant. That is, don't let the edge become a vague,
roundish, amorphous shape that looks like a sack of
wet mush. Let the white space creep into the cluster
here and there to provide different shaped "bays".

*Units may be "nested" or inter-
locked to keep the group together
and not looking like a loose,
random pile.*

PATH

Elements often touch or overlap slightly and form sort
of a continuous path for the eye to follow from one side
of the ad to another. Try to keep the negative areas,
white space, varied in size again to avoid monotony.

*Think of this as a set of stepping
stones in a garden. Can the eye
"walk" from one unit to the next
without falling into the "water"
or white space surrounding the
"stones".*

M

Many agencies feel that roughs are fresher, have more spontaneity than
comps and , therefore, use the roughs exclusively to show the client.
Their philosophy is that the client needs to judge the IDEA ... but not
the EXECUTION. However, to produce good roughs, the beginner is
often helped by having had to complete the precise details required in
a comp. Once he understands the detail, he can INDICATE it with
authority. Without this training, he covers up his lack of understanding
by multiple lines and smears.

ETHICS and POLICY

Before starting the comp on this advertisement, the artist should remember that the essence of good advertising is the TRUTH. Sometimes certain fotografic views or PARTIAL presentations will give false esthetic or false economic values to inferior products. That is, the quality of the product advertised is purported to be better than the product really is. Thus each new artist must answer for himself: Does he, the graphic artist, fulfill his purpose of presenting a product truthfully, or does he pervert his ethics by falsifying the value of the product ?

The character of the graphic artist is the key link in the entire problem. Most experienced artists and managers have discovered that products make profit for the client by REPEAT sales in a satisfied market. Advertising alone will never create a repeat market for a poor product. Good advertising CAN create larger markets for good products. Do the job truthfully, and the sales results will reflect the product image that much faster. Untruthful exaggeration in advertising often causes early spurts in sales which lead to over-enthusiasm, premature decisions, resultant overinvestment and bankruptcy in beginning businesses.

If the experienced artist or manager can educate other members on the staff to these "Facts of life.", there will be much less pressure to exaggerate product claims. Advertising must be truthful, or it is WORSE THAN USELESS !

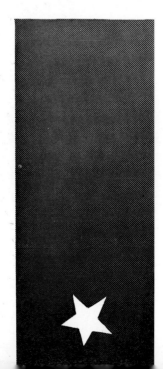

EVANS

YORK

Distributed by Brian Archer

EVANS

THERE ARE HUNDREWHEN I CARRY ON CONVERSA-
BUCKET-SEAT CHAIFTIONS OR READ, BUT THE BUCK-
THE MARKET. PERSON/ET KEEPS ME OFF THE "EDGE
PREFER THE NON-BUCKETOF MY SEAT". IT PREVENTS MY
I LIKE TO MOVE ABOUTCOMFORTABLE AFTER DINNER

YORK

DRIVER IN A VISE-LIKTHE MARKET. PERSONALLY I
WHILE HE CAROMS APREFER THE NON-BUCKET STYLE.
THE GRAND PRIX. BUI LIKE TO MOVE ABOUT A BIT
HOME — JUST AN ORIWHEN I CARRY ON CONVERSA-

DISTRIBUTED BY BRIAN ARCHER

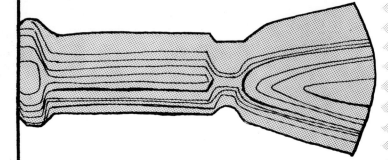

PRODUCT AD COMP (Project M – 12 hrs)

Before you start you may want to make a quick full size black and white rough (7 x 12) of the chosen thumbnail . If not, start directly on the full size comp.

Follow your chosen thumbnail layout as a compositional guide and make a 7 x 12 - inch visual, centered on your bond pad and using the following elements. Remember to keep in mind the TOTAL IMAGE of negative spaces, edge relationships, and value considerations. DESIGN as you draw.

Elements:

1. A small rendering of the product in pencil to simulate the dropout fotograf slightly reduced. (A fotograf of a product without background is referred to as a SILHOUETTE halftone, and sometimes as a DROPOUT or KNOCKOUT.)

2. A precise drafting-board line drawing of a detail in pencil to simulate ink, such as a knob, arm, or handle. This should be larger than the rendering above. (Vary sizes of images for interest.)

You may wish to emphasize textural details like woodgrain or woven cloth to add to the interest of your layout. This drawing may be a bleed also.to help split up the negative areas. Draw this detail over a swatch of your chosen SOLID color. This color should coincide exactly with the edges of the detail. This type of color usage is called REGISTERED color because its edges COINCIDE with the edges of the drawing.

3. An ELEVATION of the chair or product in an EXPRESSIVE pencil line. (Elevation means a side, back or front view, head on, with no perspective used to show depth.)

Show a different elevation of the product than is shown in the fotograf, and use an irregular, varied line that has an interesting quality instead of that even drafting – board line. This drawing may bleed off the edge if you wish. Make it smaller or larger than item 2 above so your images are not all the same size.

Draw this OVER a ROUGH EDGED pastel swatch of the same HUE as your solid but about 50% lighter in VALUE. This type of color usage is called NONREGISTERED color, because its edges do NOT coincide with the drawing.

87

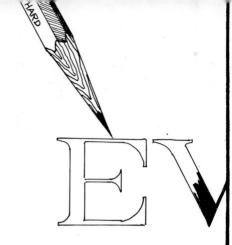

4. The headline: EVANS

Select the face from the type specimen sheets at the back of Section 10 and make a lift in pencil. When you transfer or trace this lift on to your layout remember to use a hard pencil for the outline to keep the edges clean and use a softer pencil to fill the letters BLACK. Select a size between 48 points and 96 points. This would give you capital letters ranging between one-half inch high to approximately an inch high. You will have to look for these in the HANDSET section of the specimen sheets, because the LINOTYPE section has type sizes up to 24 point only.

5. The minor head: Distributed by Brian Archer, Incorporated

This may be CAPS or Clc (Caps & lower case). Select a face about 18 or 24 points. Instead of making a lift of all these small letters, letter it in freehand by using your chisel point HB and the four 3H guidelines. Press hard enuf to be certain it is dark so it will read as TYPE.

6. Some body copy

Let us imagine that the copywriter has been told to write enuf copy to fill an area of eight square inches if 10 or 12 point type is used. This means that you must leave a space in the layout for a column 2 inches wide and 4 inches deep, or 4 inches wide and 2 inches deep, or the equivalent area. The body copy may be split into two blocks, but the total area of separate blocks must remain approximately 8 square inches.

Use drag indication with T-square and chisel point. Flush it left and/or right OR ragged both sides. Do not let the right-hand edge or left-hand edge become slanted. This STEP-DOWN type set is very difficult to incorporate esthetically into most ad layouts. The DIAGONAL edge seems to run counter to the horizontal and vertical implied design in most layouts. In general, try to avoid long 45° violent diagonals in your early layouts. A short or minor diagonal motion is fairly easy to handle for the beginning student, however. In other words , a line 5 to 10 degrees off the vertical or off the horizontal can add a little variation to the stiff checkerboard of all verticals and horizontals, but long 45° diagonals act almost like an explosion. Beware of them for a while !

7. Model name in solid color

Choose a model name for your product. Bentwood or Steelstrut might be applicable to a chair. Woodsman ? for an axe, etc. Select the face and size of the type you want to use from a COLD-TYPE catalog. Note the number of the sheet so the actual wax-backed sheet of letters can be purchased later from an art supply store. Make a lift from the catalog sample and trace the model name on your layout in the SOLID COLOR. Use sharp colored pencils here to retain the clean edges of the simulated type. (Remember the color swatches under the product drawings and the color of the model name must all be ONE HUE. You can vary the VALUE of the color under the detail drawing, but not the HUE.)

If there is a scrap box of cold-type sheets available in the classroom, you may be able to get enuf letters for the model name from it without buying a sheet. If so, make your lift from the scrap sheets.

NOTE: Advanced art schools often do not allow their students to to use cold type. They feel it is better for the student to become acquainted with the hot type faces which are used most in industry. Also, by having to trace and re-transfer letters and words by his own hand and eye without resorting to mechanical devices and aids, the student learns more about the esthetics of type design itself, and thus becomes a better designer earlier. However, students should know what cold type is, recognize its use, and realize it is used in many different instances for quick make up, operational manuals, and small jobs all over the United States. As an artist it is your job to know all things and THEN have the esthetic judgement as to what to use, where, and when !

8. Trademark (Logotype or Logo)

Logotype used to mean two or more letters cast together and from this definition gradually came to identify with the word Trademark which was often the initials or several letters of the company name placed in a design to form a mark as the company's symbol.

Trace on tissue the outline of one or two letters from the same cold type alphabet you used for the model name if you wish. Let this logo or monogram appear REVERSED in a medium gray disc bounded by a thick black circle or ellipse. This word 'reversed' means that the letters in the monogram or logo are to appear the color of the paper (WHITE in this case) against the gray of the disc. It does NOT mean to FLOP the letters from left to right and thus have them read backwards.

Use a circle template to make two concentric circles and fill in black between the circles. OR use an ellipse guide to draw two concentric ellipses. Two concentric ellipses do not parallel each other like the circles do, so if you do not want the thick-thin border, you will have to "fudge" a bit by moving the guide a bit to the right when drawing the left half of the outside ellipse, and a bit to the left when drawing the right half. One practice ellipse will make it obvious.

Transfer the logo or monogram into the center as outlines only. Now fill in between the outline of the white letters and the black border with a 2H pencil building up an even 50% (medium) gray.

NOTE: In advertising the artist is sometimes given a logo or symbol or piece of old fashioned design that is very irregular in silhouette or unpleasant in other design elements. This item is apt to be very distracting when placed with other elements in the ad. One way to cope with this problem is to reduce the obnoxious item slightly and surround it with a circle, square or ellipse. The unit can then be incorporated into most layouts with a minimum of disunity.

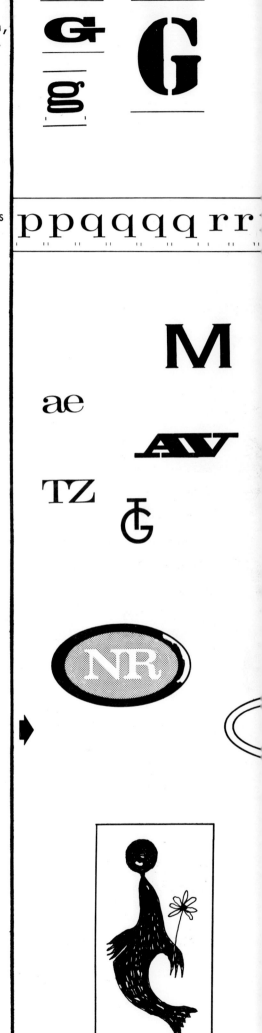

Leave this comp on the full 14 x 17 bond sheet and hand it in unmatted. Make certain it has a good thin, dark line around it as a border to divorce your layout from the extra white space around it. After being graded it will be matted later on the same mat board with the mounted MECHANICAL.

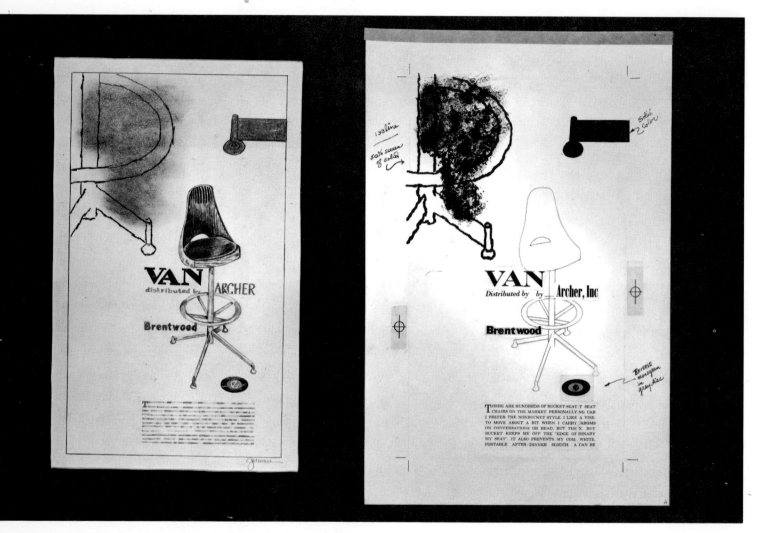

PACKAGING LAYOUTS

Packaging takes many different forms today. The graphic artist is called upon to prepare layouts for cellophane bags, cardboard boxes, bottle labels, corrugated packing cartons, metal cans, gunny sacks, and railroad tank cars. A good graphics man can handle most of the above types of design problems. The design principles are much the same as those that have been emphasized in the previous flat ads. Attention to negative spaces, grouping of positive items, implied line relationship between edges or other facets, value considerations, the ground on which it will be printed, texture awareness, and color.

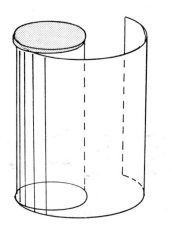

If, however, this same artist is asked to design the ENTIRE container, then he must seek outside assistance. Finding an economical method to form a special bottle, fold an intricate display package, or extrude a plastic tube, is the role of the INDUSTRIAL DESIGNER. The graphic artist must understand quite completely the various methods possible to manufacture such a container so that he can compare feasibility and costs BEFORE he commits himself or his client.

Very often the artist receives help from the client himself who has packaged similar items in the past. But if you are embarking alone on the problem of designing a unique container of any type, be warned that there are many production problems in forming three-dimensional objects that may not occur to the artist experienced primarily in the flat graphics. Machinery limitations, die cuts, molds, paper grain, stretch problems in embossing or forming paper or metal, are all areas that will have to be taken into consideration by someone who knows.

Take your time on the first job and learn more than one way to accomplish the problem. If you don't, you will have no way to determine whether you are doing it the most economical way or not. If your client's competitor comes out two months later with a similar package at one half the cost, he has a good chance of underpricing your client. Pennies are still very important to housewives buying packaged merchandise.

basic FORMS

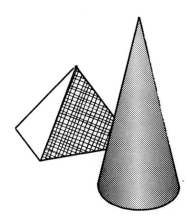

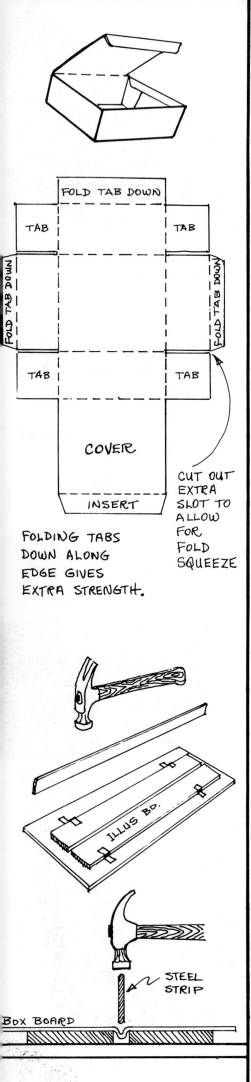

FOLD TAB DOWN

TAB   TAB

FOLD TAB DOWN

FOLD TAB DOWN

TAB   TAB

COVER

INSERT

CUT OUT EXTRA SLOT TO ALLOW FOR FOLD SQUEEZE

FOLDING TABS DOWN ALONG EDGE GIVES EXTRA STRENGTH.

ILLUS BD.

STEEL STRIP

BOX BOARD

PACKAGE COMP (Project N – 12 hrs)

If a visual or comp is supposed to be the closest approximation to the real ad that the artist can make within a given time, then an actual formed package is probably the best way to present a packaging idea. The type and design may FLOW all around the box, or each side may be a separate design facet. That is up to you. Use type lifts from the Type Specimen Sheets (Back of Section 10) or magazine pages. Do NOT make up your own letter faces. (You are not a type designer.)

Make your first visuals or roughs on the bond pad using typographic lifts plus square pastels, pastel pencils, or graphite pencils. The beginning artist always seems to use a white background with wobbly India ink lines because the box board is white and ink is handy and contrasty. In other words he doesn't SELECT, he merely does the first thing that comes to mind and thus ends up with a dull stereotype.

Therefore I usually insist that the box be any color other than white or black, and that the rough must not have India ink lines on it. Speedball pen lettering is not allowed on this problem. This is a hot type specification job and lifts MUST be used. After the instructor approves your rough, start on the comp.

Spread the box pattern out flat on a piece of BRISTOL BOARD, or RAILROAD BOARD, or BOX BOARD. (These are typical names for rather stiff cardboards which can be SCORED and bent at right angles without cracking.) Trace the pattern perimeter on the box board and then cut the pattern out of the board. On a mockup of this nature leave extra large flaps so it can be glued together without popping open after a few days. On the back of the box pattern draw a thin FOLDLINE at the corner edges and base of all flaps wherever a fold is to be made.

At this point the boxboard can be scored:

SCORING JIG

To make a scoring jig you will need two pieces of illustration board about 18 inches long and 4 inches wide; a steel strip or rule about 12 to 24 inches long, an inch wide, and 1/32 or 1/16 - inch thick; and a hammer.

Place the two pieces of illustration board side by side leaving 1/8 inch space between their edges. Tape them down on a piece of scrap cardboard to hold them in place. This leaves a groove about 18 inches long and 1/8 inch wide along the top of the jig. Now lay the box-board face down over the groove so that one of the fold lines you drew in previously coincides with the groove. Place an edge of the steel strip over the fold line and strike the top edge of the steel strip with the hammer. This drives the edge of the steel strip into the groove forcing the box board into a U shape at the fold line. Remove the steel strip and you will find that the board can now be bent at the fold line to a right angle without cracking. Finish scoring all folds.

BEFORE the box is folded, transfer your layout on to the boxboard and finish it with drymounted color paper, casein paint, or whatever media you feel will do the job. The surface of some of these boards is often very smooth. You may have to coat the board with several layers of WORKABLE FIX if you are using paints. This helps keep the paint from streaking. To prevent the paint from cracking at the corner edges during assembly, it is sometimes better not to paint over the scored edges. After assembly you may wish to touch up the corner edges or , if you wish, they can be left white. The thin white corners do not seem to detract from the presentation usually. Many package designers use the color coated papers for the large areas instead of the wet paints which tend to streak and warp the sides. Transfer-type in black, white, or color is sometimes available for use over the coated paper depending upon the instructor's specs.

It is also possible to do do your finished artwork on another sheet of ILLUSTRATION BOARD; cut around the design with a razor blade; and then carefully tear up the TOP PLY surface of the illustration —➤ board. These prepared rectangles can now be DRYMOUNTED directly on to each corresponding section of the boxboard cut-out, leaving about 1/8 inch space at all fold lines. These single-ply drymounted rectangles are thin enuf so they do not project from the surface of the box, yet they allow the scored fold lines to remain exposed and provide neat sharp corners after assembly.

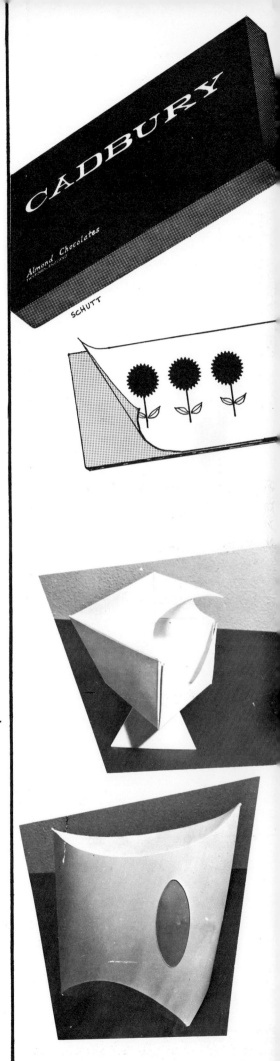

PACKAGES as SCULPTURE

Classroom experiments in forming packages are often quite helpful to the student in aiding him to understand three dimensional displays of all types. He learns to relate weight and strength of paper stock to the size of the comp. He becomes aware of paper grain and how it affects stresses in a complex package form, etc.

As an analogy to better understand this problem let us take a look at the ceramic pot. The clay pot is itself a form of packaging but in many cases has outlived its utilitarian function of water holder, cooking utensil or seed storer. It has become an object of art, a piece of design to look at and handle and approaches sculpture in its contemporary function. Visual and tactile sensation are the pot's reason for being today.

Just for fun let us apply this point of view to modern packages and assume that in 1000 years packages may have lost their meaning as containers also, and developed into a facet of sculpture known as volume enclosures which people collect like pots ??

So we start off with a few sheets of snappy white bristol board or other white board and start evolving interesting shapes without distorting or "torturing" the paper to the cracking or splitting point. The "packages" may not pack a neat dozen to the case, they may be impossible to open, the design might give a die cutter ulcers, but the students agreed that if "it" enclosed a volume and was not decorated by extraneous pieces stuck on for ornament or fins, we could define it a package.

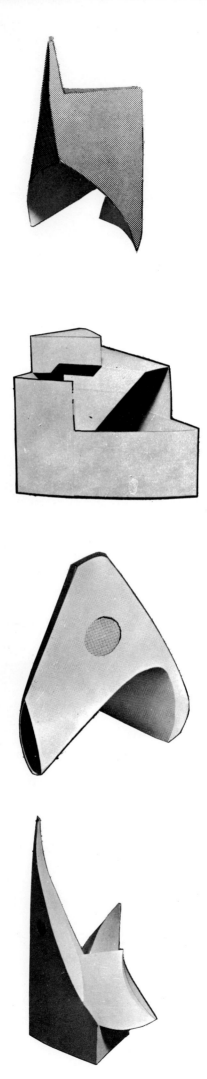

Step one should probably be using a scissors and a piece of white construction paper. Cut, score by drawing a dull table knife along the fold lines, and bend or curve to make a few small models. (Drawing is an almost useless approach to this problem.) Make these first models rather small (as construction paper is thin and weak) say about 6 inches high. The models should also be ASYMMETRICAL so a variety of folds , curves, and twists can be experienced by the student as he forms the paper. Leave tabs for joining edges and try to make the entire form out of ONE piece of paper, not more than two.

After the models have been discussed with the instructor, unfold one, enlarge it proportionately (See diagram) and transfer it to your board. This is rather easy to do if you enlarge each dimension by a simple proportion like 1/4 or 1/2 or double. Use the scoring jig on the score lines and tape, staple, tab, or glue it together very carefully. Wash those hands !

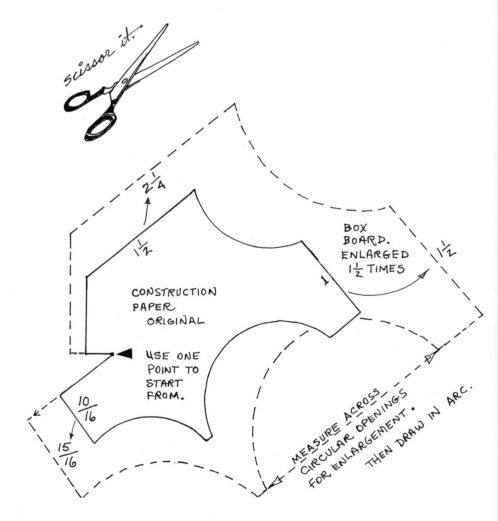

scissor it.

$2\frac{1}{4}$

$\frac{1}{2}$

CONSTRUCTION PAPER ORIGINAL

USE ONE POINT TO START FROM.

BOX BOARD. ENLARGED $1\frac{1}{2}$ TIMES

$1\frac{1}{2}$

1

$\frac{10}{16}$

$\frac{15}{16}$

MEASURE ACROSS CIRCULAR OPENINGS FOR ENLARGEMENT. THEN DRAW IN ARC.

After the shape is assembled it may be fotografed or viewed for its sculptural effect alone. If you wish to carry the project further, the various surfaces could accept fotos, type, calligraphy, drawings, or other textures. Some of the shapes and cutouts shown here demonstrate a few approaches to this package topology. Sometimes the student must consider esthetics of form completely isolated from "practical" function restrictions or he may NEVER see beyond the cube and the cylinder in packaging. Before the type or designs are transferred to the "package", a perspective rough and at least two elevations of the proposed additions must be okay'd by the instructor.

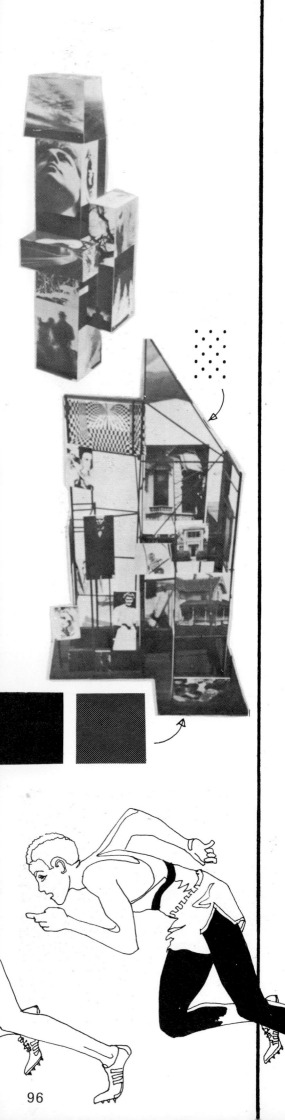

OPTIONAL PROBLEMS

1. Die Cut Display Package

Use a piece of boxboard or equivalent and package 6 spheres such as, tennis balls, lemons or Christmas tree ornaments. The package must be one piece, die cut, with handle an integral part of the construction. Package must DISPLAY spheres when hung on store rack.

2. Photographic Monument

Use black and white fotografy (your own or magazine scrap) plus a minimum of typography on a 3-dimensional surface to make an interesting KIOSK. You may use a unifying theme throughout the fotografs or stay strictly to design, that is up to you. (It is sometimes quicker to search thru magazines for interesting fotos first... then pick your theme.)

Mount the fotos neatly on flat or curved surfaces and build the structure so that it can be viewed from all sides. Neatness in mounting and STURDINESS are the main technical problems in the structure. The cardboards may be slotted or tabbed or glued to slats of wood to keep the structure rigid.

Esthetically one of your major problems will be the placement of the lights and darks in the fotos in relation to each other. As you weld many fotografs into one monument relate dark edges to dark edges; paths of grays, darks or whites with paths of similar values in other fotos to gain unity. Dropout fotos can often be interlocked with type to provide effective silhouette forms to gain attention and provide interesting areas. AMBIGUITY can be effective here also.

While you are choosing and composing the fotos you will notice how gray the blacks are and how dirty the whites look in most magazine printed fotos. Laying a piece of brilliant white paper and a coal black swatch of paint next to these fotografs will illustrate the lack of value range within most printed fotography. The everpresent white dots in the screened blacks and the black dots in the screened whites of all halftone reproduction (See Section 14 under Printed Halftones.) are the cause of the gray mushiness of most halftone reproduction.

3. Split Unit Posters

Select an event concerned with motion. Hockey, ballet, skiing, car racing, etc., might provide interesting shapes. Choose one or two performers involved in the sport or event from magazine or newspaper scrap and enlarge the shapes to poster size. Cut the shape vertically to provide two interesting silhouettes and position these two parts so that they intersect at the edge of the poster when two posters are placed side by side. See examples. State event, where and when.

When you have finished a full size rough in pencil on white background start laying in FLAT color and try to retain the impact of the positive and negative shapes on the poster plane surface. Do not try to paint in all the details of the figure or racing car. Don't model and shade and overuse perspective. Keep the shapes flat and rely upon the type to put the message across. Let the interesting shapes be the attention getters but not the interest gatherers. When you have finished the color visual, choose a toned matboard for the final two comps. This will give you a flat unstreaked color as background and save you time. Do not use poster board on this project as it accepts thumbprints too readily and does not clean up from rubber cement smears readily.

Finish the two comps by using paint or colored paper for the large flat areas and good lifts with clean edges for the heads. You will undoubtedly discover it is rather difficult to make two posters exactly alike that interlock. One poster is easier because you do not have to MATCH shapes and colors. Don't forget those negative spaces should be as interesting in shape as the positive shapes of the performers.

J. RODGERS

B. JOHNSON

4. Children Story Illustration

Choose a location that might be interesting to a child like a zoo or farm. Make a list of all the things that he might see there. Divide your page or double page spread up into various areas with the emphasis on the vertical and horizontal and within these areas place the various items on your list. Draw them flat and use geometrical shapes only. Do not try to draw a realistic horse. Construct him with a rule and compass, maybe a french curve, but keep the design flat.

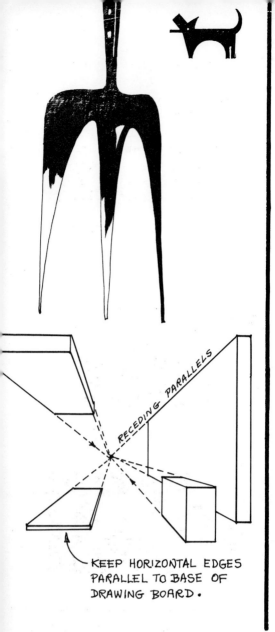

RECEDING PARALLELS

KEEP HORIZONTAL EDGES
PARALLEL TO BASE OF
DRAWING BOARD.

Now paint in the areas by using flat subdued colors such as yellow ochre, dull greens, raw umber, burnt orange, etc., with perhaps an occasional bit of bright color. This is a good exercise in mixing a variety of subdued colors and still retaining contrast for readability. The graying of all the colors gives you unity and harmony in the page. The child will still have a good time pointing out all the different items such as pitchforks, chickens, windmill, etc., that are represented as symbols of geometric form. Oftentimes a young artist has a long way to go before he draws with authority and his illustrations often have a stiff, traced look that radiates "corn". On the other hand by using his ability to compose and select color he can often come up with interesting illustrations based on design rather than relying upon his weaker talent of drawing. As the years go on he will be able to incorporate more of his drawing and weld all his talents together, but it is often helpful to the young artist to recognize his strengths as well as his weaknesses and rely on his strengths when faced with a deadline.

5. Architectural Rendering (Single point perspective)

Draw the front view of a house in single point perspective. (All para-llel lines go to the single vanishing point in the center of the picture.) Instead of thinking of a regular flat faced house, let the picture be composed of free standing walls, flat roofs, open patios, set-in vest-ibules, one or two ceramic forms, a flat tree, etc. In other words develop the picture with a set of planes both vertical and horizontal to give you the chance to draw these various planes in perspective and at the same time compose in DEPTH. Whereas in the previous Children Story Illustration or Poster you were attempting to hold the picture plane FLAT, now change and attempt to lead the eye INTO the picture and out and around. The silhouette form of the total

house or image is still important and projections of trees or chimneys etc., are often helpful in preventing the house from becoming a dull mushy square, but added to this now is the designer's job of getting the viewer's eye to wander into the picture and out again.

Use rulers and keep all vertical lines at right angles with the bottom of the page, but all lines <u>receding</u> into the picture should be drawn so they point directly at the single vanishing point in the center of the picture.

When it is completely drawn, transfer it to a piece of illustration board and paint it. Sign your name to it so that it relates to the rendering. Use some cast shadows for form definition but don't overdo it.

Note the change in type. The computer-set, fototype below is set with more precision in letter spacing. The cold-type, typewriter face at the left is more irregular. Readability ?

I'll leave that up to you.

6. Trademarks

The better trademarks, or logos, speak a universal or international language through their symbolism. (See page 116 for general information on symbols.) However, the effectiveness of a trademark usually depends upon the amount of exposure it is given by its distributor. For example, IBM is the trademark of International Business Machines. Although surveys have shown that it is one of the most recognizable marks in the world, this is probably due to its massive, world-wide distribution rather than its design symbology.

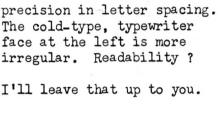

Canadian National, a railroad corporation, uses this trademark all over Canada on its trucks, rail cars, locomotives, and office stationery. Besides the initials, CN, this mark also embodies the suggestion of a railroad track or system in its configuration. Thus it has more of a symbol quality than the IBM mark does.

A mark of Southern California Edison, a company supplying electricity. The letters, SCE, in the form of an electric plug, give the company a definite image characteristic of electricity. This makes it a more powerful symbol.

This image of paper flowing over rollers becomes a symbol for the Noland Paper Co., Inc. However, it still has a faint suggestion of the letter n in its shape, which helps to identify and connect it to the Noland Company.

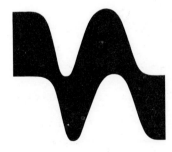

This is a pure symbol. There are no letters to tie it into the institution's name, and it might be misunderstood as a symbol for peace or a pigeon-racing club as well.

DOVE deli^very

**alaskan
enterprises**

The best logos tend to be simple and significant. The amateur designer usually tries to put too much into the mark. To prevent excessive detailing, use a wide, black, felt-tip marker and cover a few pages with quick ideas, using 10 or less strokes. Another approach is to use an X-acto knife or scissors with black construction paper and cut out letter or symbol shapes WITHOUT drawing or tracing lines on the black paper. (See page 54 for project on ambiguity.) Ambiguity, as in the Noland Paper Co. logo, can be very effective in designing trademarks. But, mainly, the scissoring or cutting first, without drawing, forces the novice to produce more significant, gutsy, graphic silhouettes. The thin lead pencil, in the beginner's hand, seems to foster too much "embroidery," and insignificant detail.

To indicate the typography that often goes with a logo on a letterhead rough, use a chisel-point pencil between light, 4H guidelines. Keep your letters small. Eight-to-ten-point lower case or small caps are best. Many young designers don't realize how small the type is on most letterheads and other office stationery.

FALCON GT 817 ALAMO AVENUE, COLUMBIA, TEXAS 77014

Printed type is about twice as powerful as your chisel will indicate, because of its crispness and blackness. So don't let your rough type indications overwhelm the page just because you haven't sanded your pencil point down narrow enough.

FALCON GT 10 WEST ROAD, COLUMBIA, OHIO 44117

When producing a comprehensive, artists often use a crow-quill or other fine ink pen to indicate the typography.

132 WEST FIRST STREET, SUITE 207, LOS ANGELES, CA 91002

132 WEST FIRST STREET, SUITE 207, LOS ANGELES, CA 91002

formosa jade

132 WEST FIRST STREET, SUITE 207, LOS ANGELES, CA 91002

✳ Note that the Alaskan Enterprises logo has a certain feeling of the carved, pole totems of **Alaskan** Indians. The typeface of Falcon GT is suggestive of the eye of the Falcon, while the negative area in the Formosa Jade trademark resembles a Chinese character. Subtle design relationships, such as these, help identity.

100

7. Action Studies

Arrange several figures in action within a 9 x 12 layout. Use touches of symbology to clarify your meaning. For example, in the sample below, even though the action is presented rather abstractly the sock stripes, the laces on the ball, the numbers on the shirts, and the shirt stripes all act to say "Basketball". Symbols of action, even though presented ambiguously, help identify and integrate the composition into a comprehensive whole. Without touches like these the layout is often apt to end up a mass of incomprehensible lines.

EDGE OF TORN TISSUE

TRACING PAPER NEGATIVE:
PENCIL LINE & SHADING
PLUS INK STOPOUTS.

COXE

9 X 12 BROWNLINE

We are going to work on tissue in this problem and make a paper "negative" which we will use over a piece of brownline proofing paper to come up with a reverse set of images.

Brownline paper is a slow fotografic printing paper with a brown tint. A package of 100 sheets, 12 x 18, may be obtained at a printers supply firm. It costs about eight dollars, so at eight cents a sheet it is a very inexpensive fotografic material for the student designer to use. Another advantage is that this proofing paper can be handled in room light, developed in water (no chemicals needed), fixed in a solution made with two quarts of water and a tablespoon of Maduro Salts (Cost about $1 per can.) and can be dried between paper towels.

Step I. Research and Separate Tracings

Select two or three figures in action from magazine scrap. Sports magazines or newspaper fotos are good sources. If the figures are too large or too small use the Lucy or freehand them down or up for better size. Sometimes parts of figures can make interesting action also. Keep all the figures from one sport or one similar action such as, all spacemen or all falcons, or all lacrosse players as this makes for more continuity of action. The figures below were chosen to show the three different techniques of stop-out, value study, & line.

a. Lay tracing paper over each figure. Use black ink and make a black & white composition of each figure by inking some areas in solidly and leaving some untouched.

b. Lay a clean sheet of tissue over each figure and make a pencil VALUE study using a variety of gray values.

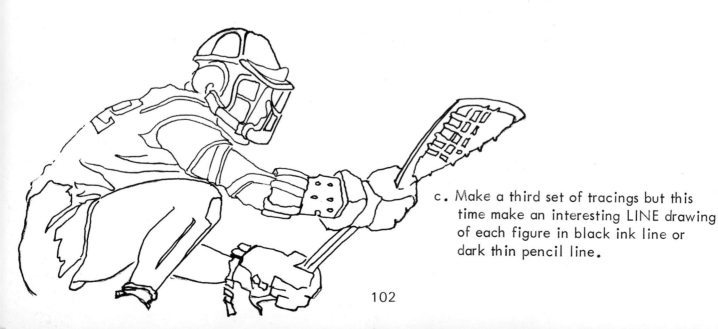

c. Make a third set of tracings but this time make an interesting LINE drawing of each figure in black ink line or dark thin pencil line.

Step 2. Composing Tracings

Draw a dark line border around a 9 x 12 horizontal rectangle on a sheet of bond. (9 x 12 is half of a 12 x 18 sheet of brownline paper.) Select several of your tracings now (Each image should be on a separate sheet of tissue.) and arrange them on the white paper within the rectangle so the action seems to flow across the page. In the example note how the basket-ball players seem to move from right to left. Overlaps or implied line relationships as well as air "streams" whisking back from moving parts can all help unify or direct the action. Realize that the final print or comp will be the reverse of your negative tissues. That is, the solid blacks will become solid whites, black lines will be white lines,etc. Once you feel you have the composition set check it with the instructor. After his ok, place a large sheet of tracing paper over the images and retrace very carefully your selected composition on the large sheet of tracing paper. You can use hard pencils, soft pencils, or ink or even paste down pieces of black paper depending on how much you want to block light. Some-times the separate tissues can be laid directly on the brownline paper without making a mast-er tracing. The overlapping torn edges of the individual tissues give interesting value chang-es between the figures.

Step 3. Exposing

The instructor will give you a small "test strip" of brownline paper. Lay a portion of your master tracing or a few of the individual tracings over the emulsion (yellow) side of the test strip, place it in the vacuum press and expose it for 3 minutes. This is standard expo-sure time for most printing trade emulsions and when you remove the test strip and place it in hot water the developed image will be a proof of what to expect when you make your final 9 x 12 print.

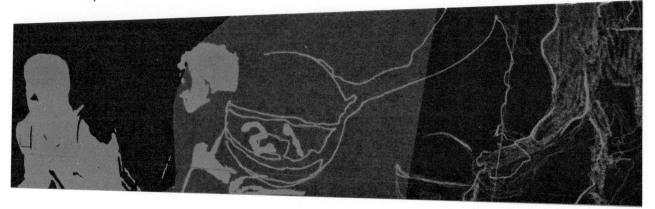

If no vacuum press is available, make one. Lay down a flat heavy piece of cardboard or chipboard; place the brownline paper, emulsion side up, on it; lay your tracing over it and place a piece of clear plastic or glass on top. Press it tightly together and expose it face up to the sun or a foto flood lamp for a minute or so and then develop the brownline paper in water.

TAPE

GLASS

CHIPBOARD

Now the sun is not as consistent as the thermal lights in the vacuum press. It is brighter at noon, weaker in the early morning or late afternoon, and haze or clouds affect its actinic strength also, so you may have to try several small test strips to see what gives you an optimum exposure under specific conditions of time and weather. To do this, lay a rather long test strip under your tracing. When you take your homemade press out in the sunlay a piece of black paper or scrap of heavy cardboard over the glass as a mask so it covers all but about two inches of an end of the test strip. Expose this two-inch end for about 20 seconds, then pull back the mask two inches more, count to 20, slide it back again exposing still another two inches for the count of 20,etc. If you do this to the end of say a 12 inch strip, you will have a strip that has been exposed 120 seconds on one end and 20 seconds on the last portion to be unmasked with 20 second interval exposures in between. When the test strip is developed it will show you what are the optimum exposures that you might want to use for your final 9 x 12 print.

Typical test strips

Exposure on sunny day

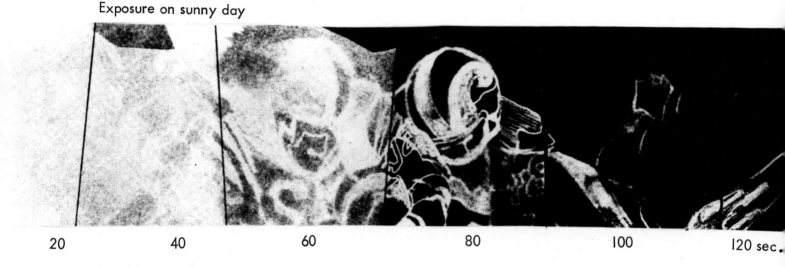

20   40   60   80   100   120 sec.

Exposure on cloudy day

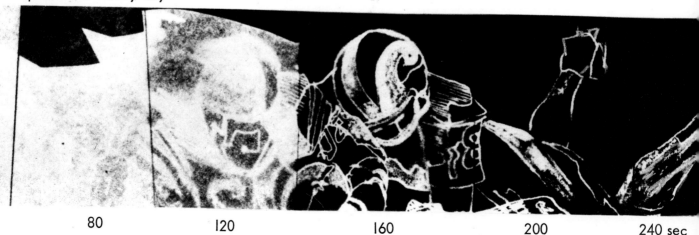

40   80   120   160   200   240 sec

Step 4. Developing, Fixing and Drying

After you have determined an optimum exposure time from test strips place your entire tracing composition over a piece of 9 x 12 brownline paper and expose it using the same exposure conditions . Place the exposed brownline paper in the sink and run hot water over the emulsion side for a minute or so until the image is clear. Then place it in the fix tray (Tablespoon of Maduro Salts in a half gallon of water.) for 30 seconds or so. Now wash off the print in the sink to remove the fix salts and dry the print between two paper towels. Keep it pressed flat until dry. If a dry mount press is available, place the print in it between several thicknesses of absorbent paper or towels and press it for 2 or 3 minutes at 225° and it will come out flat and dark. Heat seems to increase the darkness of the print. Prints placed accidently in the fix bath first or developed in cold water seem to have a more golden brown tone.

WATER   MADURO SALTS   WATER   TOWELS

DEVELOP   FIX   WASH   DRY

When the print is dry it can be drawn on or retouched with white paint. If mounted on a stiff backing it can be painted on with waterbase paints. Parts can be die cut out and replaced with another brownline strip at a different exposure. The advertising student should realize that many creative ideas occur AFTER a print is made. If your idea can be bettered by adding or subtracting forms and color, then do it. Remember the paste up is eventually shot on the process camera and evolves into a printing plate. The result you are striving for will occur on the printed page. The techniques you use to achieve this by manipulating your pasteup is entirely up to you.

Transparencies

Step 1.

Select three figures of animals in action from magazine scrap. Make a tracing of each about 5 or 6 inches in height. (If the fotos are too small, use the Lucy or grid system to enlarge them to size.)

Step 2.

Arrange the tracings so that tracing one partially overlaps tracing two, and tracing two partially overlaps tracing three. Try to achieve a progression of action as well as an interesting varied silhouette or outline shape. You may wish to use one of the tracings a second time as an overlapping fourth or fifth image to enhance the action or silhouette form. When you have the tissues positioned get a crit from the instructor.

Don't be afraid to redraw or distort the images if you feel you achieve more action or a better composition. Fotografs are not sacred images to be copied exactly. Rather they should be stimuli or springboards from which you create your own forms. At this stage you may also wish to lay in a few pencilled grays and darks on the tracings to establish a pattern or path for your later color values.

Step 3.

After the instructor okays your composition transfer it to white illustration board. Use the 3 paint primary hues, red, yellow, and blue. Paint one of the animals all in red tones, one in yellow, and one in blue. Don't paint each animal all one flat color. Instead, for example, on the red image use dark reds, medium value reds, pinks, etc. Change the CHROMA within the hue as well as the VALUES of the hue to achieve more interesting color combinations.

Where the images overlap, paint in the SECONDARY colors which would be produced by the two overlapping transparent primaries. For example, the red image overlapping the yellow image would produce various shades and tints of orange. If these secondary colors are painted in too dark they do not seem to simulate light streaming thru colored glass, which might be your objective. The lighter values of the secondaries seem to give a better illusion of transparency.

NOTE: Remember not to scrub your paint over and over and back and forth. There is a great tendency for beginners to belabor their paint and scrub it back and forth as if this enhances the color or creates better form. Actually this is one of the worst things to do. The scrubbing action does nothing but cause the pigment particles in the paint media to clog up in clusters and reduce the brilliance. Decide BEFOREHAND where you want your paint to go. Then put it on and leave it alone. Your color will then look much more vibrant & alive.

Step 4.

Mat the unit with a matboard related in color to one of the muted or dulled colors in your painting. And don't leave too much white space around the images. Always consider bringing the edges of the matboard opening in close enuf to "anchor" or almost touch the image here and there. This will help produce more significant background negative areas. Otherwise the whole unit may seem to float in a "Sea of Marshmallows". Even if you decide to leave a large area of white space, the action of always thinking and considering the negative areas in advertising units will make you that much better designer. Hand it in at deadline time.

CRI CRI MEJIA

Transparent wax-backed color sheets were laid over the black and white drawing of the totem poles. Interesting use of transparencies for a travel poster.

STORYBOARD

A storyboard is a series of pictures that describe successive situations in a story. The story can then be made into continuous action later by shooting it on film using live models, animated cartoons or puppets. (And some day the story may be shot using laser beam holograms, which would resolve into 3-dimensional photographs suspended in mid-air.)

Regardless of the method of filming, the storyboard is often the first step in initiating and communicating the idea before the expense of production is undertaken. Storyboards may vary from a few quick sketches with jotted notations to a very sophisticated matted presentation with announcer's script, sound effects and camera instructions annotated down to the last detail. The final film may be used for a variety of purposes: assembly, operating instructions and field maintenance of products; presenting a process , skill, or philosophical concept; describing a vocational field or area of study; showing advantages and disadvantages of competitive products, are all possibilities. And the clearer the storyboard concept is, the more likely the production of the film will be done with a minimum of retakes.

Usually the artist starts the storyboard by making some thumbnails until he jells a few ideas. Then he chooses a few key situations, comps them up and mats the series. Pencil, ink, felt markers or paint may be used as media. To save time the units are usually laid out on standard storyboard sheets and covered with the precut black mats. (See below.)

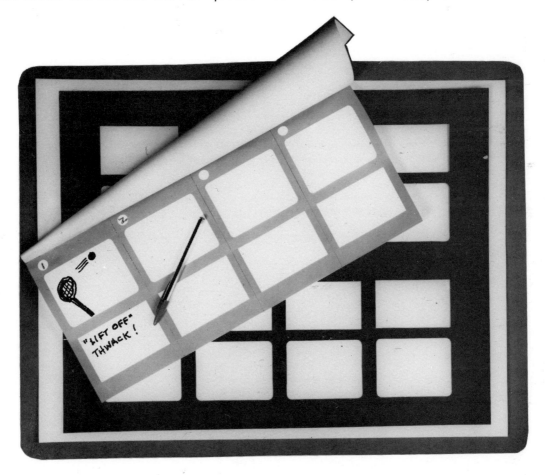

The top, round-cornered areas are used for the visuals, and the rectangular box below each one is used for the voice, action, sound and camera instructions. The voice script may be placed in quotes to separate it from the sound effects. A few of the most used instructions are defined below:

FILM JARGON

Cut – Stopping the action suddenly. "Cutting" the film.
Cut to – Stopping the action and starting another action instantly without interval.
Dissolve – Fade out the image gradually
Dissolve to – As the first image fades out the next image overlaps and fades into focus.
Establishing shot – A scene that shows where the action is taking place. Often it is a
                wide panoramic shot that is brought in to a specific field.
Long shot – Camera shoots from far away.
Close up – Camera shoots from nearby.
Pan – To sweep the camera from one side to the other or up and down.
Wipe – Masking out the scene from left to right, or right to left, etc., by obliterating
        the image gradually.
Iris in – Wiping out the image by masking in from the edges of the screen. Akin to the
        iris of the eye. Iris out would be the reverse.
Zoom in – Come in or closer to the scene thereby enlarging it.

To translate frames and footage into time:

Silent projection speed is 18 frames per sec. for 8 mm, 16 frames for 16 and 35 mm.
Sound projection speed is 24 frames per sec. for 8, 16, and 35 mm.

8mm – 72 frames per foot of film
16mm – 40 frames per foot
35mm – 16 frames per foot

EGG CRACKING.
PUFF OF SMOKE
"NEW IDEAS ARE
NEVER ACCEPTED.

PISTON PUSHES UP.
CYLINDER WALLS
MOVE IN.

6 CYCLE ENGINE
USES 2 FIRING
STROKES TO USE
UP HYDROCARBONS

YES IT MEANS
LESS POWER BUT
YOU GET CLEAN
AIR IN RETURN

Insert
2 more
descriptive
frames between
3 and 4. Ending
too abrupt.

GRAU

PORTRAITS

Portraits or figures are usually purchased from the experienced illustrator, but there are a few techniques that can be practiced by the student or beginning designer to simulate this type of finished art. These techniques also help the student understand how to develop the form of complex irregular images by analyzing, simplifying, and then defining the necessary planes. After the planes have been established by drawing, they can be shaded in grays, or painted in color with a variety of VALUES which help "turn" the form from the light side to the medium values to the dark or shadow side.

Step 1.   Choose a large fotograf of a head from magazine scrap about 7 or 8 inches high if possible. Heads only 4 or 5 inches high are too difficult to paint. Old men and women are the best subjects for this problem, because the planes are easier to see. Young people, children and babies do not make good subjects because of the smooth unwrinkled flat skin surface. "Character is lines and warts." in this case.

Step 2.   Place a piece of tracing vellum directly over the foto, or if your foto is rather small, place it in the Lucy and draw on the vellum there. Use an HB pencil and draw in each plane on the form as carefully as you can by enclosing it completely. That is, don't put a line here and a line there. Draw a line around each entire plane until the pencil meets the place where it started defining the plane. If you don't enclose each plane with a line during this step, you will not be able to paint the planes with separate values later. Obviously the planes on a complex surface like a head are not perfectly defined. You, the artist, must decide and draw the change of plane in the way you see it. Include part of the neck and collar. Otherwise the head will seem to be suspended in the center of your composition. Again, don't leave long lines or threads hanging out from the collar. Enclose each plane completely.

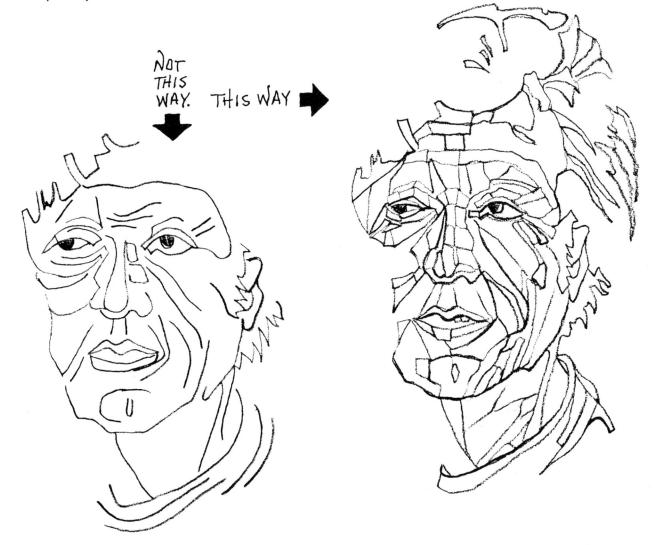

NOT THIS WAY.   THIS WAY ➡

Instead of using all straight hard lines to define a plane (See examples), let your pencil "feel" its way over the face. Soft flesh may require a lightly drawn line without a ripple in it. The gristle on the end of the nose may require a harder line with more definite changes of direction. The cartilage on top of the ear may call for a twisting, angular type of line. In other words, the face will not have a mechanical look if you use some kinesthetic sense as you draw. (Go back and review page 10 regarding drawing project A.) You may wish to leave some areas of the head blank so the background acts as part of the head composition and makes a more interesting silhouette or outline shape. (See examples.)

Step 3. After you have checked the drawing with the instructor, transfer the drawing to a piece of illustration board or toned matboard. Place it carefully. Be aware of the negative areas formed in the background. Portraits often look better if they are NOT placed in the center of the composition.

Step 4. Review pages 21, 22 and 23 regarding color and then start painting in the planes. On this first problem in portraits, let us assume a single light source, like the sun, and paint each form on the head with a light side, a medium value side, and a darker (shadow) side. If you assume the sunlight is coming from your right then paint most of the planes on that side a light value and paint the planes on the other side of the cheeks, nose, lips, head, cap, or what-have-you much darker. Use your own judgement as to what medium values you want to use for the planes in between. In general, try to keep the light values in the warm tones of red, oranges and yellows and use some of the cooler colors like blue-green, blue, or violet in the darker planes. (See full color example on the back cover.)

You can follow the lighting on the fotograf itself to a certain extent but be aware that many fotografs from magazines have been lit from several light sources or have been printed rather flat or "mushy" because of those insistent halftone dots. It is probably better to tackle this first problem by assuming your own light source and creating your OWN light, medium, and dark values as you move across the head.

Step 5. Select a matboard related in color to the portrait and mat it. Again remember to consider the negative areas around the head as you place it within the matboard frame.

115

SYMBOLOGY

As an artist you will often have to create a SYMBOL that represents a general area of interest similar to those listed in the left-hand column below. The uncreative person always settles for the first cliche' or oldfashioned idea that comes to mind: He uses a white bearded figure carrying a scythe to represent time; for Mexico he draws the sleeping peon and his sombrero under the cactus; on a music program cover he places a rippling piano keyboard, etc. The trite symbol thus becomes a dull caricature of the artist's inadequacy.

The three columns below are semi tongue-in-cheek, but they give the beginning designer an idea of what symbols of the past tend to be old hat, what is Gung Ho at the current moment, and a prediction of what future symbols might be, five or fifty years hence.

An experienced designer can use almost ANY subject and by redrawing, or even modifying the old cliche', come up with interesting results. (See photography business card in margin.) The IDEA concerning the subject is what counts ... not the subject. HOWEVER, the beginner is less likely to be trapped into designing corn if he will also explore new approaches. On the other hand, if his symbol solution is too advanced or too unreadable it leaves the audience behind and becomes useless as communication. Adam & Eve may read as a symbol for Man & Woman to most people, whereas the symbols ♂ and ♀ (Mars and Venus) read as male & female only to biologists, astronomers or alchemists . Consider your audience's sophistication BEFORE you design the symbol.

General Topics	1. CLICHE'S	2. CURRENT	3. POTENTIAL
Love	Cupid	Facial closeups	Computer matching ?
Seasons	Snowflake & sun	Signs of the Zodiac	Climate control
Weather	Raindrops & sun	Weather maps	Tiros satellite
Time	Father time	Sun dials	Equations
Optics	Prisms	Compound lenses	Electron microscopes
Music	Piano keyboard	French horn	Electronic wand
Architecture	Arch	Cantilever	Air screens
Force	Sledgehammer	$E = MC^2$	Null gravitation
Mathematics	Pythagorean theorem	Abacus	Base 2
Flight	Kites	Airplanes	Ion thrust
Sailing	Spanish armada	Sloop	Rotor catamarans
Swimming	BATHING SUITS	Bathing suits	
Children	Wicker baby buggy	Tricycle	Skateboard
Toys	Dolls	Guns & holsters	Make-a-robot kit
Armor	Crusader	Goalie	Spaceman
Weapons	Sword	Luger	Neutron scanner
Inquisition	The rack	Bare light bulb	Serum drugs
Death	Skeleton	Smashed car	Plastic organs
Writing	Heiroglyphics	Calligraphy	Sampler readout
Communication	Telephone	T.V.	Radio telescope
Photography	Tripod camera	Lens	Laser images
Precision	Calipers	Micrometer	Nanos & picos
Navigation	Astrolabe	Sextant	Loran gear
Eternity	Sphinx	Crab nebula	Quasars

✳ THANKS STEVE JOSIAS / PHOTOGRAPHER AND PETE VIOLANTE / DESIGNER

PAPER

9

While the pasteup or mechanical is being
prepared, the printing paper should be
ordered. Design characteristics of printing papers are certainly necessary in an
artist's training. The charts in this section
simplify the classifications and condense
some of the voluminous material on paper
to the extent that a beginner can grasp
the overall picture and do a more intelligent job of selection and ordering.

Two charts help the artist identify paper
by description and WEIGHT, and also by
FINISH. Some information on envelope
sizes, die cutting and perforating is also
included.

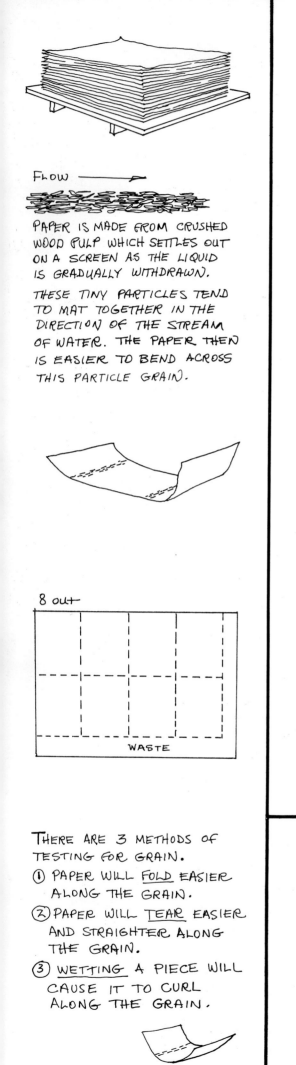

FLOW ──────➤

PAPER IS MADE FROM CRUSHED WOOD PULP WHICH SETTLES OUT ON A SCREEN AS THE LIQUID IS GRADUALLY WITHDRAWN.

THESE TINY PARTICLES TEND TO MAT TOGETHER IN THE DIRECTION OF THE STREAM OF WATER. THE PAPER THEN IS EASIER TO BEND ACROSS THIS PARTICLE GRAIN.

8 out

WASTE

THERE ARE 3 METHODS OF TESTING FOR GRAIN.
① PAPER WILL FOLD EASIER ALONG THE GRAIN.
② PAPER WILL TEAR EASIER AND STRAIGHTER ALONG THE GRAIN.
③ WETTING A PIECE WILL CAUSE IT TO CURL ALONG THE GRAIN.

PRINTING PAPERS

The chart on the following page gives the artist a general sequence from thick to thin on paper weight and quality. Bristols or boards are measured in thousandths of an inch. For the thinner PAPERS the weight of 500 sheets (1 ream) is used to express the thickness or weight difference between papers. For example, an 80 lb. printing paper is a thicker (and therefore heavier) sheet than a 65 lb. printing paper.

Paper is cut and stocked in the warehouses in many different sizes, but the weight is always determined by weighing a ream of a BASIC SIZE sheet. Printing paper's basic size is 25 x 38; cover paper's basic size is 20 x 26, etc. The GRAIN direction is usually shown by the second figure. Grain is important to a printer, as it tells him in what direction the paper will bend most easily when passing over the rollers in the high-speed presses. Thus within each classification the weight or BASIS is a good indication of relative paper thickness. Altho loosely matted fibres tend to give a thicker sheet than tightly matted fibres,

in general: The HIGHER the weight, the THICKER the paper.

The papers listed in the chart are manufactured in a wide variety of weights, finishes, and colors. The samples of printing papers in this section represent only an average weight and a typical finish within the classification. Each classification shown on the chart overlaps many other classifications in weight; and the finishes are available on almost every paper. For example, the vellum finish may be applied to bristol board or thin tracing paper.

The student artist should realize that the classifications listed are only a general expression of bulk and quality. Specific information regarding weight basis, size, how many "out" of a single sheet with a minimum of waste, finish, color, and strength must be compared when evaluating printers' bids on a printing job. A quality paper can cause a printing price to be several hundred dollars higher than a price bid based on a cheaper paper. Know paper well enough so that reasonably exact specifications can be included in your information to the printer. OR ask for paper samples and specific paper costs with each bid, so the PAPER PRICE can be separated from the total BID FIGURE. Then and only then will you be able to compare competitive printing bids.

THERE ARE REASONS FOR BASIC SIZES:

BASIC SIZE FOR BOND STOCK IS 17 X 22 BECAUSE IT CUTS EASILY INTO 8½ X 11, WHICH IS STANDARD SIZE FOR MOST LETTERHEADS. MOST LETTERHEADS DO NOT NEED REGISTRATION MARKS ON THE SIDE, AS THEY ARE PRINTED ONE COLOR, THEREFORE PAPER CAN BE CUT TO FINISHED SIZE WITH EXACTLY 4 OUT AND NO WASTE.

BASIC SIZE FOR BOOK STOCK IS 25 X 38 BECAUSE IT CUTS INTO 8 9X12½ WITH SOME MARGIN STOCK FOR REG. MARKS. BOOK MEANS IT IS USED FOR BOOKS AND MAGAZINES, MANY OF WHICH ARE 9 X 12.

BOARDS

Chipboard	Cheap gray heavy cardboard, unfinished both sides	Backing, packing inserts
Cardboard	Extremely heavyweight paper 10 ply, etc., finished one side	Street car signs, tickets, hat checks, calendars, display
Tagboard	Economical, tough, cream color	Shipping tags, job tickets, displays, record cards, inserts
Bristol	Tough, smooth surface, white, takes die cutting	Package comps, post cards, Covers, displays, drawings.
Matboard	Textured surface, usually sized sometimes glazed or pebbly. Pebble somewhat cliche' today	Used for matting or framing artwork. Can be painted on. Beware of mechanical surfaces
Illustration board	Hot press - smooth vellum finish Cold press - velvet finish, coarser	Detailed illustrations, block diagrams, watercolor, casein
Box board	Snappy, easily scored & die cut Usually white, slick surface	Package comps, point-of-sale displays, models, foldouts
Railroad Bd.	Similar to box board. Usually cheaper quality, raw colors	Posters, cut out toys Unesthetic unless modified.

PAPER

Cover	Takes scoring, folding, die cutting, embossing. Tear resistant	Book covers, menus, folders displays
Index	Smooth, stiff, wear and grease resistant, ok for pen, pencil & typewriter	Index cards, office records, Direct mail, tickets
Ledger	Surface grips machine rollers. Soft colors for identification, takes erasing, flexible	Ledger sheets, all office records
Text	Similar to book weight & opaqueness, but implies the textural surface of early handmade papers	Books, announcements, presentations, programs, annual reports, stationery, envelopes
Book	Opaque, usually takes printing both sides, smoother usually than text, resists curling, takes sharp image from type.	Books, broadsides, school annuals magazines, flyers, direct mail, labels, office printing.
Bond	Translucent. Lighter weights do not take printing both sides. OK for ink, pencil & typing.	Stationery, memos, direct mail, order forms, invoices, packing slips
Glass vellum	Transparent, medium weight, acetate-like paper.	Overlays, Magazine inserts, See throughs, backlighted displays, packaging
Onion skin	Thin, translucent, parchment-like glazed or unglazed, often with cockle finish	Typing copies, airmail stationery, Interoffice correspondence, enclosures
Tracing	Transparent, thin, usually with vellum finish for ink, pencil	Engineering drawings, visuals, lifts, overlay indications, etc.

DUPLICATOR PAPERS

Mimeograph	Rough, soft, fuzzy, absorbent	Presses against and aborbs ink from wax stencil master on cylinder
Duplicator	Smooth, hard, nonabsorbent	Presses against and receives dye impression from flat image master on cylinder.

SPECIAL PAPERS

Watercolor	Hot press – smooth vellum finish Cold press – rough wrinkled	Watercolors, casein, tempera Printmaking, chalk or ink
Construction	Rough surface, limited selection of colors, fades rapidly. Although used extensively in school rooms, the limitation of a few cliche' raw colors make it a poor aid for developing taste and color sensitivity in children.	
Color coated	Graded hues in varying values and chromas. Sample swatches with corresponding color numbers make for ease of ordering. Good for comps, collages, packaging presentations, etc.	
Pressed	Contains foreign material ranging from wood pulp roughage to straw, leaves and butterflies. Varies from the earth colored oatmeal paper to the translucent Japanese Shoji paper.	
Drawing	Many varieties from heavy, soft textures to extremely fine tooth. Accepts pencil, pastel, wash & ink in varying degrees. Wash & ink tend to dry rapidly with hard edges on the unsized papers.	
Charcoal	Toothy surface which accepts charcoal and pastel chalks. Takes erasing and rubbing. Colored as well as white.	
Layout bond	A translucent toothy bond for use in making layout roughs, visuals, and tracings. Accepts pencil, charcoal, pastels. Tends to wrinkle under ink wash. Wide ink pens leave a scratchy line.	
Rice	Thin absorbent, soft. Good for light ink washes, block printing.	
Tissue	Thin, transparent, easily torn. Protection inserts for drawings, etc.	

OTHER PAPERS (YOUR SPECS)

FINISHES APPLIED TO PRINTING PAPERS

NATURAL FINISHES

(Caused by the process used in making the paper.)

Antique	A low relief rough finish.
Eggshell	A tooth finish akin to an eggshell.
Text	Implying a textured surface with the appeal of the early hand-made papers.
Vellum	Dull velvet-like surface with a "tooth".
Machine	Dull smooth and soft.
English	Gloss smooth.

COATED FINISHES

(Made by coating the paper on one or two sides.)

Clay	Dull to glossy depending on the process.
Plastic film	Shiny and washable.
Enameled	Satin-like & similar to enamel paint surface.
Mirror	Very shiny and slippery.

PLATE FINISHES

(Machine textured AFTER the paper leaves the paper-making machine.)

Leather	Machines can make a variety of embossed or texture images to imitate any surface.
Linen	
Coral	Minute bumps
Ripple	Subtle wavy surface
Cockle	Wrinkled look
Vellum	Velvet-like tooth
Calendered	Smooth slick finish like wrapping paper.

PRINTED FINISHES

(Printed on the paper.)

Woodgrain	Printed finishes can be made to simulate a variety of materials, colors, and produce adhesive or wax backings, etc.
Cork	
Leather	
Gummed	

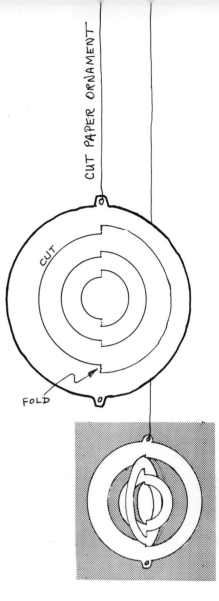

CUT PAPER ORNAMENT

CUT

FOLD

THE BASIC SIZE FOR COVER STOCK IS 20 X 26 BECAUSE THE SHEET CUTS INTO FOUR 10 X 13½. THE 13 INCHES GIVE ½ INCH OVERLAP TOP & BOTTOM ON A 9 X 12 BOOK. THE 10-INCH DIMENSION COVERS THE 9-INCH WIDTH OF THE PAGES WITH SOME MARGIN LEFT TO COVER THE SPINE. ETC.

OBVIOUSLY THESE BASIC SIZES DO NOT COVER ALL DESIGN PROBLEMS. BUT THEY DO PROVIDE A BASIS FOR MEASUREMENT AND COMPARISON. MANY OTHER SIZES ARE AVAILABLE ALSO.

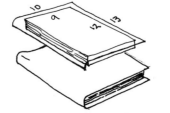

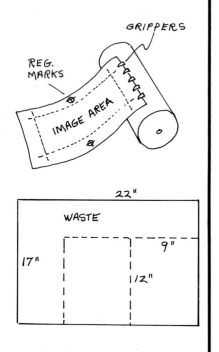

GRIPPERS

REG. MARKS

IMAGE AREA

22"

WASTE

9"

17"

1/2"

SCRATCH PAD

PAPER ORDERING   (Project O)

Select a white paper stock for your Product Ad and determine the weight basis (60, 70 or 80 lb.) that your think will work best for this mailer. Assume you want 15,000 finished mailers. Use the chart below, which is a typical price list from a paper wholesaler, and write up your order. Consider the following specifications:

Allow 3 to 5 percent of stock for makeready and waste. Allow 1/2 inch for gripper bite on the leading edge of the mailer as it goes thru the press and 1/2 inch extra on each side for the registration marks. From these job stock OUTSIDE dimensions then, figure the size of sheet to be ordered from the paper wholesaler that will give you the most number OUT with the least waste.

> For example: A 17 x 22 sheet will cut into exactly four 8 1/2 x 11 pieces of job stock with no waste. But if a job stock had outside dimensions of 9 x 12 (to accomodate gripper bite and registration marks) a larger sheet would have to be ordered instead, because the 17 x 22 sheet would cut into only two 9 x 12's with the remainder being approximately 40% waste.

From the size of the sheet you choose which seems to be most economical, figure the cost of your total order. Write down all the paper specifications and cost on a neat slip of paper and present it to the instructor for checking. This is very similar to a typical ordering situation in industry. Paper wholesalers have special salesmen who will answer by telephone or come out personally to help you on any question you have concerning paper. It is the wise manager who knows exactly what paper is included in what bid.

Offset White

Basis	Size	Sheets per Carton	Price per 1000 sheets delivered per carton	less than carton
60	17 x 22	3000	$ 16.50	$ 19.20
	23 x 26	2000	25.45	29.60
	23 x 35	1500	33.70	39.32
	25 x 38	1200	39.60	46.26
	35 x 45	800	65.40	76.30
70	17 x 22	2400	19.15	22.35
	23 x 26	1700	29.75	34.70
	23 x 35	1200	39.33	45.85
	25 x 38	1000	46.25	53.90
	35 x 45	600	76.65	89.40
80	17 x 22	2400	21.80	25.45
	23 x 26	1500	34.04	39.70
	23 x 35	1100	44.95	52.50
	25 x 38	1000	52.85	61.65
	35 x 45	600	87.90	102.50

DESIGN SUGGESTIONS REGARDING PAPER SELECTION

If a paper is to be printed on both sides it must be opaque enough to prevent the printing from showing thru the back. Press a sheet of the paper in question against a printed page. If the printing shows thru clearly, the paper is probably not suitable for printing both sides.

Consider standard envelope sizes before designing a mailing piece.

Paper for multicolor work needs weight and toughness to survive the several runs thru the press without distortion and resulting misregister.

If you are printing a light value color, like pale yellow, a brilliant (extra white) paper may give you greater contrast and readability for copy, whereas a "white" paper that has a cream colored cast may not work as well.

Colored paper can sometimes save the cost of an extra press run.

Deckled edges can give interest to cards, folders, and announcements.

Use restraint in choice of papers that have a violent pattern or texture. A sheet of wood grain bristol may be fine as a single sheet enclosure from a lumber mill but if used on all pages in an 8-page brochure might be too busy.

Black or colored screens over colored stock give interesting textures and reverse effects.

White ink on dark stocks does not usually give an image as opaque and sharp as black ink on light stock. However, the translucent irregular effect it does give should be very usable to a creative designer for block print effects, etc. (Incidently, the person or company who develops the first opaque white ink which has the same covering power as India Ink or black printers ink will have an untouched market, as at present it is unknown.)

Be aware that "Finest paper" has no absolute meaning. A semi-gloss chrome coat paper may be the "finest" paper to a printer because it can accept a fine dot four-color process with great success. The "finest" paper to a book collector may mean a soft weave Victorian text. The "finest" paper to an artist will mean the stock that is most suitable to the design job. Some cheaper papers have esthetic qualities that the more expensive ones do not have. I have seen printing masterpieces done on thin chipboard!

DIE CUTTING (OR PERFORATION)

To punch out discs and squares, or cut paper into unusual shapes, a sharp hollow die is made. It is similar to a cookie cutter in operation. The die is locked into a die cutting machine and brought down with considerable force thru the stack of paper or boxboard.

A die blade can also be affixed to a letterpress PLATEN to cut single sheets. In this case, the die can be nicked on the edge in two or three places so the cut outs will not fall out as the sheets pass thru the press. Then later the cut outs can be removed.

All that is usually necessary for the artist is to give the engraver or die maker a precise, same size, ink outline of the cut out.

STANDARD ENVELOPES

No. 1.	$1\frac{3}{4} \times 2\frac{7}{8}$
2.	$2\frac{1}{16} \times 3\frac{1}{2}$
3.	$2\frac{5}{16} \times 3\frac{5}{8}$
5.	$3\frac{1}{16} \times 5\frac{1}{2}$
$6\frac{1}{4}$	$3\frac{1}{2} \times 6$
CHECK	$3\frac{5}{8} \times 8\frac{5}{8}$
$6\frac{3}{4}$	$3\frac{5}{8} \times 6\frac{1}{2}$
7.	$3\frac{3}{4} \times 6\frac{3}{4}$
$7\frac{1}{2}$	$3\frac{7}{8} \times 7\frac{1}{2}$
9.	$3\frac{7}{8} \times 8\frac{7}{8}$
10.	$4\frac{1}{8} \times 9\frac{1}{2}$
11.	$4\frac{1}{2} \times 10\frac{3}{8}$
12.	$4\frac{3}{4} \times 11$
14.	$5 \times 11\frac{1}{2}$

OPEN END

$4 \times 6\frac{3}{8}$
$4\frac{5}{8} \times 6\frac{3}{8}$
$5\frac{1}{2} \times 7\frac{1}{2}$
$5\frac{1}{2} \times 8\frac{1}{4}$
6×9 $9\frac{1}{2} \times 12\frac{1}{2}$
$6\frac{1}{2} \times 9\frac{1}{2}$ $11\frac{1}{2} \times 14\frac{1}{2}$
7×10
$7\frac{1}{2} \times 10\frac{1}{2}$
$8\frac{1}{4} \times 11\frac{1}{4}$

If you are designing a complete envelope or printing on standards, check FIRST with your Post Office regarding minimum and maximum dimensions, address space, color, etc.

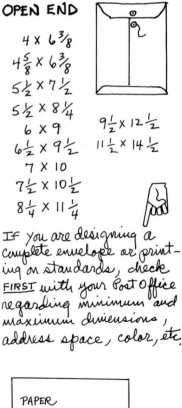

PAPER

DIE

CUT OUT

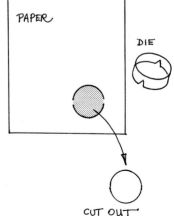

TETRAHEDRON

SNAP-OUT CUBE

89°∠

G B

I

D

F A

L

L=D

PACK FLAT IN
ENVELOPE WITH
TAUT RUBBER BAND

G F

B A

F

G

H G

POLYHEDRONS

TOP

5 1 2

6 10

5

4

TOP 3

1

8 7 6 2

9 10 BOT.

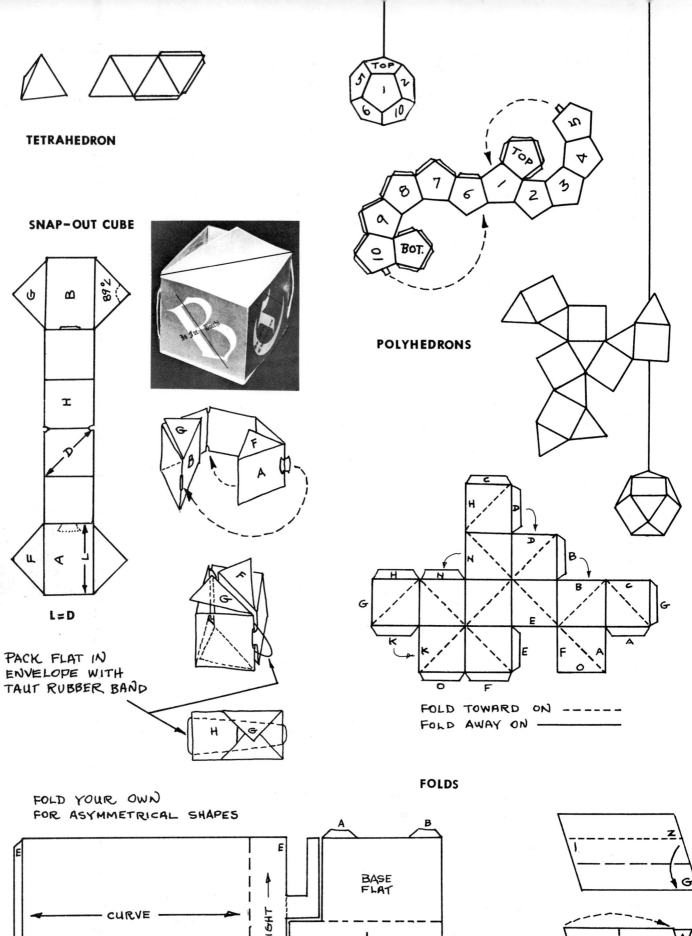

C

H D

D

N B

H N B C

G B G

E

K K E F A

O F A

O F

FOLD TOWARD ON ----
FOLD AWAY ON ———

FOLDS

FOLD YOUR OWN
FOR ASYMMETRICAL SHAPES

E E A B

BASE
FLAT

CURVE

FLAT UPRIGHT

E

C CURVE

C

FLAT FLAT

D D A B

Z

I

G

A
Z G

Z G A
I Z G

TYPE

Up to this point the artist has selected his type faces and paper, and completed his layout. We assume that he has received the "Go ahead." from the Art Director and is starting on his camera-ready art, the MECHANICAL. He must now order his type set, correct the galley proofs, and check his reproduction proofs. Examples follow which include problems such as letterspacing and leading out.

In the first part of this section is a procedure to follow for writing copy to FIT. A LINE GAGE is printed on the left-hand margin for the student's use. See Section 6 for explanation of its measure. If necessary, it can be cut off and glued on the back of a ruler or dry mounted on a strip of illustration board.

The second part of this section contains a simple explanation of the differences and use of HANDSET type and LINOTYPE. Preparation of the type specification sheet for the typographer is explained and a fotograf of a proofpress in operation and a linotype machine is included. A page of the more commonly used proofreader's marks follows.

10

An exercise for the student is presented to acquaint him with the variety of errors that are ever possible in galleys and repros. It is quite obvious in industry that when a beginning artist sees proofs he is so enamoured with seeing his "stuff" in print that he tends to merely flick his eyes over it, visualize it in pasteup and OK the whole package of proofs. Ye olde pro, however, will sit back, relax, and read it all over thoroughly, for content and meaning, for punctuation and spelling, for typographical errors, and for dimension or layout measurements. If this thoroughness can be appreciated by the neophyte artist, he will be that many months ahead in industry when he leaves school.

The exercise starts with a page of typewritten copy, doublespaced, with specifications indicated in writing. The next page is the galley proof with a number of common errors included in the copy but unedited and unmarked. The student can use his knowledge of proofreader's marks to mark the proof with a soft but sharp erasable pencil. The page following is the same galley proof with all the corrections properly noted except one. The student can now compare the proofmarks with his own to see if he found all the mistakes and whether he indicated them correctly for the typographer.

PROOFS

THESE BEARERS KEEP SQUEEZE EVEN ON TYPE

SPECIFICATION TERMS

Before writing copy or type specifications the following terms should be studied, and the type terms in Section 6 should be reviewed.

Linotype slug	A line of type produced as a single metal casting
lead (led)	A thin strip of metal used to separate LINES of type. Commonest is the 2 point. **(See page 133.)**
spacer	A piece of metal used to separate L E T T E R S.
point	A 72nd of an inch. Used to measure body size of type.

<------------- 18 picas ------------->

pica	12 points. Used to measure column width. Equals 1/6 of an inch.
set solid	Each line of type is set solidly on the line below. No leads or "air" appears between the lines.
body copy	The paragraphs of written material, or the blocks of type in an ad as distinguished from the headings or trademarks or titles.
flush	Setting the ends of lines of type even with each other.
flush left	Setting the lines of type even on the left side only. Leaving the right margin irregular.
letter space	The space on paper required to accept one character or letter.
letter spacing	Putting spacers between letters to expand the W O R D.
letter spaces per line.	Count each letter, each punctuation mark, and each space between words or sentences. (These all represent space used, whether the type body has a printing face or not.)
galley	A steel tray which holds the type that has been set.
proof	Any impression from type taken for examination.
galley proof	The first proof. Usually taken on newsprint.
repro	Reproduction proof. The final proof which is usually taken on a white coated paper and pasted in the pasteup.
CAPS	Indicates copy to be set in ALL CAPITALS.
lc	indicates copy to be set in all lower case. no capitals to be used with proper nouns or even at the beginning of sentences.
Clc	Indicates capitals to be used where they normally are used and lower case to be used in remainder of copy.
ital.	Indicates copy to be set in italics *recognized as* (slanted).

line for line

Printer
sets the copy exactly
as it is typed. No
column width is indicated.
Often used when the designer wishes the paragraph to conform
to an unusual shape to fit the layout.

WHEN WRITING COPY OR DOING LAYOUTS REMEMBER:

The customer is usually interested primarily in what the product will do for him and secondly its price and quality. So the emphasis in the majority of ads is on operation and use, particularly with new products or new designs of old products. If the product is a traditional standard (chair, screwdriver) then the emphasis is more likely to be on quality or price. Quality may be illustrated by stressing materials, esthetics, manufacturing processes, or company name prestige, which is known as INSTITUTIONAL advertising.

The economic principle behind all advertising communication is that a well in- formed citizenry will make the wisest purchase and thus use their money more efficiently. The business man who makes the better product, and makes it eff- iciently, will remain in business.

The institution of advertising then is part of our uncensored system of communication that helps keep us economically strong, AS LONG AS IT REMAINS TRUTHFUL. When people attack advertising as being "awful, gross, tasteless, and dishonest", what they really mean is that ADVERTISERS are awful, gross,etc. Advertising itself is or could be amoral. It would be as ridiculous to attack money as being wicked. Advertising is a method of communication that can be used to keep people informed by using sensitive, subtle, well designed art forms; or it can become a monster of blatant, alienating, vulgar intrusion.

There is a possibility that as customers, clients, advertising managers, and artists become better educated, they will use more interesting approaches to presentations. The ideal situation someday may be what mothers and fathers have thought for centuries: "How do my actions, MY imagery, affect those around me ?" Some agencies are already concerning themselves with this philosophy,as sensitive managers realize the awesome effect an advertising campaign can have on a nation's thought. Do we want all young people to believe that half truths, wild exaggeration, vulgar clowning, and come-ons are acceptable deportment and will lead to an enlightened personality or culture ?

If not, advertisERs and agencies will eventually have to come around to a long term viewpoint which includes "Will it inform ?" but ALSO "How will it affect the character of our young people ?". The answer lies with many people and certainly with YOU, the artist, because you are the link between the concept and the people. Educate yourself as widely and as constantly as you can. Then establish a few ethical principles for yourself and have the courage to stick to them.

"What the brain of man can conceive ... the character of man can control."
Thomas Edison

WRITE AND FIT THE COPY FOR THE PRODUCT AD   (Project P)

To make the copy interesting, you might place yourself in the position of someone who had never seen any product like it before, a Martian ?; what would an 80 year old man think of it ? ; what would the viewpoint of the product itself be ? You might consider the varieties of form, such as: monologue, dialogue, a poem, a telegram, blank verse, a dialect, beatnik slang, phonetics, statistics, a ballad, Chaucers English, or perforated tape and IBM figures.

Now comes the question:

How much copy is needed to fill the space indicated in the layout ?

Now comes the question:

HOW MUCH COPY IS NEEDED TO FILL THE SPACE INDICATED IN THE LAYOUT ?

The copy block in your product ad is, say, 2 inches wide and 4 inches deep.

Step 1   Select a Face and Point Size from the type specimen sheets at the back of this section. Probably 10 pt, 12 pt, or 14 pt.

Step 2   Lay a rule or your line gage on the selected alphabet sample and count the letterspaces (characters & spaces) within a two-inch span.
For example, this line counts out to about 28 per two-inch span (12 picas).

two-inch span

Step 3   Let us assume that you have chosen a type face. For an example we will assume that it counted out to 33 spaces per two-inch span.
Insert a sheet of paper in the typewriter. Shift the carriage to the right until it rests against the left-hand margin stop. Tap the space bar 33 times and set the right-hand margin stop at this position. The typewriter is now set to allow an average line of about 33 characters to be tapped out before its warning bell rings.   (See page 131 for example.)

Step 4   How many lines of copy must be written ?

Assume you have chosen a 10 pt type face. Use the line gage to measure the column depth in points.   As your column is 4 inches deep, the gage will show about 24 picas or 288 (24 x 12) points. (Remember , a pica is equal to 12 points.)

Divide 288 by 10 (the height of your chosen type) = 28.8 or 28 lines which must be written to fill the column. Twenty-nine would extend beyond the bottom of the 4 inch column.

Step 5   Type 28 lines of copy averaging about 33 spaces per line. The end of each line can vary in length. In other words you can end each line just short of the margin bell or a few characters beyond. This gives you leeway for correct hyphenation of long words; the lines will AVERAGE 33 spaces; a. d the linotype operator will have no difficulty fitting the copy into your specified dimensions.   (Double space between lines.)

If no typewriter is available, WRITE 28 lines of copy approximately 33 spaces per line.

Typed or written, if this copy were set as is, it would be cast as single lines of type called SLUGS. These slugs would be placed one against the other, and when the impression (proof) was taken from them, the lines would be so close together that the paragraph would look like a solid mass. This is called being "SET SOLID". That is, there is no AIR or space between the lines of copy, and in most cases (like this paragraph) it is rather hard to read. Our next SPEC will correct this.

Step 6   Leading (Pronounced leding.)

To make the copy feel a little more open and less cramped we can set the slugs slightly farther apart in the galley tray, but , of course, that would mean the copy would extend BEYOND the allowed four inches in our column depth. Therefore:

a)   Write fewer lines of copy... say 24.
b)   In the specs to the typographer, ask him to LEAD OUT the 24 lines to your column length of 4 inches.

128

The typographer will then insert a thin metal strip called a LEAD (led) between each line of type before he prints you the galley proof. (See foto of galley tray with leads. **Page 133.**) Your column will be the same length as when your 28 lines were set solid, but this time there will be only 24 lines in the column; it will look a little less jammed and be somewhat easier to read. Two-point leading is quite common in advertising copy, and many of the books you read have some leading.

To save time on large amounts of copy, the linotype operator will often CAST the 10-point face directly on a 12-point SLUG. This makes the body two points larger and saves the shop the agony of placing all those little strips of metal between the slugs of type.

MATRIX

Type faces can be cast on a regular slug or on a thicker slug.

SLUG

MATTAM   10

LEAD   2

SLUG

MATTAM   12

Step 7   On the same sheet of paper typewrite in the major and minor headlines that you wish to have typeset.

For example:

EVANS ⟩ ⎯ CAPS

Distributed by Brian Archer, Incorporated

NOTE: Leave plenty of space between heads and remember to DOUBLE SPACE all body copy when you typewrite it. This allows room for corrections to be made between the lines. It also makes it easier for the linotype operator or typographer to read it while they are setting your copy.

Double spacing

Double spacing on the typewriter also allows enough room for your BLUE PENCILLED SPECIFICATIONS to be written in clearly without overlapping or jamming the copy.

(**Page 131** is a sample of body copy and heads with typical specs.)

Copy should be typed, double spaced, on one side only, on $8\frac{1}{2}$ x 11 sheets with at least an inch margin on all sides. Type a carbon copy and number all sheets.

Put your name, address, and telephone number on the first page in the upper right-hand corner.

Call the typographer and get the deadline date established for delivered proofs. Write in today's date and the deadline date. Send the original sheets to the typographer. Retain the carbon copy for reference.

In the larger agencies there are special forms for copy, specific hours of pickup and delivery, and often direct telephone lines to the typographer for RUSH orders that must be set immediately. These are all particular modes of operation that will have to be learned by you if **you are employed by these firms.** But regardless of the size, or speed, or form, or shortcuts in the typesetting operation, the basic principles remain about the same as outlined here.

After the copy is typed, use a blue pencil or pen and HOOK a line above the copy.

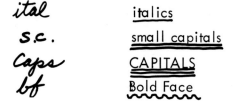

10 Fut. Clc

12 picas col. W, Flush L.

There are hundreds of bucket-seat chairs,

a) Above this horizontal line write all the information concerning the TYPE FACE you have selected, such as:

Size in points/ face/ light, medium or bold weight/ CAPS or Clc or lc or italic/ condensed or extended.

b) Below this line write all the information concerning the DIMENSIONS of the copy, such as:

Column width/ flush set/ the leading/ letterspacing.

Letterspacing means that SPACERS are placed between the letters of a word to expand it. For example the headline EVANS could be letterspaced out to approximately one inch: E V A N S

FIGURES are usually the same size as capital letters. 257483, etc. It may be necessary to have any figures, 1234, in your body copy set a size smaller, 3456, so they do not appear too large in contrast with the lower case letters.

c) If you wish certain words or letters in the body copy to be set in a SPECIAL face, indicate this by UNDERSCORING with the proper lines and abbreviating the special face in the margin opposite the underscoring, such as:

ital	italics
s.c.	small capitals
Caps	CAPITALS
bf	Bold Face

The next page is what the sheet looks like after the type specifications are written in. Ordinarily it is standard practice to typewrite copy in black, spec in blue, and make corrections in red or black pencil.

Use blue pencil to write in specs.

2 → **96 Caslon ital. Caps**

EVANS

18 Bodoni Clc
L.S. to 27 picas

Distributed by Brian Archer, Incorporated

11 Garamond Book Clc
Col w. 2", Lead out to 24 picas

18 Bodoni cap →

T̲here are hundreds of bucket-seat
chairs on the market, but personally
I prefer the nonbucket style. I like
to move about a bit when I carry
on conversation or read, and the
bucket keeps me off the "edge of
my seat" . It prevents my comfortable after-dinner slouch. It may
be great in a racing car to hold
the driver in a vise-like grip
while he caroms around the Grand
Prix but for home .... please,
just an ordinary chair. The Evans,   *bf*
Steelstrut, comes in five colors:
Sand, Ochre, Tomato, Blue & White,   *ital.*
can be nested, and retails for
about twenty-five dollars, U.S.A.

To spec copy | To specify (by writing in the margins with a blue pencil or blue pen) the type size, face, kind, width, weight, column width, flush set, leading, letterspacing and all other information necessary to set the type from the type-written copy.

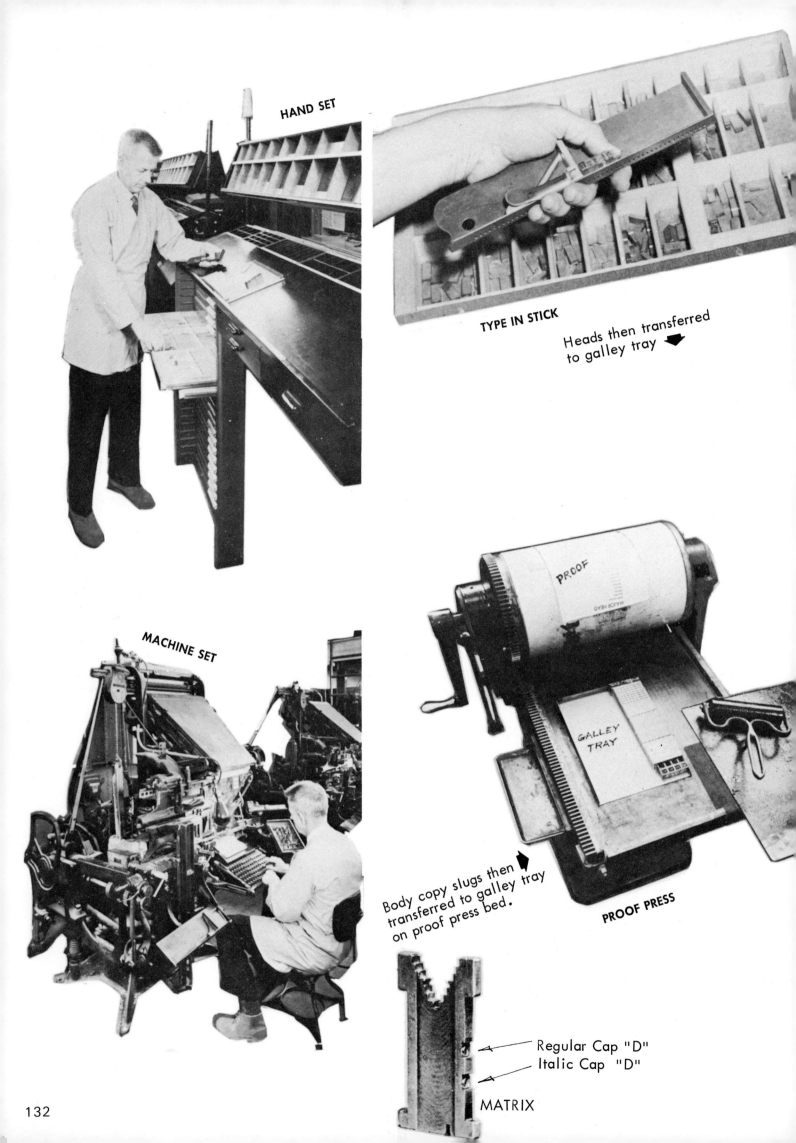

HAND SET

TYPE IN STICK

Heads then transferred to galley tray ➤

MACHINE SET

PROOF

GALLEY TRAY

Body copy slugs then transferred to galley tray on proof press bed.

PROOF PRESS

Regular Cap "D"
Italic Cap "D"

MATRIX

GALLEY TRAY

MAJOR HEAD

MINOR HEADING

Headings are usually set by hand. Working from the Artist's typed instructions, the typographer selects each type from the tray in his case and sets it in the stick in his left hand. This line of type is then transferred to the galley tray, and another line is set until the job is completed. Even though certain heads could be set by linotype, they are sometimes set by hand to save the time of changing font magazines on the linotype machine. In this paragraph the 10 point linotype slugs were set solid, so the lines of type are printed close together.

Body copy is usually set by linotype. Working from the Artist's instructions the linotype operator places the required magazines on the machine. These magazines are thin metal boxes about two feet square that contain a supply of matrices or molds which will form the type face on the slug. As the letters are punched on the linotype keyboard a corresponding matrix leaves the magazine and drops into position until the entire line is complete. Wedge shaped expanders force the matrices tightly together, and the line is moved to a position in front of the plunger. The plunger drives forward and forces molten lead against the mold faces. The slug is then dropped on the tray at the operator's elbow. The matrices are automatically returned to their original slots in the magazine. In this paragraph the 10 point linotype slugs were set with a two point lead between each line so the lines of type are printed slightly farther apart. They have "air" around them.

The handset heads and the linotype slugs are then placed on a galley and secured with leads or blocks of wood to keep the edges flush. The galley is placed on the bed of the proof press, and the type is inked by rolling the ink rollers over it. The impression roller follows and presses a piece of paper on the type just hard enough to get a clean dark image. The impression can be strengthened by adding sheets of paper as backing on the impression roller. In this paragraph the same 10 point type face was set on a 12 point slug. This eliminated the need to put a two point lead between each line. The distance between the lines of type remains the same as the two point leaded however.

While we are waiting for our galley proofs, let us practice our PROOFREADING
by marking up the practice sheet, below, and then compare it with the edited copy
on page 135.   (No peeking until you finish.)

PROOFREADERS MARKS

℘ Delete.   Take out(s)

⌒ Close ⌣ up

∧ Insert at this point the ∧ information.   *added*

\# Space. Open up

[[⟵ Carry farther to the left

] Carry farther to the right

⌐ Elevate a word or letter

� Depres^s a letter or word

▯ Insert an Em space

⊗ Broken type face. Reset.

¶ New paragraph

wf   Wrong font. Letter is wrong siZe or styl**e**

Caps   Put in capitals   =   Put in CAPITALS

s.c.   Put in small caps   =   Put in SMALL CAPITALS

ital   Put in italic   =   Put in *italic*

bf   Put in boldface   =   Put in **BOLD**

rom   Put in roman type   =   Put in character

⌢ Tranpsose   =   Transpose

/ or *lc*   Lower case   =   lower case

ld   Insert a lead between lines

stet   Restore words ~~crossed out~~.

Rules for punctuation can be found at the back of any standard dictionary

---

PROOFREADING THE GALLEY PROOF *

Use the proofreader's marks and mark this galley proof with a soft pencil
or red ink. it is not absolutely necesary fors the art ist to know or use every
proofreader mark. However the marks shown here are the most common ones,
  and if used correctly, become A cleAr quick shorthand to point oot necessary
corrrections and revisiovs to the Typographer. If you are in doubt as to what
mark to use, write the instructions in the margin, or cross out the line and
in a new one

paragraph indentsare not always necessary if the paragraphs are seperated by
extra spacing. But most important criteria is to keeep th page lay out consitent.

Galley proofs should be read several tines; for content and meaning;
for punctuation and spelling, for typographical errors and layout measuremonts.
When you have completeded marking this proof check your corrections and proof
marks with the corrected qalley on the mext page

* MOST ERRORS SHOULD BE CORRECTED ON THE TYPEWRITTEN COPY.
THERE SHOULD BE VERY FEW OR NO ERRORS ON PROOFS!

CORRECTED PROOF

[—— Use the proofreader's marks and/mark this galley proof with a soft pencil or red ink. it is not absolutely necesary for the artist to know or use every proofreader mark. However, the marks shown here are the most common ones, and if used correctly, become a clear quick shorthand to point out necessary corrections and revisioys to the Typographer. If you are in doubt as to what mark to use, write the instructions in the margin, or cross out the line and write in a new one

paragraph indentsare not always necessary if the paragraphs are seperated by extra spacing. But most important criteria is to keep the page layout consitent.

[—— Galley proofs should be read several times for content and meaning; for punctuation and spelling, for typographical errors and layout measuremonts. When you have completed marking this proof, check your corrections and proof marks with the corrected qualley on the next page.

REPRODUCTION PROOF

Use the proofreader's marks and mark this galley proof with a soft pencil or red ink. It is not absolutely necessary for the artist to know or use every proofreader mark. However, the marks shown here are the most common ones, and if used correctly, become a clear, quick shorthand to point out necessary corrections and revisions to the typographer. If you are in doubt as to what mark to use, write the instructions in the margin or cross out the line and write in a new one.

Paragraph indents are not always necessary if the paragraphs are separated by extra spacing. But the most important criteria is to keep the page layout consistent.

Galley proofs should be read several times: for content and meaning, for punctuation and spelling, and for typographical errors and layout measurements. When you have completed marking this proof, check your corrections and proofmarks with the corrected galley on the next page.

When the reproduction proofs arrive they must be checked as thoroly as the galley proofs. It is not sufficient to compare only the corrections noted on the on the galley proofs with the repro. BECAUSE, when any correction is made on a line of body copy, remember that whole line must be recast on the linotype machine and reset in the galley tray. Not often, but sometimes , the linotype operator makes the correction noted on the galley proof and inadvertently makes a different error in another part of the line. Therefore, the entire line must be proofread the second tine if a correction Therefore, the entire lime must be proofread the second time if a correction Therefore, the entire line must be proofread the second time if a correction has been made on any part of it.

A few other things to check on the repro are:
Make certain the ink image is black and not gray, that the image is not smeared, that the pressure on the type was the same, top, bottom, right, and left, otherwise the type may look a bit fatter where the tympan pressed harder. Check the lines to make certain they are not canted. Sometimes the type in the galley tray slips, and this may not be very evident until the repro is pasted in with other elements in the ad that are all level and parallel.
Handle the fresh repros carefully, as the ink is often still wet,

TWO TYPICAL COPY FITTING PROBLEMS

A.   How much space will this copy fill if you must use 12 pt type?
     (Clip out several paragraphs from magazine scrap and pretend
     they are the typewritten copy handed you by the Art Director.)

Step 1   Count the number of letter spaces in one average line of the copy.
         Multiply this number by the number of lines in the paragraphs.
         This gives you the total number of letterspaces to be set.

Step 2   Choose a column width and then select a 12 pt type face from the
         type specimen sheets at the back of this section. Use a ruler or
         your line gage and count the number of letterspaces in your column
         width span of that speciman. This is your CHARACTER COUNT
         per line.

Step 3   To get the number of lines of type that will be set, divide the total
         letterspaces in your copy (Step 1) by your line character count.

Step 4   To get the depth of the column, multiply the number of lines of
         type being set (Step 3) by 12 points. (Twelve point type is 12 points
         high from the bottom to the top of the slug.) The answer will be
         the depth of the column in points.
         Use the line gage to mark the depth of the column on the layout.
         If you have no line gage handy, divide the depth in points by 72
         to get the column depth in inches (72 points = 1 inch) and use a
         ruler to mark the depth of the column on the layout.

Step 5   If you wish to lead out the column, you must allow for leads
         (say 2 points) between all lines. This , of course, will make the
         column longer.

B.   What size type face must be used to fit THIS copy into THIS space ?
     (Clip out several paragraphs from magazine scrap and pretend they are
     the typewritten copy handed you by the Art Director.)

Step 1   Find the total letterspaces in the copy.

Step 2   Draw a rectangle to represent the size of the COPY BLOCK in the layout.

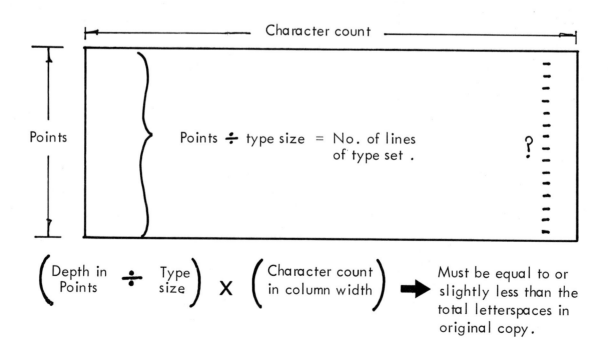

TYPE
SPECIMEN
SHEETS ❯

MACHINE SET

8 PT. CENTURY BOLD— CAPS

A TYPE FACE WHICH MEETS THE REQUIREMENTS

10 PT. GOTHIC FINE

A type face which meets the requirements
A TYPE FACE WHICH MEETS THE REQUIREMENTS

10 PT. FUTURA MEDIUM with DEMIBOLD

type face which meets the requirements of the
type face which meets the requirements of the
1234567890

A TYPE FACE WHICH MEETS THE REQUIREMENTS
A TYPE FACE WHICH MEETS THE REQUIREMENTS
1234567890

12 PT. FUTURA MEDIUM with BOLD

type face which meets the requirements of the
type face which meets the requirements of the

TYPE FACE WHICH MEETS THE REQUIREMENTS
TYPE FACE WHICH MEETS THE REQUIREMENTS

12 PT. NEWS GOTHIC CONDENSED with BOLD

type face which meets the requirements of the
type face which meets the requirements of the

A TYPE FACE WHICH MEETS THE REQUIREMENTS
A TYPE FACE WHICH MEETS THE REQUIREMENTS
1234567890

12 PT. CENTURY EXPANDED with BOLD

type face which meets the requirements of
type face which meets the requirements of

FACE WHICH MEETS THE REQUIRE
FACE WHICH MEETS THE REQUIRE

18 POINT BODONI ITALIC

ABCDEFGHIJKLM

abdefghijklmnopvrstuvwxyz

18 POINT FUTURA DEMI-BOLD

ABCDEFGHIJKLM

abcdefghijklmnopqrstuvwxyz

18 POINT FUTURA DEMI-BOLD ITALIC

ABCDEFGHIJKLM

abcdefghijklmnopqrstuvwxyz

HAND SET

30 POINT ONYX

ABCECFGHIJKLM

abcdefghijklmnopqrstuv

48 Pt. Craw Modern Bold Caps

ABCDFGHIJN

48 Pt. Copperplate Caps

ABCDFGHIJKN

60 Pt. Stencil Caps

ABDEGKNPS

72 Pt. Stymie Bold Caps

ABCEGNSW

84 Pt. Franklin Gothic Extra Condensed Caps

ABCFGJKMNRSW

96 Pt. Onyx Caps

ABCDEGHJKMNRST

HAND SET

96 Pt. Caslon Caps

ABEGNRS

96 Pt. Caslon Lower case

abefgikmrst

108 Pt. Gothic Condensed No.1 Lower case

abefgikmprstxy

14 Line Gothic Regular No.2 Lower case

abefgnst

PASTEUP

11

While waiting for his reproduction proofs to return from the typographer, the artist starts preparing his PASTEUP for the printer's COPY CAMERA. The Product Ad Comp problem from Section 8 is used as the example from which the paste up is made. The BASE of the pasteup contains the majority of the typography and all the BLACK artwork. Over this, in register, appears a transparent overlay sheet containing the COLOR images. This overlay is called the COLOR SEPARATION because it separates the color images from the rest of the ad. The printer can now fotograf the images separately.

A JOB SHEET is included which parallels the pasteup and color separation steps above but allows the student to work from his own original layout. His completed pasteup is then mounted on the same matboard with his Product Ad Comp. The two items make a good unit for his portfolio.

Although a portfolio should contain items which show the interviewer a student's FUTURE potential in design, it must also have items which show the student's technical skill at present. "Have you done any pasteup?" is often the key to that first job opening.

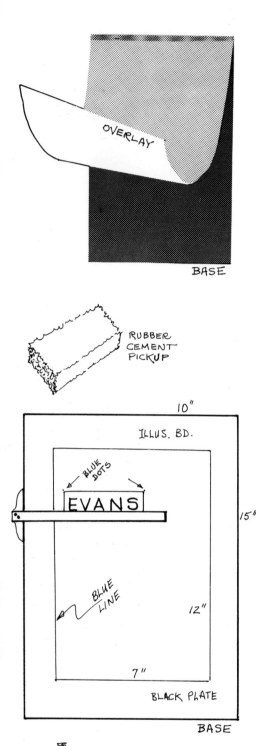

OVERLAY

BASE

RUBBER CEMENT PICKUP

10"

ILLUS. BD.

BLUE DOTS

EVANS

15"

BLUE LINE

12"

7"

BLACK PLATE

BASE

RUBBER CEMENT

ORTHO FILM IS NOT VERY SENSITIVE TO BLUE. THEREFORE WE USE A <u>BLUE WAX PENCIL</u> FOR GUIDE LINES, ETC.

BLUE PASTEL PENCILS OR BLUE CHALK TEND TO SMEAR OR RUB OFF.

MECHANICAL FOR PRODUCT AD (Project R - 10 hrs.)

The MECHANICAL may also be called the PASTEUP or CAMERA-READY ART, and sometimes the COPY or COLOR SEPARATION, depending on usage. It is usually composed of a piece of illustration board which has on it all the typography and artwork which is to appear in black, plus one or more OVERLAYS or separations. These overlays are acetate sheets. Each sheet contains all the typography and artwork which is to appear in a particular color. A second overlay would contain all the typography and artwork which would appear as another color and so on.

With some exceptions, as many overlays are necessary as there are separate HUES in the ad. However, any lighter VALUE of the same hue may be placed on the same overlay sheet. As the ad we are preparing for camera has only one hue plus black, we will need only one overlay sheet.

I BLACK PLATE

1. Borders

On a 10 x 15 piece of cold press illustration board draw a thin blue line defining the 7 x 12 inch layout of the ad. Use a right triangle and T-square to insure 90 degree corners. Precise measurement is absolutely necessary at this point, or you will add to the difficulty and COST of printing. (USE A BLUE WAX PENCIL NOT A BLUE PASTEL)

2. Trim repros

Select and cut out your repros from Section 23. When trimming reproduction proofs, leave at least 1/8 inch margin around the body copy and heads. Handle by the edges and keep fingerprints off the copy.

3. "EVANS" repro

Position the EVANS repro on the illustration board in the same position as you indicated it on the comp. Level the word EVANS with a T-square (Do not guide on the cut edge of the repro as it is probably not square.) and place a blue pencil dot on the illustration board at two corners of the repro. Turn the repro over on some scrap paper and smear the back with a thin coating of rubber cement. Pick it up and position it on the board again to coincide with the blue dots. Check the level of the word once again with the T-square and press the corners down with the tip of your knife. Lay a clean sheet of bond over the repro and press it tightly to the board by burnishing it down with your fingernail or BURNISHER. This bond paper prevents the repro from twisting or smearing, as sometimes the ink on the repro is not quite dry. Pick up the dry rubber cement around the edges of the repro by rubbing with a RUBBER CEMENT PICKUP or a clean fingertip.

4. Body Copy repro

Position and paste in the BODY COPY repro and level as above.

5. "Distributed by Brian Archer, Incorporated." repro

Position and paste in. If you wish to use "Inc." only to shorten the line, cut off the "orporated." and make a black period after Inc right on the repro.

Altho rubber cement is a handy material for many pasteup uses, large pieces of repro copy and artwork with white backgrounds can be mounted faster by using pieces of white tape on the corners. This white tape has a slick surface which is easily cleaned up; it is opaque and thus can be used to cover unwanted copy or smears; its adhesive backing is not as sticky as transparent tape and thus allows copy to be lifted and moved once it is down.

When MORTISING (adding or correcting) copy on the pasteup it is better to mount the new copy right on top of the old. This makes for no shadow problems when the pasteup is shot. If copy is butted together (see drawing) the valley shadow will usually show on the negative. The layer method, however, allows the light from one side of the copyboard to eliminate the edge or layer shadow.

6. Photo position

With your ~~blue or~~ sharp black pencil draw a silhouette OUTLINE only of the reduced fotograf without detail, on the illustration board. This will show the STRIPPER (the person who assembles the negatives.) exactly where the reduced fotograf of the product is to appear. Do not draw or render the product again, as this only wastes time.

Note: Fotografs must be kept separate from the other black art
        work because when they are copied on the copy camera
        they will have to be screened to preserve the intermediate
        gray tones.

7. Black artwork

Draw in all the other BLACK artwork on the illustration board. This will include the half-product drawing in ink, detail drawing in ink, and the trademark. Allow 1/8 inch BLEED over the blue line border for all lines or areas that print to the edge without margin. This overlap of the blue line allows for some cutting error when the page is trimmed after printing. If the ad were not going to be trimmed, the bleed would not always be necessary.

8. Trademark

Ink the circle with a ruling pen compass, or use a circle template and a cylindrical nib pen. If the trademark is to be an ellipse, use an ellipse template. See Section I for descriptions and suggestions on the use of these instruments.

Use the ruling pen compass EMPTY of ink or a circle template and cut a disc from the wax-backed sheet of 50% screen dots so that the edge of the disc LAPS the black circle. Position the zip disc over the circle, place a sheet of bond paper over the disc and burnish the disc down tightly. When completed you will note that the rough dot edge of the zip disappears against the thick black circle. If the trademark is to be an ellipse, use the ellipse template to cut the elliptical shape from the zippatone screen.

PRODUCT OUTLINE

OR LAY ZIP OVER THE AREA
AND CUT OUT WITH KNIFE.

reverse

FLOP

BLUE
LINE

IMAGE
AREA

This preprinted dot pattern appears gray to the eye because the dots are so small the reader cannot distinguish the individual dots. The light bouncing off the tiny black dots and the tiny white spaces between the dots intermingles and appears "grayish" to the retina.

When this trademark is made into a negative, into a printing plate, and finally printed on white paper, the dots still remain, of course, and give the same gray appearance.

The monogram or letters which are to appear REVERSED in the gray disc will be added later on the acetate flap. A reverse means the image is defined by the ink surrounding it, or the areas that are ordinarily black become white. Obviously the color of the paper that the reverse is printed on will be the color of the image. If you intend to print an image backwards... that is, really reading from right to left.... you call for a FLOP. The stripper then flops or turns the negative over when he strips it in. A reverse in advertising does not mean printing the letter backwards.

9.   Trim marks

Ink in 2 trim marks at each corner of the blue line border. Make them l/4 inch long and very fine. They are extensions of the borders and should be l/8 inch AWAY from the corner. These marks are used by the printer to line up his knife blade when he trims the printed piece.

10. Registration marks

Registration marks are preprinted on a roll of scotch tape about an inch apart. Burnish one on each side of the ad in the margin about l/4 inch outside the blue line. (If you do not have these cold-type registration marks, you can make a fine ink cross.) These marks are printed with the ad right on the paper stock. There is a similar set on the color plate, and as the job runs thru the printing press the pressman watches the reg marks. If the black registration marks do not coincide with the color registration marks, the press and paper must be adjusted. Later these marks are trimmed off with the trim marks and excess stock.

The black plate or BASE of the mechanical is now finished. The next step is to attach the acetate flap and complete the color separation.

II SILHOUETTE HALFTONE or DROPOUT

Although most photographs are shot and printed as rectangular half-tones, sometimes the subject looks better if it is printed without a background. If so the following procedure is used.

1. Put a flap of acetate over the mounted foto of the product. Hinge it at the top with masking tape.

2. Press ruby red on the acetate covering the product.

3. With a sharp knife cut lightly around the product edges and strip the excess red aid away from the background.

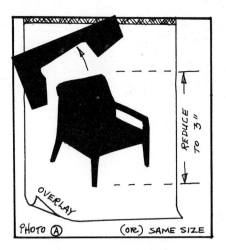

PHOTO Ⓐ   (OR) SAME SIZE

This red silhouette of the product will be fotografed by the printer to make a negative film MASK. The negative will be opaque except for the transparent WINDOW of the product shape. When the fotograf of the product itself is SCREENED there are usually some unwanted background areas or dots that appear on the neg. This mask can then be placed over the halftone negative of the product and will block out the background areas leaving the product image without a background.

SAME SIZE NEG. MASK

4. With WITNESS lines and DIMENSION lines in blue pencil, indicate the height of the product as it will appear IN THE AD. For example: The notation, "Reduce to 3 inches." written in the margin between the dimension lines, means that the foto-graf must be reduced to that size when the negative is made. (If the fotograf or other artwork is to appear the same size as the original, with no reduction, merely write "Same size." in the margin.)

5. If there are many fotos, they should be numbered or lettered in sequence and keyed to their positions in the mechanical.

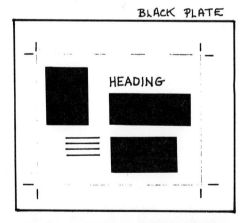

BLACK PLATE

HEADING

WINDOWING

If your ad includes a few rectangular halftones either same size or reductions, rectangles of black or the red artist aid can be pasted in position on the black plate or base of the pasteup. When the black (line) copy is shot, the rectangles will appear as transparent windows in the black negative. After the halftones are shot they can be pos-itioned under these windows and burned into the printing plate right with the line work. Of course if the halftones are to be reduced, the artist must figure the scaling to make certain the width and length of the pasted rectangles are proportional to the reduced halftone neg. Using a mechanical scaler is one of the quickest ways to do this.

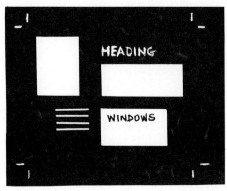

HEADING

WINDOWS

NEG.

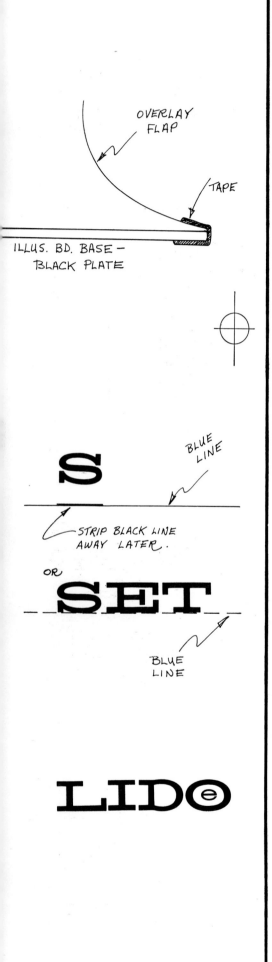

ILLUS. BD. BASE —
BLACK PLATE

OVERLAY FLAP

TAPE

S

BLUE LINE

STRIP BLACK LINE AWAY LATER.

OR

SET

BLUE LINE

LIDe

III   COLOR OVERLAY

All elements of one HUE, regardless of VALUE, go on the same overlay. The lighter values are achieved later (when the printing plate is made) by SCREENING those images so indicated on the overlay.

1.   Acetate flap

Attach a piece of 10 x 15 frosted acetate, frosted side up, as a flap to the top of the black plate with masking tape all the way across. Cut the ends neatly. The acetate should be free to fold all the way back. The masking tape should act as a hinge and should not be folded around the sides of the board.

2.   Registration marks

Strip in two registration marks on the acetate flap directly over and coinciding with the two on the black plate below. Trim marks are not necessary on overlays.

3.   Model name

Lay the sheet of wax-backed cold type face up. Use a sharp knife or single edge razor blade. Cut out each letter of the model name and include the fine black guideline underneath it, but be careful NOT to cut thru the backing sheet. Lift each letter away from the backing sheet gently.

Draw a fine blue line just below the position of the model name, so that when the black guide line on each wax backed letter is laid on the blue line the base of the letter is in exact position with that of the comp. Many artists do not use this system , as it is hard to fig-ure the correct spacing between guideline and letter base, so they cut the guide line away from the letter and place the base of the letter directly on a blue line which is drawn at the base of the word.

Use T-square and a good ruler. Keep the letters almost TOUCHING and level each letter by eye. When the word is tacked into position, lay a piece of bond over the letters and burnish the letters down on the acetate. If you have used the black guide line, trim it and strip it away.

Note: The wax-backed cold-type letters are only being used in this problem for the experience in handling cold type. Actually, reproduction proofs could be pasted down on the overlay as readily as was done on the black plate. If no cold type is available, cut out one of the typical model names in Section 23 and rubber cement it into position on the acetate overlay.

Although the model name will be printed in color, it is only nec-essary to give the copy camera an image of the shape of the word. The color will come from the ink on the printing press. Further questions on this will be explained in the section on printing.

4. Monogram in trademark (Reversed)

Cut out one or two wax-backed letters from the sheet of cold type and burnish them down on the acetate flap directly over the gray disc. This is a good example of using a SEPARATION flap for something besides color. Use a blue wax pencil (the blue pastel pencils smear) and run a zig-zag line from the monogram to the margin. Write in the margin "Reverse monogram in gray disc.". Any label or instruction, such as this, is known as a CALLOUT.

5. Registered color

For the color in exact register under the detail drawing, remove the backing from a piece of ruby red artist aid, position it on the acetate over the detail drawing, burnish it down gently, and trim the excess away with a knife very carefully to avoid cutting into the acetate flap. Red reads as black to the ortho film used in the copy camera, and yet can be made transparent for the very purpose you used it here. We can see thru it to trim to exact edges. It would be rather difficult to make the same shape as the detail drawing if we had to use an opaque black material , right ? If the image extends to the edge (bleeds), the ruby red should overlap the blue line border by 1/8 inch. Run a zig-zag blue line into the margin from the red shape and write in the margin "solid color" on the acetate.

6. Nonregistered color (Rough edged)

In this case the ruby red will not lend itself to simulating rough edges (unless we purchase a special kind with a chemical softener) so we will use another method. Use black ACETATE India ink with a sponge or brush or rag dauber, and coat the frosted surface for the effect desired immediately above the drawing on the black plate.

Again allow 1/8 inch bleed over the blue border line if the image overlaps the edge of the ad. When daubing a bleed, lay a piece of paper 1/8 inch outside the blue line border to keep the margins clean. This extra overlap allows for any trim errors made by the trimming knife. If the image was NOT extended over the edge of the ad, and the knife cut slightly outside the edge of the ad, there would be a white space or LEAK along the edge of the ad that would be unsightly. Remember that the printer trims stacks of paper at one cut and the stacks may be slightly uneven as the blade comes down under tons of hydraulic pressure.

This rough edged area of color is to appear lighter in VALUE than the solid color. (The darkest "color image" on an overlay is known as the SOLID, because the ink is mixed to match the darkest hue, and any other lighter values of this ink are SCREENED to a pattern of dots to simulate a lighter color.) Therefore, indicate with blue wax pencil in the margin of the overlay the particular SCREEN or percent of the solid you desire to have this color area printed. For example, a 50% screen of solid would mean the color would come out on the printed page about 1/2 as light as the solid color. A 10% screen would produce a very pale, almost white, color. A PERCENTAGE SCREEN SCALE is a handy thing to keep in your kit box. (SEE PAGE 180.)

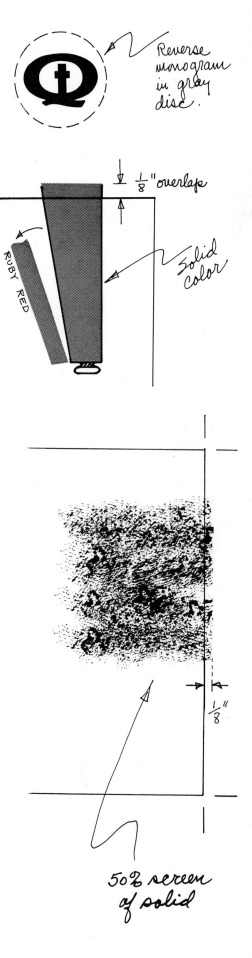

Reverse monogram in gray disc.

↓ 1/8" overlap

RUBY RED

Solid color

50% screen of solid

70%		30%

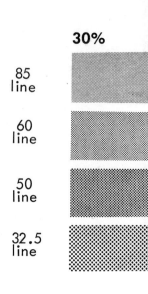

85 line

60 line

50 line

32.5 line

color swatch

To control the size of the dot in the percentage screen you may indicate the LINE used, such as: Coarse   85 line

Medium   133 line

Fine   300 line

An 85 line screen means there are 85 dots to the linear inch, etc. See Section 13 for further explanation and production use of VELOXES.

7.   Color swatch

Label the overlay by its color in the lower right-hand corner with a blue pencil: For example, "Yellow Plate". Make a swatch of your solid color about 3 inches square. You may use chalk, paint, or colored paper, but it must not be streaked, as the printer cannot tell which streak to match ! If you use more than one color overlay, you must provide a different swatch for each overlay. Always give the printer a good sized swatch, because he taps the ink out on paper with his fingers to compare with the swatch. Tapping ink directly on the swatch is a good way to see if the value and chroma are just right. If there is no room for his dabs on the sample, it is difficult for him to match the ink to the artist's swatch.

Note: Color separations are usually done in black or ruby red (ACTINIC black) artist aid because all that is necessary for the camera is an image of the shape and texture for the negatives. The COLOR will come out later on the printing press when the colored ink is mixed and printed in that image on the paper.

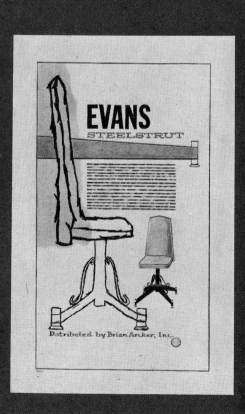

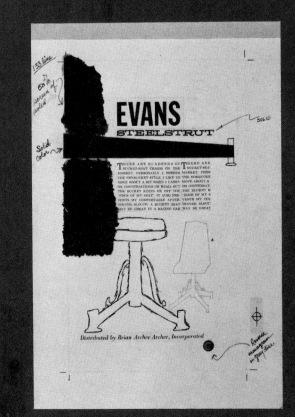

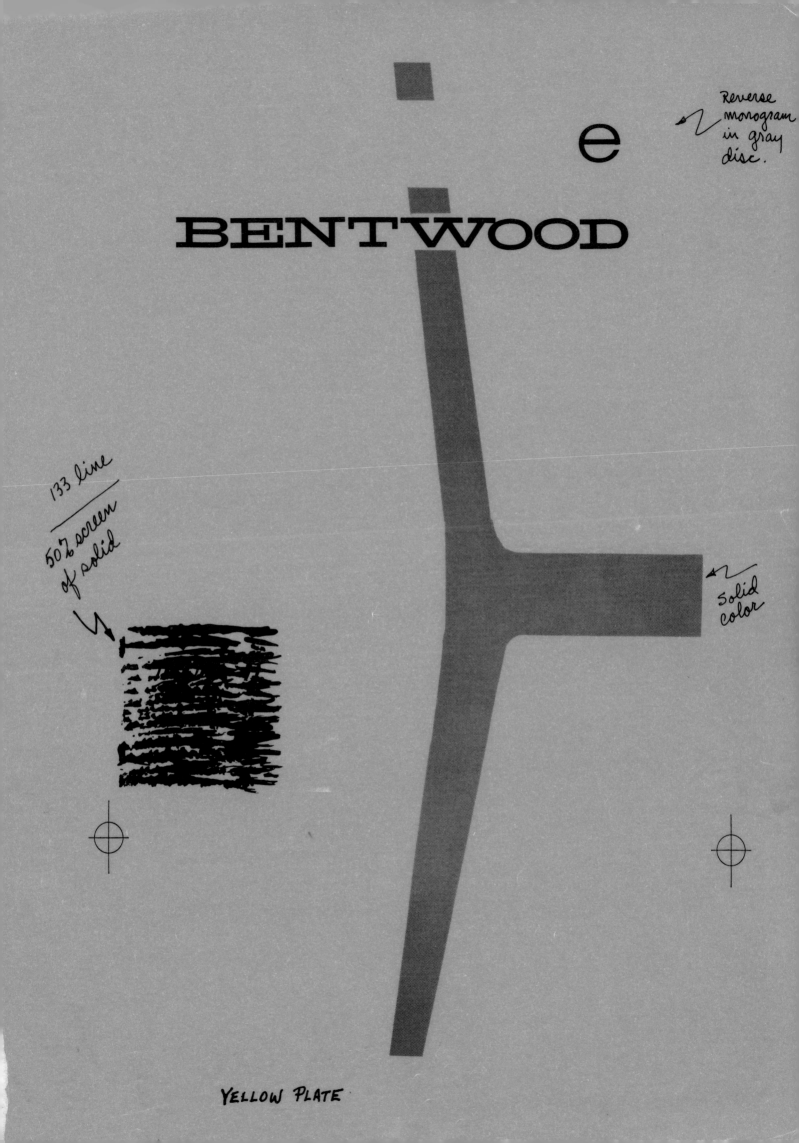

e

Reverse
monogram
in gray
disc.

YELLOW PLATE

BENTWOOD

133 line
50% screen
of solid

Solid
color

YELLOW PLATE

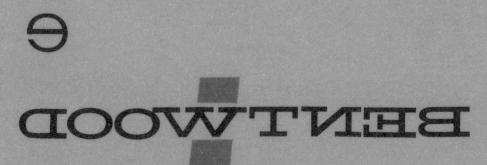

BENTWOOD

e

Solid color

133 line
50% screen of solid

YELLOW PLATE

EVANS

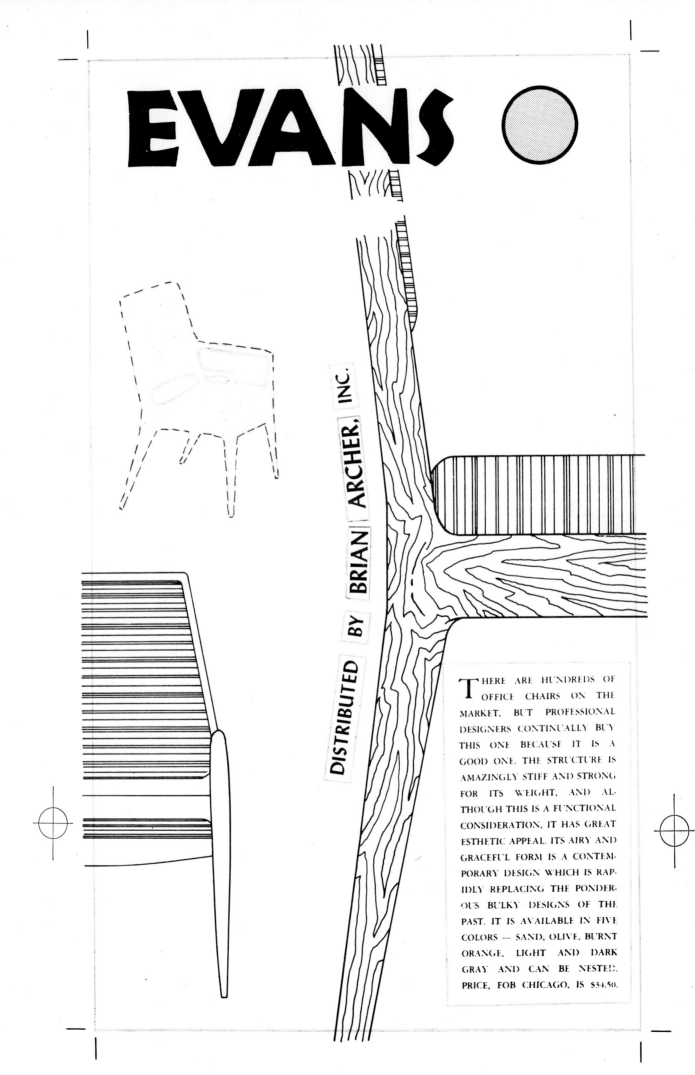

DISTRIBUTED BY BRIAN ARCHER, INC.

THERE ARE HUNDREDS OF OFFICE CHAIRS ON THE MARKET, BUT PROFESSIONAL DESIGNERS CONTINUALLY BUY THIS ONE BECAUSE IT IS A GOOD ONE. THE STRUCTURE IS AMAZINGLY STIFF AND STRONG FOR ITS WEIGHT, AND ALTHOUGH THIS IS A FUNCTIONAL CONSIDERATION, IT HAS GREAT ESTHETIC APPEAL. ITS AIRY AND GRACEFUL FORM IS A CONTEMPORARY DESIGN WHICH IS RAPIDLY REPLACING THE PONDEROUS BULKY DESIGNS OF THE PAST. IT IS AVAILABLE IN FIVE COLORS — SAND, OLIVE, BURNT ORANGE, LIGHT AND DARK GRAY AND CAN BE NESTED. PRICE, FOB CHICAGO, IS $34.50.

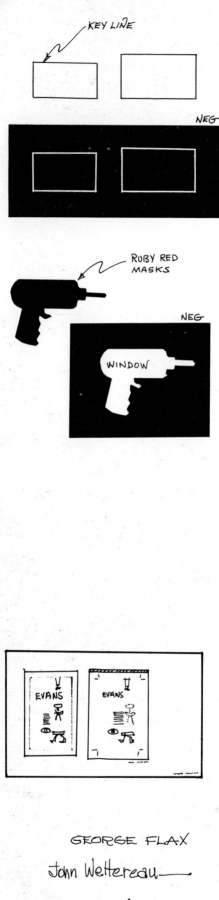

KEY LINE

Another method often preferred by the professional stripper is to have the artist show the position of the rectangular halftone by a thin red line on the pasteup. This thin ~~red~~ line then appears on the negative, and the stripper can use his precision metal T-square and square light table to cut the windows very accurately in the line negative or in the flat. The rectangular halftone negs can then be KEYED or registered exactly in place under these windows.

Suggestion:

If you are working on a job like a catalog with numerous reductions and dropout fotos, have all the halftones shot first. Then have the printer give you brownline contact prints from the halftone negatives. Cover the brownline prints with wax-backed ruby red; cut dropouts to size, and burnish down these red MASKS in position on the black plates of the mechanicals. When the black plate negatives are made, the reds will appear as transparent windows in the negs. The stripper can then place the halftones of the fotografs or original artwork exactly in position over the windows in the black negatives and thus save the time and expense of shooting and stripping separate dropout masks. This method also has the advantage of allowing the artist to place the fotos EXACTLY where he wants them.

IV PRESENTATION of COMP and MECHANICAL

(See Section 4, Matting, step 4 and 5.)

MAT the Product Ad Comp on the LEFT side of one of the 20 x 30 matboards leaving about a 3-inch matboard margin on the left. Cut the opening in the matboard large enough to allow an inch margin around the comp border. (See page 148.)

MOUNT the mechanical on the FRONT of the matboard about one and one-half inches to the RIGHT of the comp. (See page 148.)

Tape the foto dropout and color swatch neatly on the back of the mechanical.

Place your identification neatly on the back in the lower right-hand corner of the matboard in black pencil gothic caps, 1/8 inch high between 3H fine light guide lines. If you wish to put it on the front, use a white wax pencil, needle sharp, and print your name the same size (1/8 inch high) in the lower right-hand corner or in a position where it will be unobtrusive, yet relate to the total layout.

Hand in the entire unit at deadline time.

After the mechanical is completed, the black plate, color overlay, product fotograf and dropout mask are all fotografed separately on the COPY CAMERA. A negative is made of each of the four items.

The following 8-page sequence of copy board, lens-board, camera back, and inside of the vacuum door allows the student to actually place his job on the copy board, read the lens setting, check the image on the ground glass, position his film & expose. He can then "develop" the film in the trays on the page. This functional presentation thus helps the student understand this rather complex process visually.

camera lens **12**

The "black" negative, the "color" neg, the halftone neg, the masking neg, & the monogram positive film are shown drying over the darkroom trays. The development process is described simply to make for basic understanding by the artist. No attempt is made to give a complete explanation of the myriad judgements and calculations facing the camera man or printer.

If the artist understands the principles of production, he sees the necessity for precise registration and sharp separations. He begins to use the machines as creative tools in their own right. Line resolutions, bleached brownlines, etching on negs, drawing directly on grained plates become areas for experimentation. Otherwise printing machines remain a vague, bewildering, "necessary evil" of production.

film

contact screen

vacuum-back door

shutter

aperture control (f-stop)

lens board

PRODUCTION TERMS

Before starting the explanation of production processes the following terms should be studied. These terms will help the student understand the complex steps in printing production. They will also assist him in writing technical instructions to production personnel who will be producing his artwork.

Same size	No reduction or enlargement. Item is reproduced the same size as original.
Solid	Solid black or solid color. All one tone.
Flat color	Solid color. All one tone.
Pasteup	The base (usually of illustration board) and the acetate flaps which contain the artwork, typography and indicated fotografy in register.
Register	Correct alignment. An edge or line coinciding exactly with another.
Mechanical	Used interchangeably with Pasteup.
Copy	Used interchangeably with Pasteup. Also means the written material or body copy in the ad.
Halftone	Any intermediate gray between dark and white. Any artwork or photograph containing gray tones.
Halftone negative	A negative containing tiny dots which simulate gray tones.
Screen	A printed black or printed color that has been broken into a pattern of tiny dots to SIMULATE a lighter tone. (Assuming it is printed on white paper.)
Ruled screen	A transparent plastic sheet with fine lines ruled on it in opposite directions. The lines on some screens are 1/150 th of an inch apart, so the screen is referred to as a 150-line screen.
Percentage screen	A film base containing a fine dot pattern which holds back a certain percentage of light. A 10% screen, for example, is one that allows only 10% of the light to pass through.
Texture screen	A film base with a textured surface. Cross hatching, wavy lines, mezzotint or similar techniques are produced on the base photographically or mechanically.
Square halftones	Any rectangular halftone picture.
Silhouette halftone	Any halftone image printed without a background
Reverse	A letter or image made by printing ink around it. Similar to a knockout. A negative print.
Dropout	Used interchangeably with silhouette halftone and knockout.
Knockout	Used to denote a word or section cut out of the halftone.

CALCULATOR CUTOUT

Cut out the two circles and glue or drymount them on a stiffer paper if you wish. Cut out the black windows. Place the disc with the window openings over the other disc. Coincide the centers and make a pin hole in the center dots. Push a small brass fastener through the hole.

Or straighten a paper clip, push it through the center and tape the short end to the front. (See page 157 & 162 for its use.)

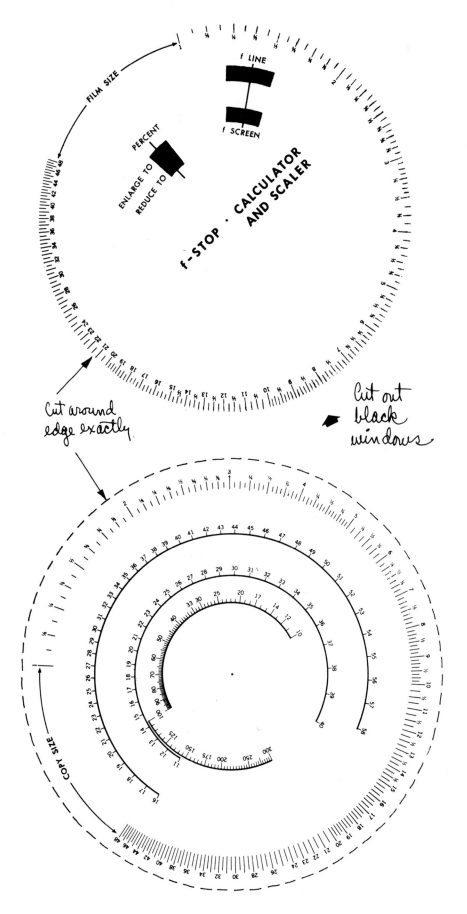

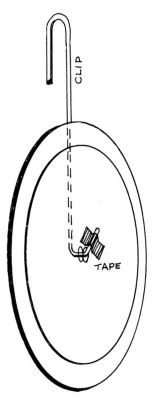

The process described in this section of measuring and focusing by eye has been replaced by cameras which focus and measure automatically.

These newer cameras use percentage scales on the copyboard track and on the lens board track. Thus the cameraman merely sets the copyboard to 100% and the lens board to 100% for same size copy, or any other percent reduction or enlargement and sets the f-stop aperture to the same percentage reading and the camera is ready and in focus..

However, this section describes the older and more direct method of measuring and focusing by eye so the student can understand better the actual camera process.

A   SHOOTING A LINE SHOT (Same size)

Making a negative from your mechanical without placing a screen over the film in the camera is known as a LINE SHOT. The objective in a line shot is to reproduce the blacks exactly and leave the white areas white. There are no subtle, interwoven areas of gray on this black plate (the base of your mechanical); therefore a line shot will give us more fidelity by keeping the black areas solid black and white areas solid white. Neither area will have a dot pattern which would gray its surface. (Turn page to Step 1.)

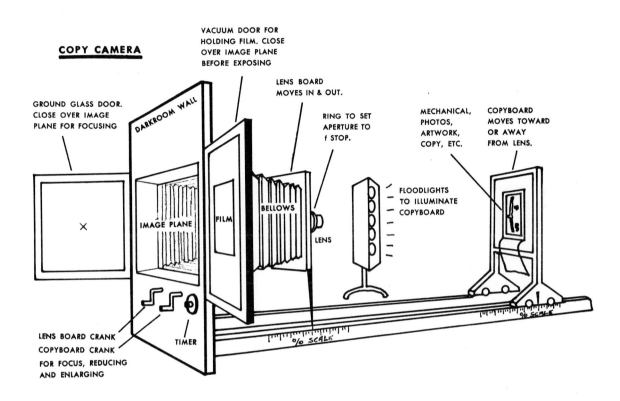

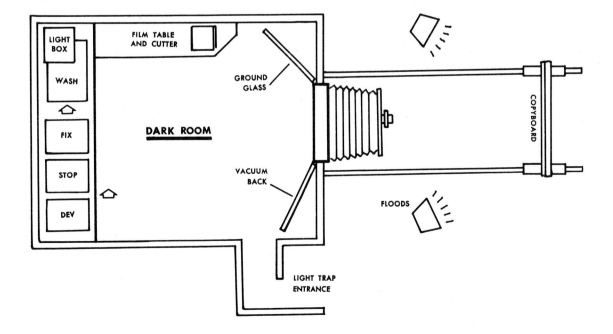

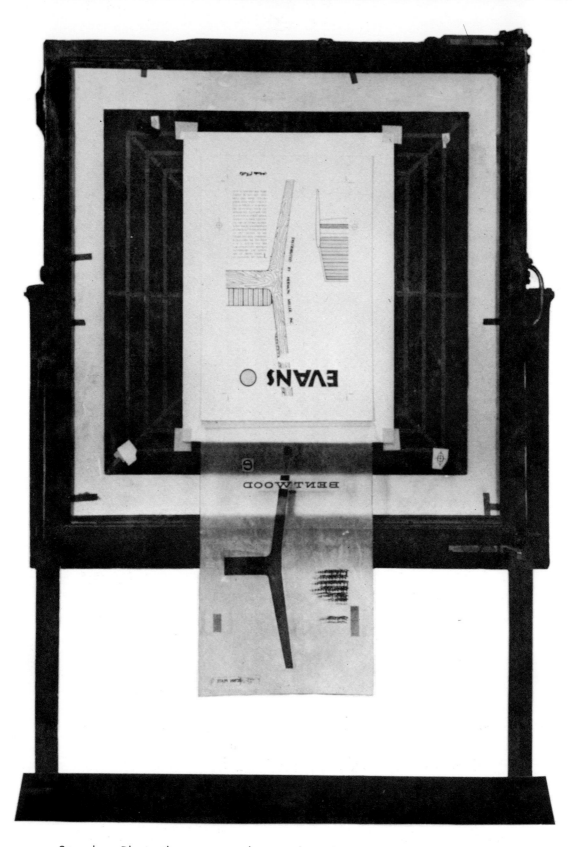

Step 1   Place the copy on the copyboard.
The base (black plate) and the acetate overlay (color plate) must be
shot separately. Assume the base will be copied first. Fold the acetate
overlay back flat and place the pasteup under the glass on the copyboard. If the pasteup is bulky, tape it to the glass. Center it. If
you put the top side down, the ad will appear right side up on the
ground glass focusing door in the camera and make it that much easier
to focus and measure.

Step 2   Make the lens setting

This shot will be same size. That is, it will not be enlarged or reduced.
The Ratio Scale & EXPOSURE CALCULATOR (See page 153.) when set
for same size (l to l) shows f-32 in the LINE window as the proper lens
opening to use for a line shot , same size. Therefore, set the lens
aperture to f-32 by moving the pointer on the scale just above the lens
on the front of the copy camera. This changes the lens diaphragm
(similar to the iris in your eye) to the correct size opening for same-
size copy. Now step thru the light trap to the back of the camera.

A

B

LENS BOARD CRANK

COPYBOARD CRANK

Step 3 Ready the camera

Turn off the white overhead lights. You are in darkness now except for the red SAFE lights. Close the translucent ground glass door over the back of the camera. Switch on the flood lamps which illuminate the copy board. Flip the jack switch to open the lens shutter. This allows the light to pass from the copy, thru the lens diaphragm to the ground glass surface where the image can be examined by the operator.

Step 4 Focus the image

Check the height of the image. A transparent plastic ruler is easy to read on the translucent illuminated glass. Use the lens board crank and copy board crank to move the two boards in and out until the image on the glass is the same height as the subject on the copy board, twelve inches in this case, and in sharp focus. Focusing is now completed. Flip the jack switch to close the lens shutter and open the ground glass door wide.

Step 5 Load the film

Remove a piece of sheet film from the film box and cut it to a size slightly larger than the pasteup, because it is necessary to copy all the trim marks and registry marks which lie in the margins of the pasteup. Place the piece of film in the exact center of the vacuum door, emulsion side out and switch on the vacuum back. This starts a pump which sucks the film against the vacuum door. Close the vacuum door over the back of the camera.

TIMER

0 5 10 15 20

FLOODLIGHTS

on off

VACUUM BACK

on off

SHUTTER

open close

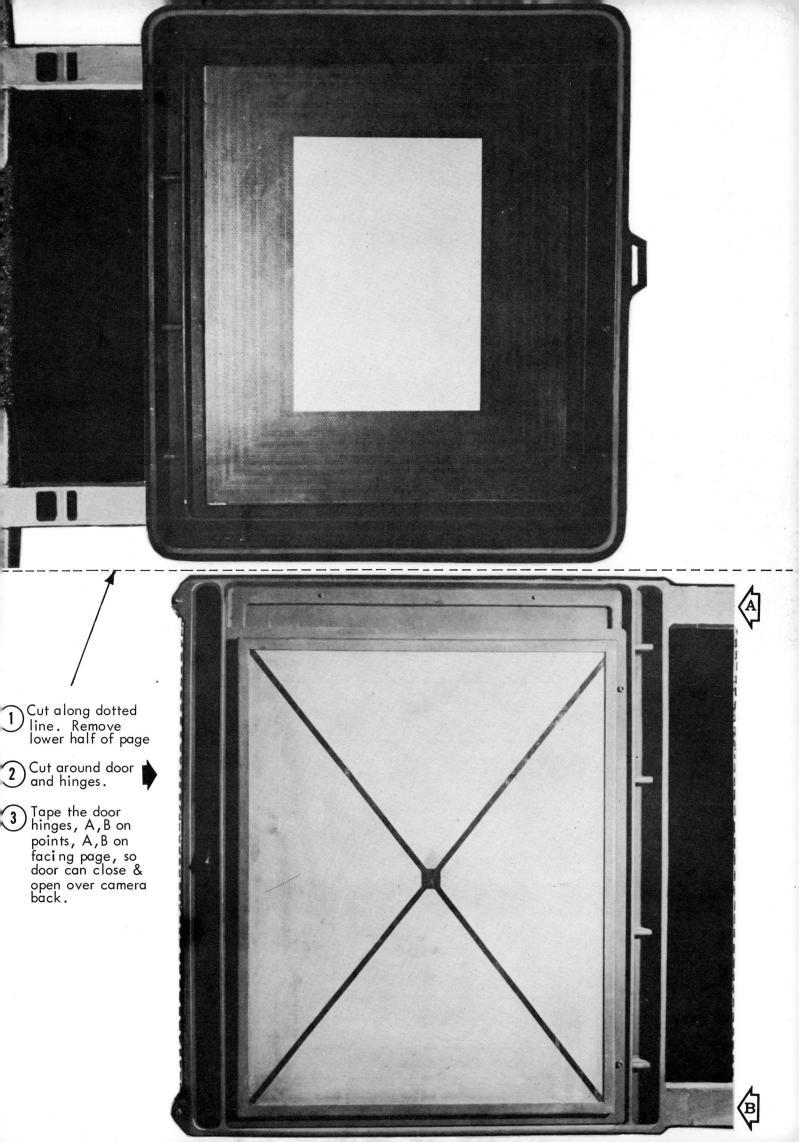

1. Cut along dotted line. Remove lower half of page

2. Cut around door and hinges.

3. Tape the door hinges, A,B on points, A,B on facing page, so door can close & open over camera back.

A

B

Step 6   Expose the film

The emulsion side of the film is now in the same position as the
surface of the ground glass was, so the image transmitted thru the
lens will be at the correct size and in focus on the film when the
shutter is opened. Set the pointer on the shutter timer to 14 seconds.
(This is standard exposure ordinarily used with ortho film.)
Press the timer button. This opens the shutter, exposes the film for
14 seconds, and closes the shutter, all automatically.
Turn off the flood lamps; open the vacuum door; switch off the
vacuum back, and remove the film from the door.

Step 7   Develop the negative

Slide the exposed piece of film into the developer tray and agitate
the developer by tilting the tray up and down. After a minute or so
the latent image will start to appear on the film. Hold the negative
(as the film is now called) up to the red safe light and examine it
carefully. The background areas should become dense and dark
without pinholes. However, any fine transparent lines or lower
case letters should not be allowed to "fill in". It thus becomes a
matter of judgment to prevent under or over development. When the
negative appears to be of the right density, slip it into the STOP
tray which stops developer action. Then place it in the FIX tray
for several minutes which hardens the emulsion and allows the excess
to be washed off later. Now place the negative in the flowing
rinse water and wash for at least 15 minutes. Hang it up to dry on clip.

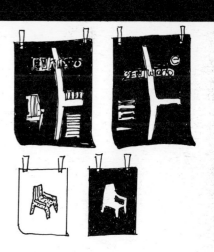

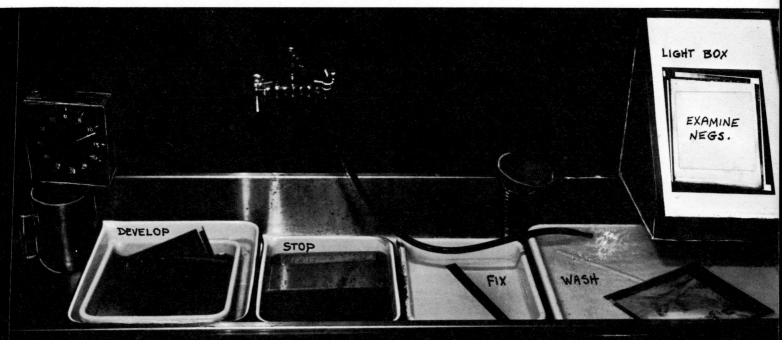

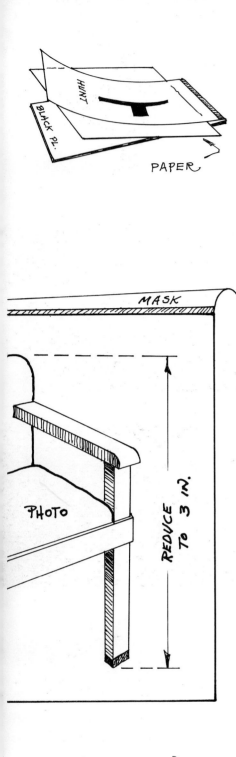

PAPER

MASK

PHOTO

REDUCE TO 3 IN.

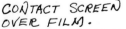
CONTACT SCREEN OVER FILM.

B   SHOOTING A COLOR OVERLAY

Place the acetate flap of your mechanical over a white sheet of paper when you center it on the copy board. The final "color" negative must be the same size as the "black" negative to register correctly when printed. Therefore no changes in camera position are made. This becomes just another same-size LINE shot. The same procedure is followed as in part A above until the "color" negative is hanging alongside the "black" neg. The area on the color overlay with the " 50% screen of solid" indication will be screened separately when the negative image is burned into the plate (Section 13.)

C   SHOOTING A HALFTONE (with reduction)

Making a negative from a photograph or artwork which has grays in it, by placing a RULED screen over the film during exposure, is known as a HALFTONE shot.

Step 1   Place the photograph on the copyboard.

The photograph and the dropout mask must be shot separately. Fold the mask back and center the photograph on the copyboard upside down.

Step 2   Calculate the f-stop from the indicated reduction.

Photos are usually reduced slightly for clarity in printing. In this example, the photo of the chair is assumed to be 5 inches high and the reduction dimensions written on the margin indicate it must be reduced to 3 inches high to fit the layout position. The EXPOSURE calculator (Cutout, page 153.) shows f-27 in the SCREEN window when FILM size (3 inches) is lined up opposite COPY size (5 inches) on the outside scale. Therefore, set the f-stop on the copy camera lens to f-27. This is a slightly larger opening than f-32.

Note: In general, reductions need less light than same size; screened shots need more light than line shots, because the screen interrupts some light after it passes thru the lens. The balance is automatically computed on the logarithmic scale of the f-stop calculator.

Step 3   Ready the camera as in the previous LINE shot.

Step 4   Focus the image

Turn on the floods. Open the shutter. Close the ground glass door over the back of the camera and reduce the image of the chair to 3 inches on the ground glass by cranking the lens board and copy board in and out. Use the plastic ruler to measure the image height. Make certain the image is centered and in sharp focus. Swing the ground glass door away. Close the shutter & turn off the floods.

Step 5   Load the film and screen

After centering the film on the vacuum door, place one of the ruled screens[1] over the film emulsion to emulsion to prevent halation. Close the door over the back of the camera & turn on the floods.

1. THESE SCREENS ARE ALSO CALLED CONTACT SCREENS BECAUSE THEY LIE FLAT AGAINST THE FILM.

Step 6   Expose the film

Set the timer and press the timer button. There are other techniques used by the camera man to increase detail in shadow areas, or build up highlight areas, but we will discuss general principles here only.

During the 14-second exposure the light must pass through the screen before it strikes the light sensitive emulsion on the film. Each tiny square space between the crisscrossed lines of the screen may be likened to a funnel with the center being clear and the edges being almost opaque with a graduated density between. A light gray area on the photograph will reflect more light through its section of spaces in 14 seconds than a dark gray area will. Thus the rays of light coming from the lighter areas on the photo sensitize the emulsion on the film faster and build up a larger DOT on the film than the weaker rays coming from the darker areas. This happens in proportion all over the film with the differences <u>accentuated</u> by the fact that the weaker rays have a tougher time getting through the denser parts of the screen holes and thus tend to leave a small tiny dot in the center of each square while the stronger rays from the lighter parts of the photograph tend to bull their way through the denser parts of the screen holes and leave a much larger dot. Soon the latent image is built up on the film as a pattern of microscopic DOTS of various sizes which simulate the entire tonal range of values in the fotograf or other continuous tone art.

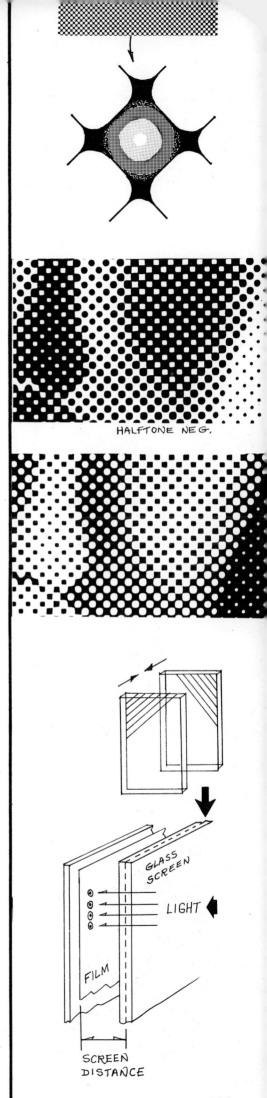

HALFTONE NEG.

Below the halftone negative is the printed image. Note the tiny <u>white</u> round dots (center of funnel) in the darks; the larger <u>white</u> round dots in the gray areas; and the overlapping <u>white</u> dots in the highlights. The black squares left in these lighter areas are the dense line intersections from the screen.

NOTE: The older types of screens were made by etching parallel lines on two pieces of glass and filling the grooves with pigment. The two sheets of glass were then sealed with the pigmented lines in contact and at right angles to each other.

This screen was positioned a short distance away from the film on the vacuum back door. Each small opening in the screen grid acted like a tiny pinhole lens. As the light came thru, it was projected as a tiny DOT on the film surface. Further theory had this tiny dot of light surrounded by concentric rings of light of diminishing intensity. At any rate, the pattern of dots simulated the continuous tones of photographs quite satisfactorily.

GLASS SCREEN

LIGHT

FILM

SCREEN DISTANCE

Step 7   Develop the negative

Turn off the floods. Open the vacuum door and remove the film. Follow the previous development procedure until the HALFTONE negative is hanging alongside the "black" negative and the "color" negative.

MASKING NEG.

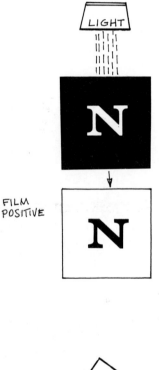

LIGHT

FILM
POSITIVE

D   SHOOTING THE DROPOUT MASK

Place the dropout mask over a white sheet of paper when you center it on the copy board. Do not change the position of the lens board or copy board, because the negative of the dropout mask must be shot exactly the same reduced size as the fotograf. Make the line shot of the dropout mask. Use the Exposure Calculator to determine your f-stop. (Remember you are not using the screen over the film this time.) Hang the masking negative alongside the other 3 negs.

E   MAKING THE MONOGRAM POSITIVE

The monogram appears as a transparent image in a dense opaque background on the "color" neg. Cut this out as a square of film. Place it over a similar size piece of ortho film in a contact printer and expose it to white light for a few seconds. Remove the ortho film and develop it like the other negatives. You now have a film POSITIVE. That is, the monogram is opaque and the background is transparent. (It is the reverse of a negative.) When making up the "black flat" (Section 13) this positive will be placed over the trademark disc to hold back the light in the monogram area. Hang it up to dry beside the other four negatives.

DUPLICATING FILM is another light sensitive film which develops as a duplicate image (In other words , a positive.) instead of a negative. This is used, for example, if you want the entire ad reversed. The heads, copy and art all show as white lines or white halftones on the printed page.

DOT PICKUP (Copy dot)

Art work often comes to the printer as a printed halftone. The original (continuous tone) photograph may have been lost, and the printed picture, cut out of the company's old catalog, is the only available print. As it is already separated into dots, the camera man needs only to shoot it LINE to get his halftone negative. However, if the halftone printed piece is to be reduced, he usually has to RESCREEN it. This he does by placing the contact screen squarely over the film in the camera and cocking the printed piece at a 30° angle on the copy board. The angle helps prevent a moire' pattern from forming on the new negative.

If the copy were reduced without rescreening,too much detail is lost, as the reduced negative can not hang on to the tiny dots, black or white, in the original,and the reduced neg goes flat.

FOR REDUCTION KEEP ART AND SCREEN AT 30° ANGLE.

30°

STRIPPING

The "black" neg, the halftone neg, its masking neg plus the monogram positive will be used to make the black printing plate.

The "color" neg plus a piece of percentage screen will be used to make the color printing plate.

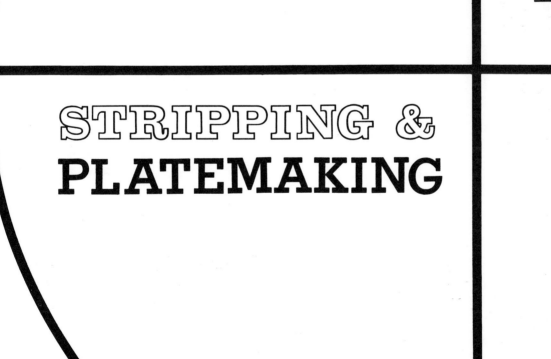

STRIPPING &
PLATEMAKING

13

FLAT

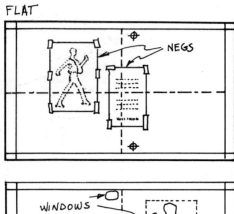

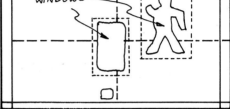

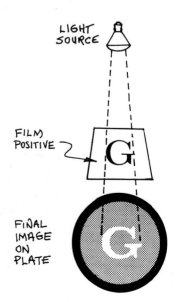

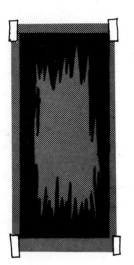

LIGHT
SOURCE

FILM
POSITIVE

FINAL
IMAGE
ON
PLATE

STRIPPING ✳

1.   Goldenrod flats

A FLAT is a rectangular piece of rather heavy orange (goldenrod) paper. It is almost opaque but on a light table will let some of the orange light pass thru. Thus the images on the negatives can be seen quite easily thru the paper. These flats are made the same size as the printing plates. Their purpose is twofold: to provide a base on which separate negs can be registered and taped in place, and to provide a mask which holds back unwanted light in the nonimage areas. Grid lines printed on the flat show margin limits, paper edge, and center lines to assist the STRIPPER in positioning the negs.

2.   Stripping the Product Ad color flat

The color negative on the Product Ad is laid emulsion side up over a 10 x 15 goldenrod flat, squared up with the edges of the flat, and centered. It is then taped to the flat. The flat is turned over and WINDOWS (openings) are cut thru the goldenrod paper opposite the image areas. Care must be taken not to cut into the negative surface. Windows are cut to expose the registration marks also.

3.   Screening a SOLID

The artist has indicated on the mechanical color overlay that he wants the rough-edged color under the drawing of the product to be 50% screen. Therefore, the stripper takes a PERCENTAGE screen from the 50° screen drawer, cuts a piece just large enough to cover the transparent "color" image on the negative and tapes it over the image area.

When the printing plate is burned thru this flat, the film screen will leave a pattern of microscopic dots on the plate in that area. When this particular color area is printed from the plate it will receive only about 50% the amount of color ink that the SOLID areas will be receiving. The paper spaces between the colored dots will be reflecting white light which will mix with the color light from the dots and make the area appear much lighter in value. Thus the color will look much lighter than the solid colors printed on the same sheet of paper.

The reason this screening is not usually done on the copy camera when the halftones are shot, is that it is difficult to register small pieces of percentage screen in particular areas on the film on the vacuum back.

4.   Stripping the Product Ad black flat

The black negative is taped emulsion side up on the flat. Windows are cut to expose images, trim marks, and registration marks.

The monogram film POSITIVE is laid over the gray disc, centered, and taped in place. The black monogram of the positive will hold back the light when the plate is burned. There will be no image in that area, and when printed, the monogram will be white surrounded by the gray disc. The transparent background of the positive, however, still allows the light to pass thru the surrounding area of gray and the transparent bounding border of the trademark.

✳

STRIPPING is a trade term which means assembling negatives and masks into a paper FLAT to get the job ready for platemaking.

Another window is cut in the place where the product fotograf has been indicated. A hole is cut into the black negative at the same place and the HALFTONE neg of the product foto is positioned over it and taped in place. The dropout mask negative is now laid over the halftone negative to coincide exactly with the edges of the product foto. This MASK allows the light to pass thru the product image but holds back the light in the background areas. Thus the product will appear as a SILHOUETTE halftone (dropout) with no background.

An alternative method would be to strip the halftone into a separate flat. The line flat is burned into the plate first and removed. Then the halftone flat is laid over the same plate in exact register and burned into the plate. This method is known as a DOUBLE BURN and is often used when the halftone fotos are close to type or artwork and there is very little space around images for level stripping. Any edges of film stripped too close to an image create a bump which may allow light to creep under the edge of the image and cause halation or TELESCOPING.

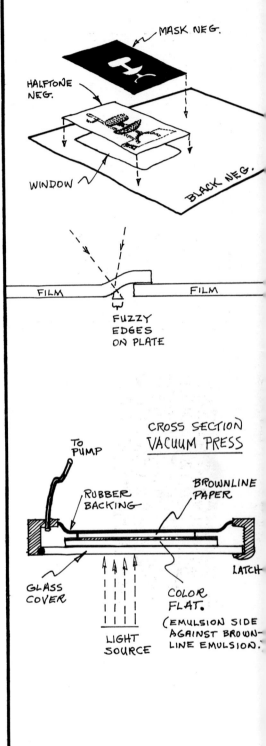

BROWNLINES and COLOR KEY

I. Making a brownline

Brownline paper is an inexpensive paper coated with a slow light-sensitive emulsion that can be developed in hot water. The emulsion is not very sensitive to ordinary room light and thus can be handled and developed without darkroom facilities. It can be purchased in standard paper sizes, such as 8 1/2 x 11, or in rolls. When developed and dried, the image is a dark brown.

The color flat is laid emulsion side down against the emulsion side of the brownline paper in the <u>vacuum</u> press. The glass cover is closed against the flat and presses it tightly against the brownline paper. The air is pumped out of the press cavity. The rubber backing then squeezes the brownline paper and flat firmly against the glass cover. The arc is set for a 1-minute burn instead of the regular 3-minute burn. The "color" image on the brownline paper will thus be somewhat lighter in value than the black image which is burned in next.

The color flat is removed and the black flat is positioned and lined up with the same piece of brownline paper exactly, so that the black image will be in register with the color image. The arc is set for a 3-minute burn this time.

The brownline paper is removed from the vacuum press, laid face up on a tray and rinsed with hot water until the total image appears quite readable. The paper is then placed in a Maduro Salt fix solution for a few minutes, rinsed again in water, and hung up to dry. When dry, the color images will show as light browns and the black images will show as dark browns.

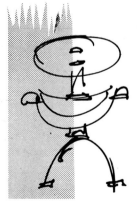

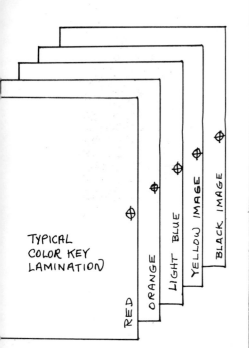

TYPICAL
COLOR KEY
LAMINATION

RED
ORANGE
LIGHT BLUE
YELLOW IMAGE
BLACK IMAGE

"Chaos is but unperceived order; it is a word indicating the limitations of the human mind and the paucity of observational facts."

Harlow Shapley —
"Of Stars and Men"

CHECK LIST:

CONTENTS
REFERENCES
CONTINUITY
SPELLING
PUNCTUATION
LAYOUT
TYPOGRAPHY

2. Color Key

Whereas the brownline proof shows differences in color location and registration by a difference in the VALUE of the browns, there is another type of proof which shows the actual color.

This type of COLOR KEY proof is made up of two or more thin acetate sheets registered or keyed carefully one over the other. The acetate sheets are similar to positive film. That is, the image appears as a color surrounded by transparent film after the sheet is exposed thru a flat and developed. Each acetate sheet develops as a single color. A typical color key proof for our Product Ad would have one sheet containing the black images laid over another sheet containing the color images in true color.

The color sheets are transparent, so laying a blue color over a pale yellow would simulate a blue with a slight green quality, etc. A variety of combinations can be developed so that the majority of color separations can be reproduced as a laminated color transparency for approval by the artist before the printing plates are made.

3. Checking the proofs

The artist and printer both examine the proof and note any corrections or registry problems right on the proof. Most of the time the corrections can be made by shifting the negatives slightly in the flat, or opaquing out blemishes on the negative. The more serious corrections may have to be made by reshooting the mechanical, or even redoing the artwork, to gain the total effect desired. The brownline or color key are excellent check points for most jobs. If a serious error was not discovered until the job had started running thru the press, or worse yet, if the entire job was run before the error was discovered, it could cost the client, or the artist, or the printer (depending on whose fault it was) a considerable amount of money.

The following are some naturals that have tricked the best artists, clients, and printers in the country. Don't initial those proofs too quickly. Look, think, and relook. It is always a good idea if the artist can get the copywriter, the engineer, and others in on a "quick look" basis. Even the office secretary sees the layout from a different viewpoint.

A secretary once pointed out on a brownline proof that the street address of our branch office in San Francisco was really the address of our Boston branch, and vice versa. This would have been printed on 25,000 four-page brochures going to engineering firms all over the world. I can still picture the "No such address" return mail! Br-r-r-r-r. She saw the proof with a different viewpoint: Mailing, not layout.

Another time an engineer noticed that the fotograf of a machine he had designed had somehow become flopped in the stripping process. The controls all appeared as though designed for a left-handed operator. This would not have made for good Sales Engineer – Advertising Dept. rapport if it had been printed. He saw it with a different viewpoint: Function, not layout.

Trademarks printed upside down make clients froth at the mouth. Many modern trademarks are somewhat abstract. Stripping in an elliptical or rectangular shape on a dim halftone negative can lead to some unique results.

Salesmen may not have the slightest idea how a brownline is made, but they look at the proof with company image in mind. Credit policies, sales contract clauses, proposal schedules are all areas that a salesman will check automatically because it affects HIS job. The artist cannot know all areas.

After the reproduction proofs are checked, it is assumed they get pasted in correctly. Sometimes, however, blocks of copy that are similar in shape get pasted in the wrong position. The copywriter always enjoys reading his own copy, and nine times out of ten he will catch **discrepancies** in continuity or position of paragraphs that otherwise may go completely unnoticed. He sees the ad from a different viewpoint: Words, not pictures.

Obviously in a large agency there are qualified people who are well paid to see that these errors do not happen. But many of you students will be working alone with small firms, department stores, job shops, even running your own business. Suggestions like the above help keep errors to a minimum. Remember – change your VIEWPOINT when you proofread and proofread 5 or 6 times.

Another thing I like to point out to students is that, in general, people are fascinated by the things the art department does. If you can include them occasionally, without interfering with their own work, you establish a good rapport. Asking those concerned to help check some proofs from their viewpoint gives them a sense of importance and gets them interested in helping you keep standards up. Granted, they sometimes point out picayunish items, but there is no harm in this. There are many gray areas of solution where the kind of decision depends completely upon "who"s in the saddle." All told, however, the philosophy of letting others understand your work and working WITH you while you as the artist still make the FINAL decision , is a great way of living and working as an artist in the business world.

At the other extreme, some artists tend to regard the art area as sacred property. "Nobody gets to see that brownline but us. We'll do the job, and we'll take the blame if it's not done right. Keep that chain up. We lost a mat knife last week. Sorry, you're not supposed to see the roughs. Now , look Joe, you're in the photo department. You just make the prints... we'll do the layout. Sally, when the typographer calls, tell him if I want to order 6 point italic caps, that's my business ... so he thinks it isn't going to read ? That's my business, I repeat, not his."

The difference between these two points of view lies more in the tact and manner of dealing with suggestions than in the philosophy you subscribe to. Esthetics and layouts may be your forte, but there is no reason to rub people the wrong way in production, sales, and administration when your art dovetails into these departments every day.

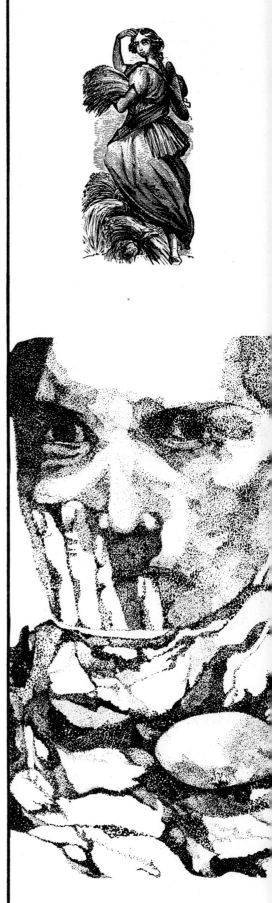

When things get a little hairy, keep your sense of perspective (humor). Remember at 2 AM during a rush deadline, sometimes, that the universe was created for people — not advertising!

169

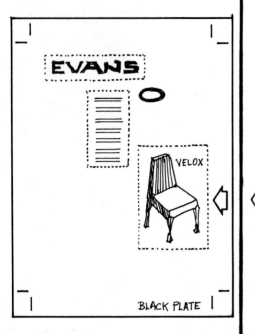

BLACK PLATE

A 30 LINE 40% TINT REDUCED 50% BECOMES A 60 LINE 40% TINT

A 30 LINE 10% TINT REDUCED 50% BECOMES A 60 LINE 10% TINT

VELOX PRINTS

A VELOX is a screened print somewhat similar in appearance to a brownline. The halftone negative is laid over a high contrast fotografic paper (emulsion to emulsion) in the vacuum press and exposed for a few seconds. After development the image appears in black dot form on the semi-glossy paper. This print can then be pasted directly on the mechanical with the other LINE material. (When the continuous tones of the original foto have been separated into dots , the print may be considered LINE material.) For example, let us assume the halftone neg of our chair in the product ad was used to make a velox. The velox could then be pasted on the black plate (base of the mechanical) in the exact position indicated for the chair foto. The cameraman can now make a single LINE exposure for the black plate, recording the dot image of the chair velox and the other line typography and artwork simultaneously. This eliminates part of the time-consuming job of stripping the halftone negative in position on the line negative in the flat as was done before.

Another advantage of using velox prints on the mechanical is that the artist can see the entire composition. He can also judge the quality of the halftone negs by the appearance of the screened prints.

There are limitations in using velox prints, however. One is that they require coarser screens at present than are normally used, so that there will be enough separation between the dots.

The choice of screen used to MAKE a velox is also somewhat critical. If the mechanical (with pasted on velox) is going to be shot same size, the screen used to make the velox should be between 85 to 120 line. If the velox is going to be pasted on a mechanical which will be reduced 50%, the screen used should be coarser, perhaps 65 line. Then after reduction, the velox print will show no finer than 130 line. Top notch printers can handle 150-line veloxes, but ordinarily it is safer to stay with slightly coarser dot patterns.

One other check before the entire job is run can be the COLOR proofs. These proofs are the first few sheets that roll off the printing press when the color run has actually started.

This section does not attempt to show the many details, judgments, and technical skills that are inherent in stripping and platemaking. It does attempt to give the artist some knowledge of the principles and working problems involved in processing his artwork. By understanding WHY, he will be able to produce less expensive and better mechanicals. By understanding HOW, he may be able to use these tools to further his own expression. Negatives, emulsions, screens, masks, developers, positive and negative plates should be as exciting to an artist as watercolor, stencils, oils, engraving tools, or charcoal.

LITHOGRAPH PLATEMAKING

Color plate

A litho printing plate is a thin sheet of metal coated with a light-sensitive emulsion. The "color" flat (that is the flat containing the negative of the color images) is laid emulsion side down, face to face with the emulsion side of the plate and placed in the vacuum press. (If the percentage screen has not been taped in place, a piece of percentage screen is now cut out and laid over the image area that is to be screened.) The glass cover is latched tightly against the flat and plate, and presses them against a flexible rubber backing. The air is pumped out of the cavity between the cover and the backing, and the rubber backing squeezes the plate and flat firmly together against the glass cover. The negative and the plate are now in perfect contact. There are no wrinkles and light cannot fan out or creep under areas of the negative.

The glass front of the press cover is faced toward an arc lamp about 24 inches away, and the arc timer is set for about a 3-minute burn. The rays from the arc pass thru the transparent images of the negative and burn a similar image on the surface of the plate.

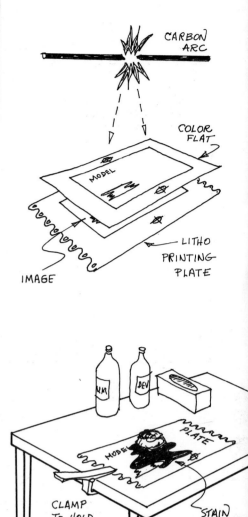

The plate is removed from the press and placed emulsion side up on the developing table. The surface is rubbed with process gum, then with a pad soaked in liquid developer and stain. The image gradually appears, and the red stain helps it become more visible. The image that appears on the plate is READ RIGHT. That is, the copy can be read, and the fotografs appear in natural left-right relationship. The chemistry of the surface of the plate has been altered by the development process. The image area is NOT receptive to water. The non-image area IS receptive to water. The color plate is now ready to be placed on the plate cylinder in the printing press.

Black plate

The black plate is made from the "black" flat and another printing plate in exactly the same manner as the color plate was made. We now have two printing plates ready to go.

GO

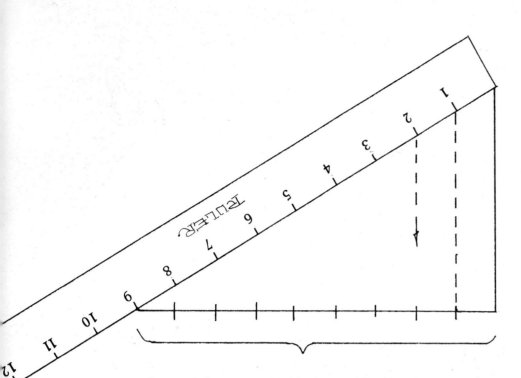

One quick way to divide a specific line into equal parts is to angle a ruler above the line after selecting the number of parts on the scale. Then drop parallels to the line.

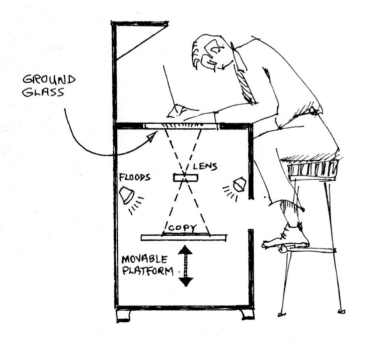

GROUND GLASS

FLOODS

LENS

COPY

MOVABLE PLATFORM

A LUCY (CAMERA LUCIDA) IS ANOTHER DEVICE FOR PROPORTIONING, ENLARGING OR REDUCING ON A GROUND GLASS PLATE. THE ARTIST OR STRIPPER CAN THEN TRACE, DRAW, OR MEASURE FROM THE IMAGE.

The artist must also realize he is part of a TEAM. The papermaker, the copy writer, typographer, fotografer and printer are often artists in their field also. And only complete rapport with the best of these will produce that subtle quality and feeling the designer searches for.

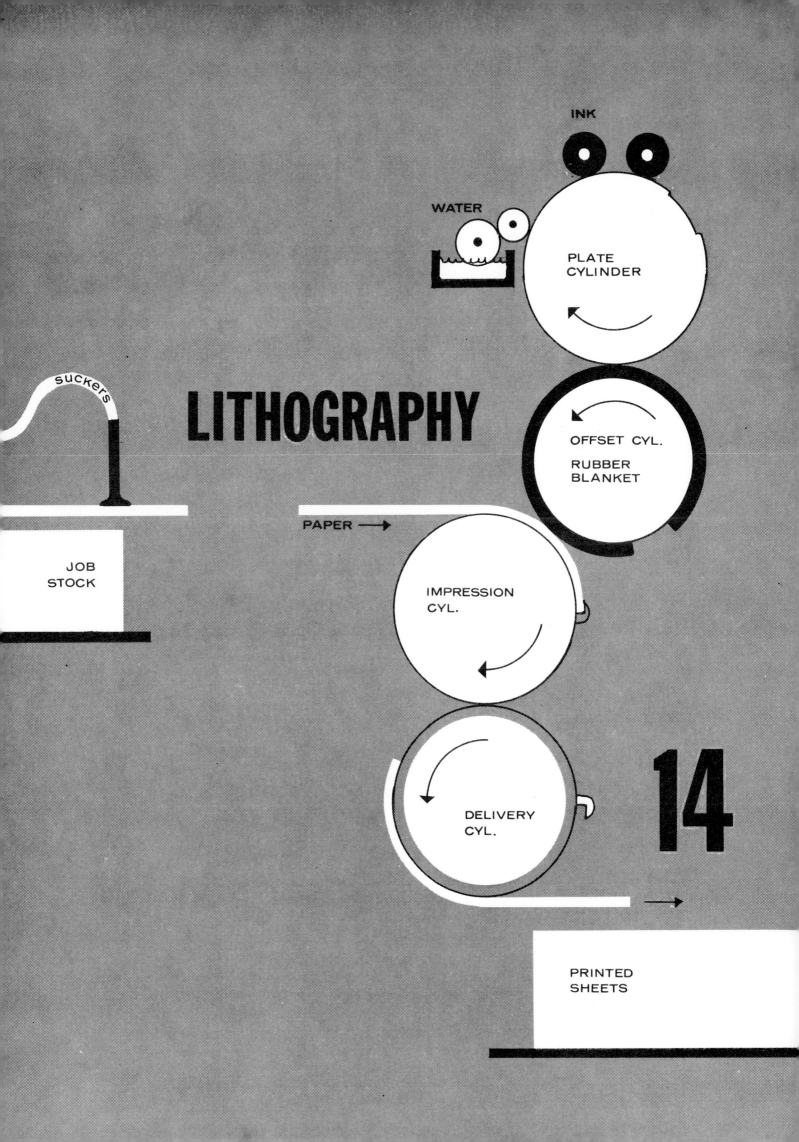

INK

WATER

PLATE
CYLINDER

LITHOGRAPHY

suckers

OFFSET CYL.

RUBBER
BLANKET

JOB
STOCK

PAPER →

IMPRESSION
CYL.

14

DELIVERY
CYL.

PRINTED
SHEETS

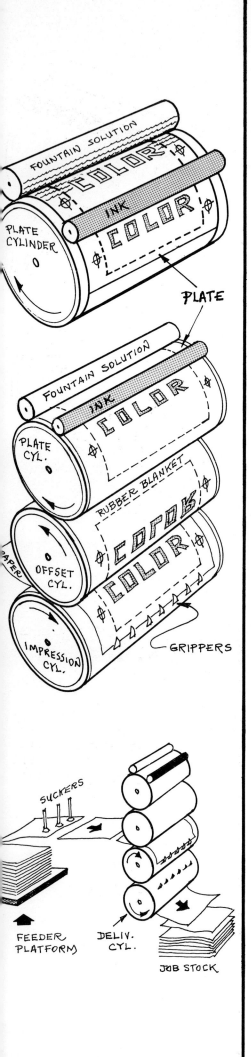

THE COLOR RUN

1. Inking the plate

The color plate of the Product Ad is wrapped around the PLATE CYLINDER in the printing press. The colored ink that has been mixed to match the artist's color swatch is put on the INK ROLLERS, and the press is started.

As the plate cylinder turns, the plate is bathed with a thin film of moisture as it passes under the FOUNTAIN SOLUTION ROLLER. This film of moisture is attracted to the NON image areas and the image areas remain dry. The plate then passes under the ink roller. The ink, being greasy and tacky, adheres to the dry image but is repelled by the film of moisture lying on the nonimage areas.

2. Image transfer

If the READ-RIGHT image on the plate were now transferred directly to the paper, the copy and art work would all be printed backwards and would READ WRONG. Therefore another cylinder covered with a rubber blanket is placed between the plate cylinder and the paper.

This OFFSET cylinder presses against the plate cylinder as it revolves and receives the ink image on its rubber surface. It makes a half turn and transfers this color image to the paper. The image is now Read Right on the paper, with the registration marks printed in the margin.

3. Paper feeding

The paper stock is cut to a size slightly larger than the ad and stacked on the FEEDER platform at one end of the press. As the sheets are sucked off the top to be fed into the press, the platform raises automatically. Several SUCKERS pick up the top sheet of paper and start it along the conveyer system to the GRIPPERS on the IMPRESSION cylinder. The grippers open and BITE down about 1/4 inch over the forward end of the sheet. As the impression cylinder turns, it presses the paper against the offset cylinder, and the paper receives the color image from the offset cylinder. The grippers then open and pass the edge of the sheet to the grippers on the DELIVERY cylinder which pulls the sheet free and releases it on the stack at the other end of the printing press. The stack of paper with the printed image on it is referred to as the JOB STOCK.

4. Clean up

When the run is finished, the JOB STOCK is stacked to one side and allowed to dry. The color plate is removed from the plate cylinder, cleaned, coated with a thin film of process gum to protect the image, and stored. The colored ink is removed from the ink rollers by washing them with thinner. One of the printed sheets is often placed with the stored plate as a proof. A series of these proofs are called the PROGRESSIVES or Progs.

THE BLACK RUN

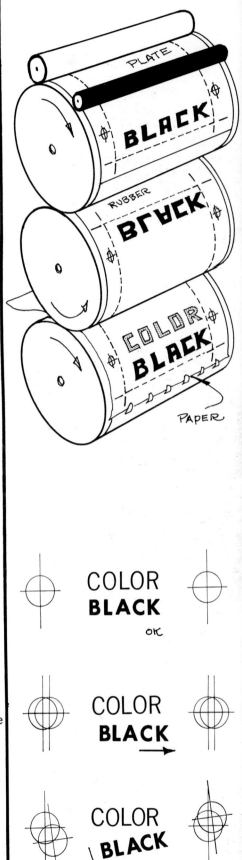

PAPER

1. Inking the plate

The black plate of the Product Ad is wrapped around the plate cylinder in the printing press. Black ink is put on the ink rollers, and the job stock (with color image on it now) is stacked on the feeder platform. The press is started.

2. Image transfer

As before, the image on the plate is inked (in black this time), and as the plate cylinder turns, it transfers the image to the offset cylinder which transfers the image on to the paper. Registration marks and trim marks are printed in the margins. Remember that the impression cylinder is under the paper, and that its only function is to press the sheet against the offset cylinder as they revolve together. There is no image or ink on the impression cylinder... all it does is impress the paper against the ink on the rubber blanket.

3. Paper feeding

A certain amount of adjustment on the press is necessary before the ink is printing satisfactorily. This time is often called MAKE READY. To avoid wasting the job stock, the pressman usually runs thru some scrap sheets of paper for make ready. When the ink is printing evenly on all sides, without specks or doughnuts ⊙ appearing, the press is ready. At this time, one of the black progressives (this is just the black image now without the underlying color image) may be put to one side to be stored later with the black plate.

The job stock is now started thru the press. Four or five sheets are run thru the press first. The fifth or last sheet is then examined by the pressman particularly for REGISTRY. If the black registration marks coincide exactly with the previously printed color registration marks, all is well. However, if the black image is above, below, right or left, or cocked at an angle to the color image, then adjustments have to be made in the conveyer system to correct the paper position. Once the adjustments have been made, the job is run off as rapidly as possible with the pressman standing by to watch for any variation from normal.

COLOR
BLACK
ok

COLOR
BLACK
→

COLOR
BLACK
↓

4. Clean up

When the job is completed it is usually stacked on a palette or dolly and moved near the cutter for later trimming. The black plate is removed from the plate cylinder, cleaned, coated with a thin film of process gum to protect the image, and stored with the other plate and progressive proofs. The press is cleaned and made ready for the next job.

TOP PIECES AND EDGES OF
DAMP STACK MAY DRY & CURL.

STIFF PAPERS
TEND TO WHIP
GOING THROUGH
PRESS.

SUCKERS
HAVE DIFFICULTY
PICKING UP
POROUS PAPER

WHO ?

Changes in humidity sometimes cause paper to shrink or expand, and other technical matters give printers many many problems. As an artist, be aware of these, and learn to compliment printers on well-done jobs, as often, or oftener than you criticize jobs which need correction. If you do, you will have a shop that enjoys working with you. The artist who is complimentary to others will never be begrudged the perfectionist attitude in his search for excellence. Artists must be critical. And as the criticism almost always involves other people in advertising, the surest way to get them working WITH you is to let them feel they have been part of the final solution. The easiest way to do this is a verbal " Thanks, Joe. Without you fellows I'd never make it." Sometimes an informal letter to a man's supervisor, or a more formal letter to the manager of a plant expressing your appreciation for the past year's efforts can do wonders in personnel relations or in just having more fun working with people you like.

5.   Reruns

The flats, a set of untrimmed progs, and a few of the trimmed complete ads are usually packaged and returned to the artist. Ordinarily the printer keeps the plates, altho there are many different arrangements made between agencies, printers, and clients as to who keeps what.

Let there be one caution here: When a policy is established, make certain all parties are aware of their obligations and DO keep a complete file and know the length of time production items are to be kept. If a client wants a reprint on a certain brochure after 6 months have passed, it is very embarrassing not to know where the plates, negs, or mechanicals are stored. The game of "Oh, I thought you were to keep them !" ruffles tempers and causes many an overtime hour without profit. In the larger well-run agency, certain departments take care of total accounts over a long period of time. But for the starting artist in small business, it is a good idea to WRITE down some of the responsibilities of people working with you. A monthly check of this responsibility list, with an occasional memorandum or question to parties concerned, will save many a dollar in your first three years in industry.

Roughs, Comps, Orig. Art . . . . .   Client ——— ?
Mechanicals, Repros . . . . .   Agency ?
Negs and Flats . . . .   Agency ?
Printing Plates . . . .   Printer ?

PRINTED HALFTONES

The fotograf of the product has now been reduced, shot as a halftone negative, burned into the black plate as a halftone image, and printed on our final ad as a halftone picture. The dark grays and light grays of the original fotograf are reproduced as well as the lights and deep darks. Further explanation of this OPTICAL ILLUSION is necessary at this point to help the artist make judgements concerning the various SCREEN RULINGS or SCREEN PERCENTAGES. These judgements can be useful in producing original prints for fine art exhibitions as well as commercial copy work.

The printing press cannot produce light gray ink or dark gray ink from black ink. However, it can print microscopic DOTS of black that are unrecognizable as dots to the eye. The light reflected from these tiny dots, when mixed with the light reflected from the white paper, appears gray to the eye.

Dark grays are simulated by a pattern of large microscopic black dots with lesser areas of paper showing thru. Light grays are simulated by a pattern of smaller microscopic black dots with larger areas of paper showing thru. Deep blacks are made by printing the ink as much like a solid as possible.

Ordinary halftones have certain peculiarities. Because the ruled screen covers the entire image area, there will always be some tiny black dots in the pure white or HIGHLIGHT areas, and there will always be some tiny white paper spaces showing thru in the supposed pure black or solid areas. Use a magnifying glass and examine some pictures in magazines. You will probably discover the whites in the picture are not quite as white as the paper in the margin. Also the blacks in the halftone picture have a pattern of tiny white dots, whereas the black in LINE copy, such as typography, is solid black. The typical reader does not even notice that the blacks in the pictures are rather grayish, so this is not a very critical problem in most publications. However, to an artist who is attempting to produce a print with deep soft blacks and snow white areas for contrast with subtle grays, this is a matter of real concern.

CORRECTIONS

There are a number of techniques used by the camera man, the stripper, or the platemaker to give the artist what he desires in the final printed piece. A thorough talk with the production man before the job is processed saves many a rework.

FLASH or BUMP are terms used by the camera man to describe overall exposure of the film either thru the screen or without the screen to intensify certain qualities desired in the negative, such as more detail in the shadow area.

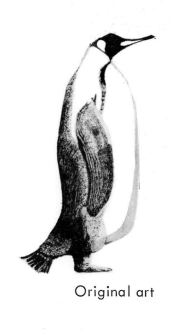

Original art

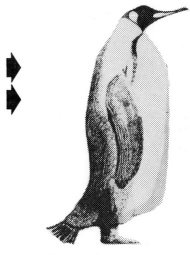

Untouched halftone

CYANIDE ETCH CORRECTED NEG. HAS MOST OF DOTS ELIMINATED TO GIVE BETTER DARK IN HEAD.

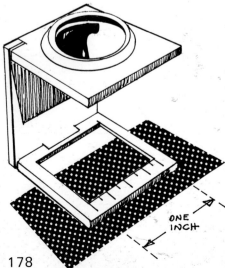

Corrected halftone

CYANIDE ETCH is a process which can be used to decrease the size of the white dot in the blacks. The stripper usually does this by soaking a piece of cotton in a cyanide solution and rubbing the transparent areas of the negative on the emulsion side. The cyanide eats away the tiny dots of emulsion left in the transparent area. Then, when the plate is made, the black image is burned in as a solid and no white dots appear to make it look grayish.

OPAQUING out the highlights is another technique. The red or black opaquing fluid is used on a fine brush to opaque out the transparent dots in the dense areas of the negative. Then when the plate is made, the dense area holds back the light completely. No light hits the plate in that area, and the highlight remains pure white with no tiny black dot pattern to make it look grayish.

POCKET MAGNIFYING GLASS FOR EXAMINING DOT PATTERNS AND COUNTING.

ONE INCH

Opaquing out or drawing freely with opaquing fluid on a neg produces some very interesting work. By understanding and doing some of these techniques you can broaden your own areas of expression. The hiss of arc lamps, the eerie glare from the light tables, the semigloom of the stripping room, the rattle and roar of the presses can become an atmosphere of creativity. Learn to use the complex machine as a creative tool in its own right. Too many artists regard these processes as a vague mass of bewildering "necessary evils" of printing.

There is really no reason why the intelligent artist cannot understand and control these tools in the same manner that he controls the sable brush on watercolor paper, oil paint on the canvas, or the graver on the metal plate. Painting, etching, or scratching on a negative film base, drawing directly on grained or DIRECT IMAGE plates, can give the final print a fresh, unique look that is as original as it is different from the more traditional methods.

To produce these works, however, the student's attitude must be broadened. He must believe that production processes can be used not only to copy PREVIOUSLY DONE art work, but can be used to actually create new images. This attitude change will come if the student is encouraged to try new methods and has the nerve to experiment. Results will not always be satisfying, and many an eyebrow will be raised by the nonadventurous kibitzers watching the "messes" pile up on the paper. But every now and then interesting things happen, sometimes accidentally, sometimes with forethought and planning. When an exciting result does arrive, announced or unannounced, it is the greatest feeling in the world to a creative person, especially if he has concocted it himself.

RULED SCREENS (Also referred to as CONTACT SCREENS)

In Section 12, Copy Camera, we placed a ruled screen over the film when shooting the halftone foto of the product. This screen was a clear, flexible, acetate sheet covered with a grid of fine lines ruled in opposite directions (That is at a 90°angle to each other.)

Each tiny square in the grid varies in density from the opaque lines around its edge , thru decreasing density to a tiny transparent hole in the center of the square. Thus during a short exposure the light travels easily thru the clear hole in the center of each square and tends to get held back in the denser areas around the hole. If the exposure is longer, however, the light finally wades thru the denser areas and builds up a larger dot. The longer the exposure is, obviously, the larger the dot becomes, and as the tiny dot in the center can never get blacker than black the dot remains uniform in value.

As the black round dot on the neg gets larger, it tends to fill up the grid. The intersections of the lines on the screen, however, are very dense and squarish and thus leave tiny transparent squares on the negative. These tiny transparent squares then become the tiny black squares in the printed light areas.

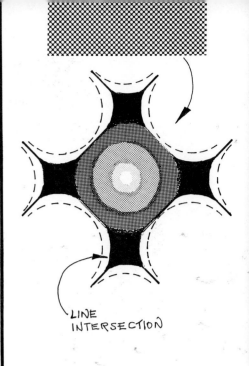

LINE INTERSECTION

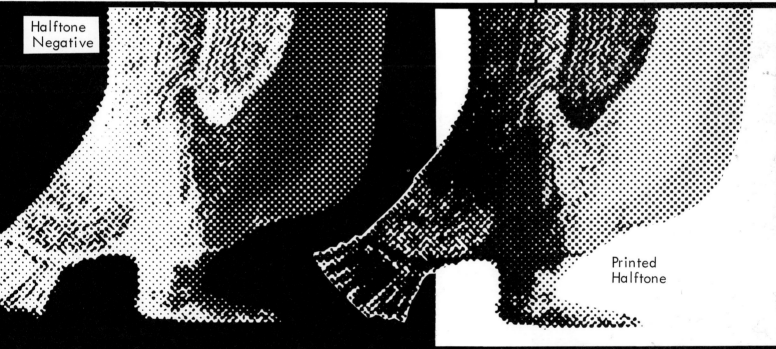

Halftone Negative

Printed Halftone

The lines on the coarser screens are 1/65 of an inch apart. The lines on a very fine screen may be 1/300 of an inch apart.

65 line	Newspapers or coarse textured papers
85 line	
120 line	
133 line	General offset lithography or letterpress
150 line	
300 line	Usually requires special papers to prevent dots from smearing.

The screen RULING used on a particular production job is determined by the printer and artist who usually discuss the paper texture, effect desired, and cost.

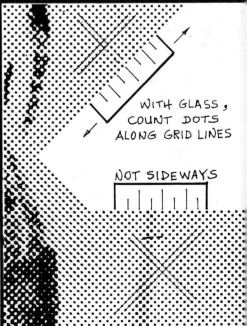

WITH GLASS, COUNT DOTS ALONG GRID LINES

NOT SIDEWAYS

179

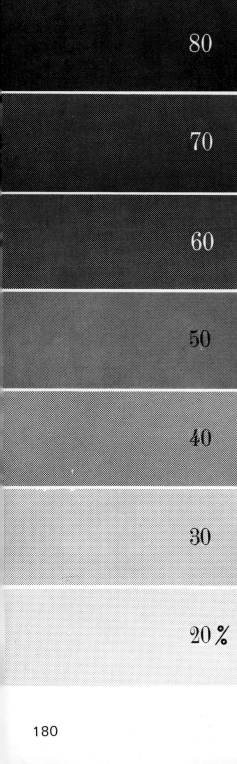

PERCENTAGE SCREENS

In Section 13, Stripping and Platemaking, we placed a small piece of 50% screen over the "rough-edged color" image on the color negative. This was done to make the color image 50% lighter than the solid color being printed on other portions of the ad. These percentage screens are similar to the halftone screens but do not have the density gradations. They are made from the halftone screens and have a different function. They are used to HOLD BACK a certain overall percentage of the printed image, allowing the white paper to show thru, which lightens the image.

The printer often prepares these screens himself. He chooses an average rule screen, say 120 line, lays this over a piece of film, and exposes it to white light for a short length of time to get a tiny dot pattern. Using another piece of film, he exposes for a longer period of time to get a slightly larger dot pattern, and so on. After the pieces of film are developed, he may have as many as 9 percentage screens running 90%, 80%, 70%, etc., thru 20% & 10%; each having a slightly larger dot pattern, therefore a greater capacity for holding back light. A 10% screen would thus hold back 90% of the light. This type of home made film screen is much cheaper than the precision ruled original halftone screen and can therefore be cut up into odd shapes to conform to certain images on the flat which have screen percentage callouts. These film scraps are usually kept in separate drawers and labelled by percentage so the stripper can find them easily.

The artist must realize that percentage screens can be made from fine or coarse ruled screens. For example, the 50% screen mentioned above could be made from an 85-line ruled screen or a 150-line ruled screen. Paper and artwork would be the determining factors as to what size line was required.

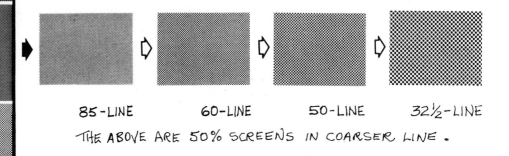

| 85-LINE | 60-LINE | 50-LINE | 32½-LINE |

THE ABOVE ARE 50% SCREENS IN COARSER LINE.

A black screen <u>scale</u> is printed on the edge of the page. When choosing a screen to simulate a lighter color, place the printed tonal scale near your layout. You can then make value decisions and choose the screen PERCENTAGE required. Obviously a 50% screen of Yellow will be lighter than a 50% screen of black, so you must make some allowance when screening the lighter solids. To do this, place the light solid opposite its corresponding value on the screen scale. Then you will be able to determine better the screen percentage BELOW that value.

TEXTURE SCREENS

There are a variety of thin acetate or film base screens on the market that have textures on the surface instead of density grids or dots. Thin stripes, heavy stripes, wood grain, spiral, mezzotint, and many others are available. One process known as POSTERIZATION , can transform the continuous tones of a fotograf into 4 or 5 definite shades of gray. This has the effect of making the subject appear as though it were silk screened or painted in flat grays like a poster. Other screens have the capacity to make certain artwork look similar to a line engraving or scratchboard. Section 18 describes how to make one.

The quality of these screens is becoming better, and there are places where they can be used effectively. However, they can also make artwork appear very "busy". Unrestrained use of screens in advertising for screen's sake is the mark of a poor designer. If you are going to use a texture screen process of any kind, include it in your planning from the VERY START. Design with a reason for using it. Don't break up an excellent fotograf merely because you'd like to see what a screen texture looks like this week. Cooks don't throw in an extra teaspoon of baking soda in the batter at the last minute. Designers should consider the TOTAL design by balancing the relationships of all the elements in the ad from the start. (A half-truth perhaps, but the beginner can well profit by it for a while.)

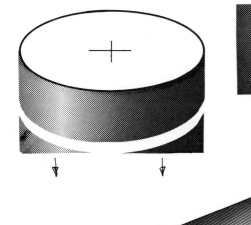

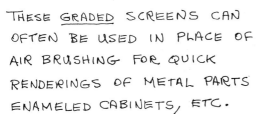

THESE GRADED SCREENS CAN OFTEN BE USED IN PLACE OF AIR BRUSHING FOR QUICK RENDERINGS OF METAL PARTS ENAMELED CABINETS, ETC.

VARIETIES OF PEOPLE AND TREES ARE AVAILABLE FOR QUICKIES.

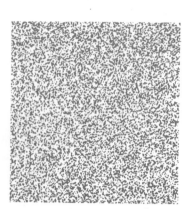

UNDER MAGNIFICATION, THE
SURFACE OF THE GELATIN
LOOKS LIKE LITTLE WIGGLES.
(LESS MECHANICAL THAN DOTS)

COLLOTYPE

A planographic method of printing similar to lithography is called Collotype. This is also a photomechanical process in which the print is made from a hardened gelatin film. There are no dot patterns in this method. The gelatin film is more or less impervious to moisture depending on its exposure thru a continuous tone negative (a negative with no dots). Photographic negs are typical continuous tone examples.

The areas that are impervious to moisture retain more of the greasy ink; the areas that retain moisture are less receptive to the ink and thus the plate produces a tonal image without the dot patterns of the foto offset method. Temperature and humidity control are very critical factors in this type of operation, but expert printers can reproduce remarkable color fidelity.

A TYPICAL PRINTING PRICE QUOTE

Regardless of the method of printing, a printing bid is usually based upon a single specific art job. The table below, however, gives an overall scale which shows the student how the cost PER SHEET decreases as the run becomes longer or if several sheets can be printed at once. (Such as 4 up) The costs of camera, negatives, stripping, plates, and press make-ready are, of course, spread over a greater number of pieces.

		One sheet 2 sides	per sheet	Two sheets 2 sides		Four sheets 2 sides	
100	1st run	40.35	.404	74.20	.371	147.90	.369
	rerun	12.35	.124	20.00	.10	22.30	.056
500	1st run	42.75	.086	79.60	.08	158.70	.079
	rerun	14.75	.030	25.40	.025	33.10	.017
1000	1st run	47.60	.048	87.00	.044	176.10	.044
	rerun	19.60	.020	32.80	.016	50.50	.013
2000	1st run	58.80	.029	104.20	.026	215.25	.025
	rerun	30.80	.015	50.50	.013	89.65	.011
5000	1st run	106.25	.021	157.16	.016	312.55	.016
	rerun	75.80	.015	102.96	.01	186.95	.009

Printed black ink
8 1/2 x 11 (2 sides)

PHOTO - OFFSET LITHOGRAPHY TEST (Sections 12, 13, & 14)

Use ink on 8 1/2 x 11 ruled paper and write in LEGIBLE script. This means that your handwriting should not slant more than 20°and the letters should be kept close together. (Poor handwriting is the result of 3 easily corrected factors: Stretching words out by leaving large gaps between letters; Slanting letters at a 45° or greater angle; and not following the base guide line.)

Tell in your own words the processes, in sequence, that a printer goes thru after he receives your mechanical until the ad is printed in two colors. (Remember that black is counted as one "color" because it means one press run.)

Below is a list of terms to assist you. Each term must be used at least once in your description, and each time it is used it must be underlined. This will help the instructor determine whether you have covered the various steps in the printing process. Write in the headings at the beginning of each new section, as this will define each section clearly.

It is assumed that you know what the terms are, so do NOT define them. Tell how they are used in the process. You will be allowed one and a half hours. At the end of that time please hand in your paper. Do not write on the list of terms, and you will not be allowed notes during the test.

Stretching
Slanting too muc
Forgetting base lin

Fold back the
acetate overlay and
place the mechan-

The following paragraph (1) is an example of how NOT to describe a process. Too many definitions are superfluous and confuse the reader. If the aim of the technical writer is to describe a piece of equipment, the definitions might be in order, but in this case, your job is to describe a PROCESS, not things.

(1) Take the mechanical which is a piece of illustration board with the art work on it plus an acetate overlay with the color images on it and put it on the copyboard. The copyboard goes back and forth on a steel track depending on whether reduction or enlargement is desired. The lens has a scale of figures over it and an indicator with which you can set the lens opening, which is f 32 in this case. Etc.

This paragraph (2) is a sample of better technical writing. Most tech writers have a gift of presenting ideas clearly and quickly in the simplest language possible.

(2) Fold back the acetate overlay and place the mechanical, top edge down, on the copyboard. Set the lens diaphragm to f 32. Turn on the floods. Close the ground glass door over the back of the camera and use the lens board crank and the copy board crank to focus the image on the glass , same size. Etc.

OFFSET LITHOGRAPHY TEST

List of Terms

1. Shooting the line copy

Mechanical
color overlay
black copy
copy board
same size
lens aperture
f stop 32
arc lights
ground glass door
lens board
cranks
focus
centered
image

Safe lights
vacuum door
vacuum switch
Ortho film
set timer
timer button
shutter
15 seconds

2. Developing

vacuum switch
film
developer
safelight observation
negative
dense background
sharp detail
good contrast
stop bath
fix
wash
dry

3. Shooting halftone copy

fold back dropout mask
product photograph
copy board
reduction from _ to _.
f-stop calculator
aperture set at f _.
arc lights

ground glass
focus
measure image
safe lights
Ortho film
vacuum door
ruled screen
timer
timer button
15 seconds
develop

dropout mask
white sheet of paper
line shot
develop

4. Stripping

Goldenrod flat
black negative
halftone negative
masking negative
monogram positive

Goldenrod flat
color negative
light table
red tape
windows
emulsion side down
opaquing fluid
pinholes

5. Brownline proof

Brownline paper
color flat
emulsion to emulsion
vacuum press
flip table
arcs
1 minute burn

brownline paper
black flat
3 minute burn

hot water
Maduro Salts fix
wash , dry
artist's approval
artist's initials

6. Plate making

color flat
piece of percentage screen
emulsion to emulsion
zinc plate
light-sensitive emulsion
vacuum press
flip table
arcs
3 minute burn

remove plate
process gum
developer with red stain
wipe & dry

7. Printing

Job stock
feeder platform
color plate
plate cylinder
colored ink
ink rollers
start press

plate cylinder revolves
fountain solution roller
nonimage areas
ink roller
image areas
offset cylinder
rubber blanket

suckers
conveyer system
grippers
impression cylinder
paper
finish of color run
color prog
washup press

black plate
plate cylinder
black ink
black prog
registration marks
finish of black run

trim, fold, stitch,
package

LETTERPRESS 15

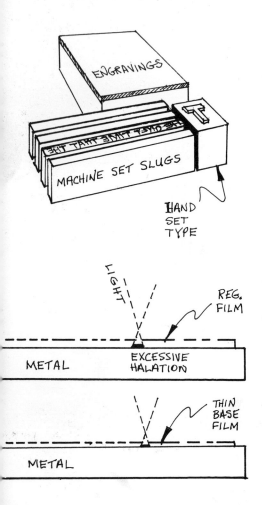

LETTERPRESS

Preparation of mechanical

Mechanicals and artwork prepared for letterpress printing are very similar to those prepared for lithography. In some cases reproduction proofs of the typography are not necessary, because the actual type is set in the bed of the press and locked in with the engravings which have been made from the artwork. In other cases the mechanical does include the type repros which are pasted in, shot with the art and and processed as part of the engraving plate.

Making the negatives

When a neg is laid against the LITHO plate its emulsion side is down and held firmly against the light-sensitive emulsion of the litho plate. This makes for perfect contact and a read-right image on the plate.

However, the image on the letterpress plate (the engraving) must be READ WRONG, because the engraving will be printed directly against the paper surface. If the negative flat is flopped so that the read-wrong image gets burned correctly on the engraving, the emulsion of the neg will be up and thus the thickness of the film will be between the emulsion of the neg and the emulsion on the engraving. There will not be perfect contact, and the light from the arcs will fan out under the emulsion of the neg and cause HALATION or a soft fuzzy look around the edges of the image on the engraving.

To prevent this then, the camera man uses a film that is very thin to keep halation at a minimum. So, altho the mechanicals are prepared the same way, the negatives for making engravings must be shot on THIN-BASE film.

Making the engravings ✳

A letterpress engraving is made from a stiff piece of metal plate about 1/16 - inch thick, coated with a light-sensitive emulsion. The thin-base negatives are stripped into flats, positioned over this plate, and the image is burned into the plate, much like the litho plates were made. Instead of developing the surface of the plate, the plate is placed into an acid bath. The acid etches or eats out the nonimage areas. The recessed areas are sometimes deepened by hand graving or routing out the metal by machine. The image areas (solids or dots) remain level with the top surface of the plate, because they remained protected by the emulsion which was fixed by the burn from the arcs. A LINE engraving has no dot patterns. A HALFTONE engraving has dot patterns. Engravings are often called CUTS.

The engraving is then mounted on a block of hard wood so it will be TYPE HIGH when it is placed in the bed of the press. Type bodies, including linotype slugs, are all .9186 of an inch high (2.33 cm). This height is standard so that engravings and type remain level and can be used on most FLATBED presses. The paper and TYMPAN or backing under the paper then make up the remaining space between the face of the type and engravings (FORM) and the impression cylinder which rolls the paper against the ink.

*See page 237 for picture of engraving and its print.

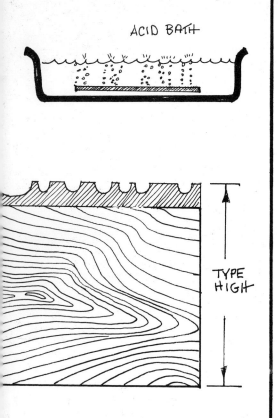

Locking up the FORM

The COMPOSITOR places a CHASE, which is a hollow, rigid square of metal, on a flat stone table and in it assembles the type and engravings to conform to the layout specifications. Rectangular wood blocks of varying sizes called FURNITURE are used with metal wedges called QUOINS to hold the composition in place so tightly that the chase can be carried to the bed of the press without the type or engravings dropping out. This locked up unit is known as the FORM.

FLATBED printing

The form is placed on the flat bed of the press and locked in position. The bed with the form on it then moves <u>under</u> the ink rollers. The ink rollers deposit a layer of ink on the type-high surfaces of the form. As the bed returns to its former position the fixed impression cylinder rotates and brings with it a sheet of paper which is rolled over the inked form. The SQUEEZE or impression can be changed by varying the thickness of the packing on the impression cylinder. The printed sheet is then delivered to a stack at the other end of the press and the process is repeated. Gas flames and talc dusting are used to help dry the ink, prevent sticking between sheets, and eliminate static electricity. When the ink from one sheet sticks to the back of the sheet above it is called offsetting, but modern day inks have eliminated much of this problem.

The majority of newspapers are printed letterpress. The majority of magazines and brochures are printed by lithography. Each process has advantages and disadvantages which must be considered when selecting the method of printing. Lithography still depends upon the letterpress method for its reproduction proofs.

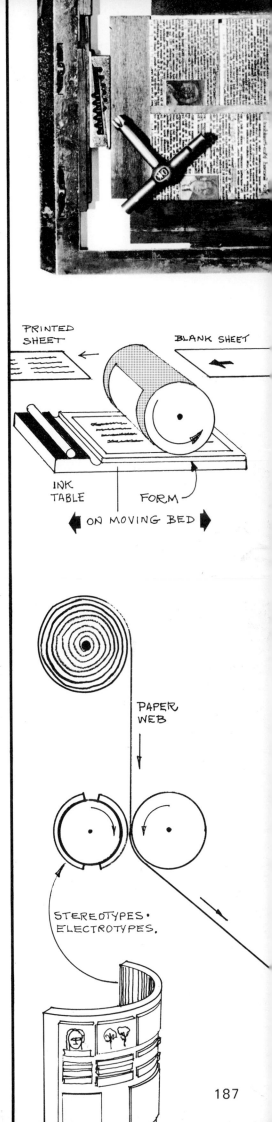

WEBFED printing

Single sheet feeding in the flatbed presses is too slow when the edition of a large city newspaper has to be printed within hours. Instead the paper is fed into a press from continuous reels of newsprint and then cut and folded automatically. To print on these fast moving webs of paper, the flat FORM must be made into a duplicate curved plate and fastened to a cylinder which rotates at high speed.

STEREOTYPING

To make the curved duplicate plates, a mold is made of the flat form by covering it with a slimy fibrous papier-mache material which dries as a female mold with the exact impressions of the type and engravings in its surface. This MAT is then held in a concave curve and filled with molten type metal. When the metal cools the mat is removed, and the STEREOTYPE or duplicate curved plate is locked on the cylinder in the webfed press. As many plates are locked in as can be accomodated by the press, each printing a separate page, simultaneously on opposite sides of the paper. The paper itself runs thru the press at speeds up to 30 miles per hour.

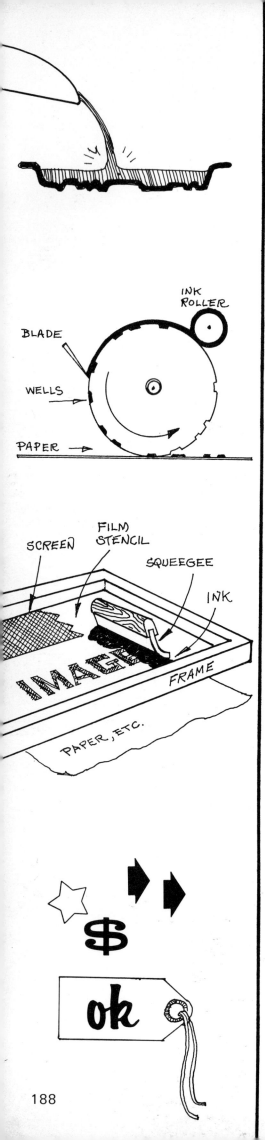

MATS

The papier-mache' described above is also used to make MATS from the flat form which are sent to smaller magazines or country newspapers all over the U.S. A manufacturer or large chain, for example, may want an ad to appear the same day all over the country. Rather than have each small newspaper set a separate ad, several hundred mats may be made from the original form. These are lightweight and can be sent thru the mail very cheaply either to the store in each city or directly to the newspaper. The newspaper casts the type metal into the flat mat and then locks the cast duplicate plate into the form on his flatbed press.

ROTOGRAVURE

Whereas lithography is printing from a flat surface and letterpress is printing from the high part of a relief surface, Rotogravure is printing from the low part of a relief surface. Ink is spread over the plate and then wiped off by a blade as the cylinder turns. Ink remains in the depressions or wells but not on the high parts of the plate, and as the paper is pressed against the plate it picks the ink out of the wells in the plate. This method lends itself to long runs of quality printing, because the printing image is low and does not get worn even tho the cylinder turns 500,000 or 1,000,000 times.

SILK SCREENING

Recent developments in photomechanical stencil films have revived this method of printing. It is being used successfully in industry to do precision work that previously could be done only by skilled engravers. Essentially it is a stencil thru which the ink is pressed directly on the poster, milk bottle, industrial panel, or printed circuit board. The screen is incidental to the printing and is only a means of supporting the stencil. The stencil can be a photomechanical film, a glue residue, or simple paper cut out which is supported by a silk, nylon, or metal mesh fabric in a rigid frame. The screen is then pressed on to the surface and ink is squeegeed thru the stencil. Metallic inks are used to form electronic circuit boards, and in some cases material can be sifted thru the stencil to be hardened later into ridges (thermal setting).

Electrostatic Printing is a recent development in which a thin flexible screen sifts powdered ink on to the surface. The ink particles are held by electrostatic attraction until fixed. As the screen does not have to touch the surface to be printed, curved items like sacks of potatoes, fruit, or drums can be labeled with ease.

An old axiom

Regardless of the method of printing there is a saying among production men that artists should remember: "There are 3 factors in printing: Speed, price, and quality. Only two of these are at optimum in one job." In other words, you may be able to get a rush delivery and low price, but you won't have quality. You may be able to get high quality and a low price but you won't get a quick delivery also, etc. Rush deadlines can not be met with quality unless extra help, overtime, and sometimes interrupted press runs are part of the process -- all of which make the price go UP.

COLOR 16

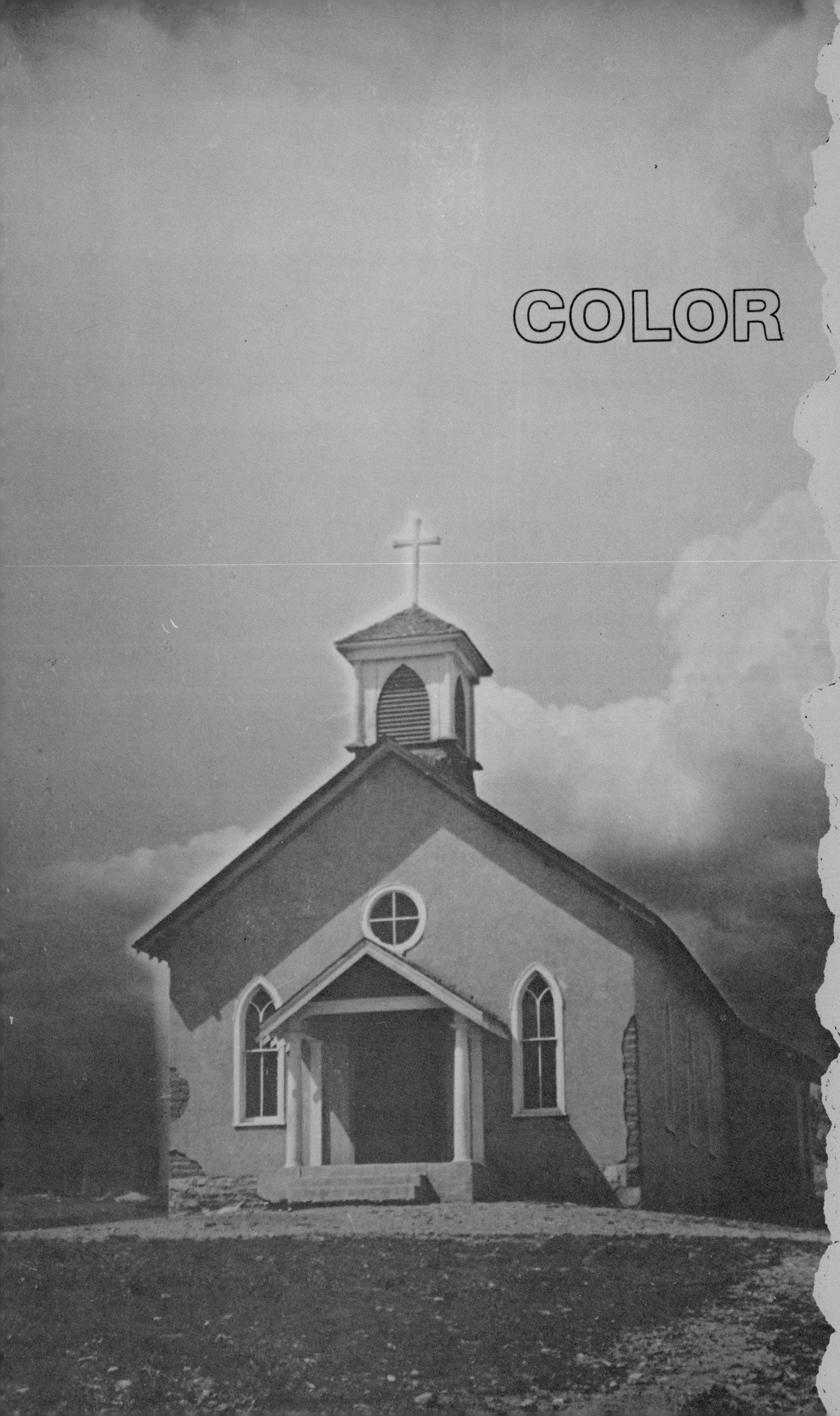

30°

FULL COLOR PAINTING ON COPYBOARD.

MAG. CYAN YEL.

FLOODS

BLUE FILTER BLOCKS YELLOW LIGHT.

TRANS-PARENT IMAGE AREAS LEFT BY BLOCKED LIGHT

FILM ON CAMERA BACK

DUOTONES (See page 185.)

Printing a black and white fotograf in two colors can add more interest to the design or quality to the fotograf in some cases. **(Example, page 185)**

The foto is shot twice as a halftone. The second exposure is made with the ruled screen angled about 30° from the first shot. Then when the second image is printed over the first, the dots are more apt to arrange themselves in random patterns. If both negs are shot with the screen at the same angle, the printed dots tend to cluster in lines or symmetrical groups which are very apparent to the eye. This is referred to as a MOIRE' pattern and is usually unwanted.

A black on black duotone or DOUBLEPRINT tends to increase the value range by giving the printed halftone deeper darks. This is also called a Duoblack.

Printing a halftone image over another color is referred to as an OVERPRINT or FAKE DUOTONE. The preceding page is of that type, and you will notice a considerable amount of contrast is lost in this method, because the solid color makes the light areas or highlights darker than the normal white paper.

FULL COLOR PRINTING — NEGATIVES

Full Color means that the image is reproduced by printing four overlapping images in 3 light primary PROCESS (transparent) inks + black: Magenta (purplish red), Cyan (greenish blue), Yellow, and Black.

This means the paper has to be run thru the press four different times in perfect register. To make the four different printing plates, the artist's work is placed on the copyboard and shot as a halftone four different times, through four different light filters, to make four different halftone negatives.

For example:

A blue filter (sometimes referred to as a violet filter) placed just behind the lens of the copy camera allows Magenta and Cyan light to pass thru to the film, but it BLOCKS the yellow rays. As the film becomes dense where it is struck by light, the Magenta and Cyan rays leave the dense pattern. The blocked Yellow image remains as the transparent portion of the film or negative. When the printing plate is made, the light burns thru the transparent parts of the negative to make the image on the metal plate. Yellow Process Ink is therefore used to print from this "Yellow" plate. Remember it is the BLOCKED light that provides the transparent image on the negative, which in turn makes the image on the plate which accepts ink.

A green filter allows Cyan and Yellow light to pass but BLOCKS the Magenta light. The resultant plate is inked with the purplish red ink called Magenta.

A red filter (sometimes referred to as an orange filter) allows Magenta and Yellow light to pass but BLOCKS the Cyan. The resultant plate is inked with the greenish blue ink called Cyan.

All 3 filters are used to make the fourth or "black" negative. The film is exposed first thru one filter for a set interval, then thru the next, and then thru the other. This filter arrangement is known as a SPLIT and results in all the DARKS in the original full color mechanical appearing as transparent areas on the negative. The resultant printing plate is therefore inked with the black ink and gives the final printed piece its deep darks that the primaries themselves cannot give.

Each negative is screened as a halftone, and to avoid having the dots of each neg coincide with the printed dots of the other negatives, the screen is placed at a 45° angle when the black neg is shot; 75° for Magenta; 105° for Cyan, and 90° for the yellow neg.

When the image is printed then, the dots are spread more randomly over the surface of the paper. If the screens are not placed at these different angles, the dots tend to arrange themselves in clusters which resemble a faint plaid pattern on the image. This MOIRE' pattern is distracting and usually unwanted. However, these Moire' patterns could be interesting if planned for and integrated into a design.

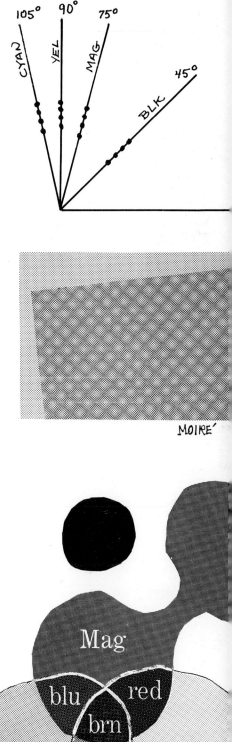

MOIRE'

FULL COLOR PRINTING

Full color jobs are printed in PROCESS colors, which means the inks are transparent. Thus a variety of colors can be "processed" by overlapping the three pigments; Magenta, Cyan, and Yellow.(If the inks were OPAQUE they would almost obliterate the underlying color.)

Let us assume the four Litho printing plates or the four Letterpress engravings have been made. Usually the yellow plate is printed first. The press is then washed and this time Magenta process ink is applied to the ink rollers. As the transparent Magenta dot image is printed over the Yellow dot image, some of the dots overlap to make Red. On the third or Cyan run, the transparent Cyan dots then produce Blue where they overlap Magenta; Green where they overlap Yellow; and Brown or Gray where they overlap Red. The final or black plate adds the darker values by overlapping some of the color dots and reproduces any BLACKS that were in the original copy. The entire range of HUE, VALUE, and CHROMA (intensity) of color is thus achieved to simulate the original artwork. Keep in mind that the above is based on the theory of LIGHT PRIMARIES.

Most artists understand the PIGMENT PRIMARIES (Red, Yellow, and Blue) and the fact that when red is mixed with yellow, the result is an orange pigment, etc. To get a similar result from the printed page we are forced to overlap TRANSPARENT inks (not mix them on the printed page) and then rely upon the light that is reflected from the white paper to pass thru each thin layer of ink.

Dots in four color process print in a microscopic circular pattern known as a ROSETTE. Even if some of the dots do not overlap they still simulate the spectrum because the wavelengths tend to merge and form the secondary colors on the way to the eye.

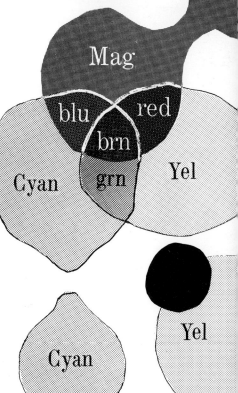

An interesting experiment might be made using Burnt Sienna, Yellow Ochre, and Blue Gray process inks on the press instead of the bright primaries.

Altho the principles of full color printing can be explained rather simply, there are many many observations, judgements, technical adjustments, and plate corrections that must be made by the Camera Man, the Platemaker and the Pressman to arrive at the final printed piece. The majority of artists find themselves knowing very little of this highly technical process. They can be of the greatest assistance by examining the color proofs with the printer and discussing the the color relationship. But they should not try to tell the craftsman HOW to correct.

Keep in mind the following philosophy: Listen to the other members of the team in THEIR fields. But be firm in decisions that pertain to DESIGN - - - that is YOUR field. Even though your are a beginner, the design idea is your baby. Technicians should not tamper with your layout any more than you should tamper with their equipment. "Illigitimi non carborundum."

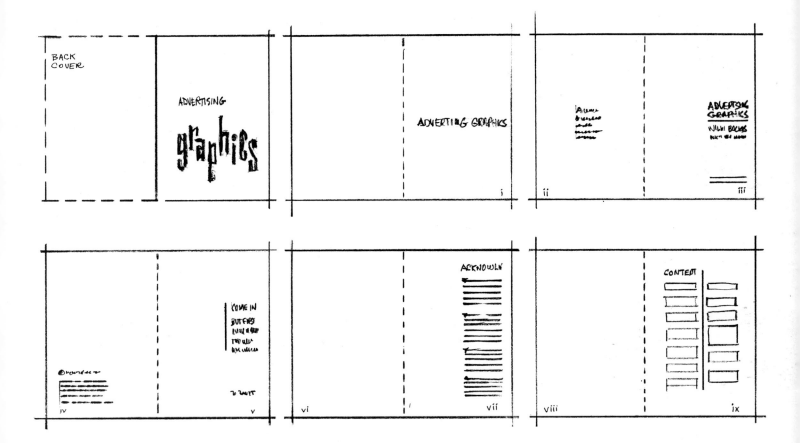

BACK COVER

ADVERTISING graphics

ADVERTING GRAPHICS

i

ii

ADVERTISING GRAPHICS WITH BACKS

iii

COME IN BUT FIRST ...

TO SWIFT

iv

v

vi

ACKNOWLN

vii

viii

CONTENT

ix

DUMMY 17

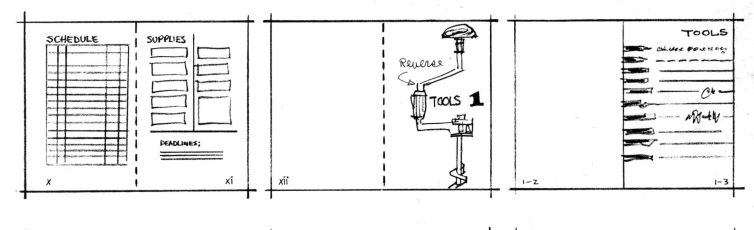

SCHEDULE

SUPPLIES

DEADLINES:

x

xi

xii

Reverse

TOOLS **1**

TOOLS

1-2

1-3

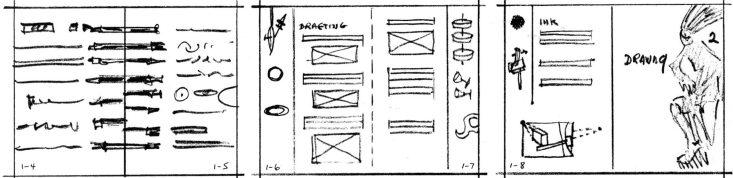

1-4

1-5

DRAFTING

1-6

1-7

INK

DRAWING

2

1-8

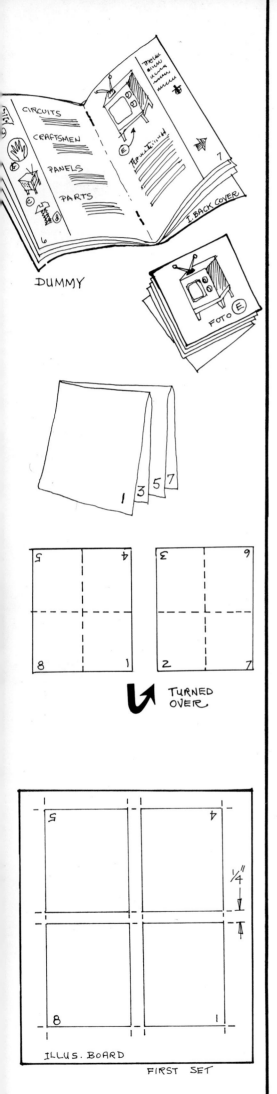

DUMMY

TURNED OVER

ILLUS. BOARD

FIRST SET

THE DUMMY

When the stack of mechanicals and masked fotografs for a multi-paged catalog is delivered to the printer, it usually helps him understand the job if you provide a rough or DUMMY of the finished piece which he can use as a page - layout guide.

Ordinarily this dummy comes into being while the catalog or brochure is in the first planning stages. Certain pages are alloted certain products; the company's capabilities may be explained in a certain section; a list of well-known customer corporations might be indicated on the inside back cover, etc. Later revisions may cause whole pages to be torn out or covered with another sheet of paper. Eventually rough layouts and indicated copy blocks start to appear on the pages. These "worksheet" pages in the dummy finally show the exact amount and location of art work, copy, and fotografs on each page.

A dummy can be a very neat professional job approaching a comp in its detailing, or it can be a hastily thrown together folded sheaf of papers with page numbers and a few instructions scrawled here and there. It serves the artist as an overall plan and helps the printer visualize the sequence of the completed brochure. Sets of comps prepared for client visualization are sometimes stapled together later and used as a dummy.

SIGNATURES and IMPOSITION

To save time and money many jobs are printed in multiple, back to back, on a large sheet. The sheet is then folded, stapled, and trimmed to form the finished booklet or catalog. This large sheet is called a SIGNATURE. The relation of the pages on the printing plate is called a PRESS PLAN or IMPOSITION.

As an example, let us prepare the layout positions for a typical 8 page brochure: Fold a piece of paper in half toward you and then half again to the right endwise. Number the pages 1 thru 8 as in the diagram. (Number 1 is always a right-hand page.) Odd numbers should fall on right hand pages. Now unfold the sheet and lay it flat. The pages 8, 1 and 4, 5 are now in their relative positions as they will be printed FOUR UP on a large printing press. Turn the sheet over and the imposition of pages 2, 7 and 6, 3 will be indicated similarly. Obviously the top of the page numbers point toward the HEAD or top of the layout on each page. Note that consecutive pages are back to back on this signature.

Four-Up Pasteup

The layouts or mechanicals are prepared in 2 sets of 4 each. The four pasteups can be made on one piece of illustration board about 1/4 inch apart in the same position as indicated by the signature dummy. (See diagram) The 1/4-inch space allows for any 1/8-inch bleeds for trim allowance on adjacent pasteups. The page numbers of adjacent right and left pasteups should always add up to one more than the total number of pages in the brochure. For example:

8 + 1 = 9 or 4 + 5 = 9 are quick checks against placing a page in the wrong location in an 8-page brochure.

Each set can now be shot as one large neg, stripped into a flat, and made into a single printing plate. After one side of the signature is printed, the other set of four is printed on the back side of the sheet in exact register. This lining up page 2 directly behind page 1, and page 3 directly behind page 4, etc., can be checked by holding a makeready sheet up to the light.

Numbering

Page numbering always starts with number 1 as a right-hand page not counting the cover. On some brochures, especially when using a heavier paper for the cover stock; the front cover, back cover, and inside front cover, inside back cover are printed as a separate press plan – – a two-up, back to back run with no page numbers. As the larger brochures are usually printed in signatures of 8, those with 8, 16, 24, or 32 pages are easily assembled. It often costs more per page to print and bind brochures with odd numbers of pages because the printing, folding, and binding operation is complicated by having to introduce two-up signatures with four-up or eight-up, etc.

Terms

A layout that covers any two facing pages is called a DOUBLE PAGE SPREAD. The two pages which face each other in the middle of the booklet are referred to as the CENTER SPREAD. The line where pages meet at the binding in the center of a double page spread is called the GUTTER. The outside of the binding on which titles are sometimes printed is called the SPINE. An extra length page is known as a FOLD OUT and any special insert is often called a TIP IN.

Press SIZES

Time on small printing presses costs less money, but the larger presses can print more UP and thus may be cheaper per unit produced. Because of the need for gripper bite space and to prevent the paper from rubbing the sides of the press, the image areas are slightly smaller than plate size. Under certain conditions the image size may be expanded slightly. For example, the 9 x 12 indicated image size indicated for the 10 x 15 plate size below, might be enlarged to 9 1/2 x 13 with careful pressmanship but, in general, the 9 x 12 and 17 x 22 image sizes are modules of the standard paper sizes, 6 x 9 or 8 1/2 x 11.

	Plate Size	Maximum Image Size
Small Press	10 x 15	9 x 12
Medium Press	20 x 23	17 x 22
Large Press	42 x 58	40 x 56

The image sizes listed above give the artist a rough idea of how many UP can be imposed on the printing plate. For example, a 2 x 5 label for a can of Tuna might be printed 8 up within the 9 x 12 image area on the small press, or it could be printed approximately 220 up on the large plate if an extremely large number were required.

If you only learn one thing from this section, let it be this: Check your press plan with the printer BEFORE you make your signature or mechanicals. It will save many a headache.

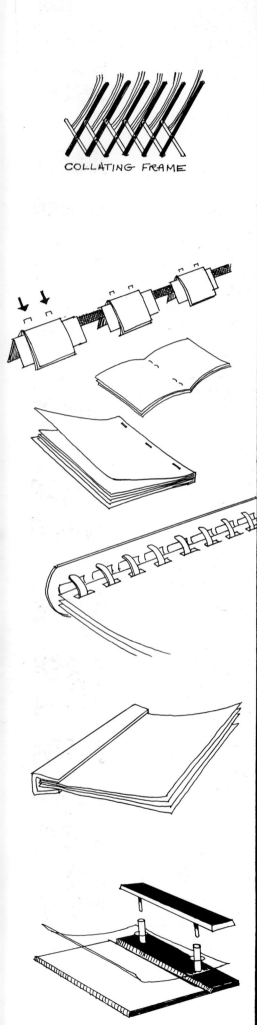

COLLATING FRAME

COLLATING

The placing of pages in correct sequence is known as COLLATING. In offices where product bulletins, catalog pages, resumes, etc., are kept in stacks, there is often the need to make up a quick sales folder, or proposal booklet from these preprinted items. The stacks are placed consecutively around the edge of a table. The secretary then walks around the table taking one sheet off each stack until she has a complete set which is then placed in a folder or hand bound. Sometimes the whole office staff joins in to make up the required number of sets. There are also collating frames in which separate packs of pages can be placed on edge to save space and walking distance.

BINDING

Saddle stitch

On small brochures the printed signatures are folded and usually they are SADDLE STITCHED by machine which drives staples into the gutter fold from the outside. The name derives from the fact that the signatures are folded and laid over a metal form similar to a saddle while the staples are inserted.

Side stitching

As the booklet gets thicker, SIDE STITCHING is used. The wire staples are driven in from the front cover about 1/8 inch from the spine edge and clinched on the back.

Plastic spine

PLASTIC SPINE binding is a simple method of binding that can be used to prepare office or agency publications of 20 or 30 copies. First a series of square holes are punched in the binding edge of the pages. The teeth on a plastic spine are held apart in a hand operated machine, and the pages are then dropped over the teeth of the spine. When released, the plastic teeth curl thru the holes in the paper. The spines come in different colors and sizes to accomodate various thicknesses. One other advantage is that the pages lie flat when opened.

Slot binding

Another type of hand binding for inplant publications or small business reports is the plastic SLOT binder. The pages are merely slid into the spring slot which binds the booklet edge together by compression.

Post

POST and RING binders are used for binding thicker volumes of punched sheets. Architectural reference manuals and hardware supply catalogs are usually bound in this fashion.

The more complex methods of binding which involve gluing, stitching and heavy covers are handled by professionals in a bindery.

PRINT MAKING 18

PRINTMAKING POSSIBILITIES

An advertising artist prepares most of his art on a rather small scale. The 1/4 page ads in newspapers or magazines, two-fold 6 x 9 mailers, letterheads, company logos, 9 x 12 catalogs, signs for that Fall Sale, are fairly typical. He often finds that his sense of composition in these small areas is excellent. He has an innate feeling for typography placement and spacing. His drawings have more of the carefree and intuitive feeling of personal expression than the more consciously composed designs made during his student days.

As an artist he has been very aware of watercolors, photographs, oils, and prints in gallery exhibits. And undoubtedly he and his wife have a an excellent collection of work done by fellow artists ranging from furniture and stitchery through pottery and steel sculpture to prints and children's drawings. Over the years he has learned that beauty appears in the "eye of the beholder". An assortment of beach shells, smooth stones, a butterfly wing, a coin, a child's top, a porcelain egg cup, a hot-rod model, pebbles, purple egg cartons, an old transit telescope, a photo of Galaxy M-345, a mounted cover from a Westways magazine, a friend's Christmas card, a dried red pomegranate... are very apt to occupy more wall space in his home than formal oils. He rarely judges a piece of art by "Whoo signed it ?" , but rather by his own feeling. As a result his home has character, not because it is expensive, but because it reflects his creativity and individuality of choice.

However, an artist likes to create art that is completely expressive of his own personality as well as to SELECT things which please him. There usually comes a day when he decides to try a watercolor or start an oil. Now if he had been working as hard at 3-foot watercolors or 5-foot oils during the years , as he had at 11-inch comps, he would come up with something reasonably good. But at this late date he usually discovers his design concepts and "taste" are way ahead of his ability to execute. The size has changed, the media is different and most important, the scale of the tool in relation to the finished work has changed. The sable brush that washed in a whole head of hair with one flick on the six by nine inch illustration board now barely makes a mark on that huge white expanse of 400 lb. Arches. There is a tendency to end up with paintings that are overdetailed and have a "labored" look. He recognizes this immediately and diagnoses the problem in even less time. He changes the size of the tools. He starts using wide bristle brushes, or a palette knife. He is on the right track, but alas, that track is usually a very very long one.

As most instructors realize, it takes years to understand a new media. For every artist trying another field there is always some design knowledge as well as kinesthetic sense that gets lost during the transfer. This is not necessarily so for the ORGANIZING designer. For example the art director, the designer of exhibits, the world's fair pavilion designer, are in a sense men who make SELECTIONS. Their attributes are that they can select items or designers that work well together and come up with an integrated answer. They would be the first to admit that they themselves could not have done the photography, the structure, the drawings, the copy, the sculpture, the animation, the color, as well as the experts within those areas. Thus, although it sometimes appears as if this designer jumps from field to field with equal facility, there is usually one difference. He is not DOING the artwork in the pieces. He does put the pieces together in a larger framework, which in turn is his artwork. This is not to imply he is lesser or greater than the DOER of the smaller pieces. It is to imply that the doer in any single field has a different track to follow before he sees his own expression flower. One's capacity to appreciate or select is often far ahead of one's ability to create with basic materials.

The moral of all these paragraphs is that before the typical advertising artist will be seeing positive results in his new painting experience, he will be considerably older. However, there is an area for immediate expression in which he is well versed already: Printmaking.

Prints are generally smaller and therefore closer to the scale in which the advertising artist has been working. Printmaking, like the ad man, is concerned with PAPER and the smash of metal into its fibres or the delicate kiss of ink on its surface. This is the lifeblood of a good advertising designer, and he doesn't have to practice for 10 more years to get the feel of it. He may never have thought of commercial engravers, typographers, letterpress men, printing paper salesmen, or photo-offset men as sources of fine art. Distributors ? Yes. Reproducers ? Yes. Actual creators of esthetics for the sake of esthetics ? Not yet. The esthetics are there in advertising: the color, the spacing, the feel of the line, the paper, the total visual image. But so far they have been used mainly to sell things, sometimes noble ideas, but not self expression.

It is very interesting that in the rush to make an industrial nation, the advertising designer and printing craftsmen have been largely ignored by museums, foundations, art galleries, people in general, and strangely enough by the advertising people themselves. Oh, there are advertising design exhibits here and there attended by the agency clientele who got "in", but after all, "Who wants to hang a picture of a bottle of catsup on your bedroom wall ?" The public could care less. Until today.

Painters of Pop Art capitalized on this very gap in appreciation. They adapted the 1/4 page tire ad and the comics to canvases 6 feet by 20 feet in their own familiar media, oils and spray paints. Again it was the artist searching for expression and areas of visual esthetics in our culture that stumbled upon advertising. Advertising had been so inextricably bound up in our economic system and life, that no one could see the forest for the paper mills. It has been so close to the average American that he never considered calling it art. Thank goodness. He couldn't possibly see its esthetic uniqueness until a hundred years or so had rolled by. Well, the hundred years and then some have rolled by since a woodcarver hung the first tavern sign up in New England. Since then the complex of process cameras, photo emulsions, engravings, dies, high-speed presses has become an entire new area for expression; if the artist is willing to work IN it, not AROUND it; if the artist will use the tools to create - not just copy.

The painters of Pop Art had the nerve to drive the first wedge. All they did was say, "LOOK !" But they said it publicly, loudly, and shockingly. The majority of people answered, "OK, so I looked." Most ad people probably thought, "Ugh, they've blown up the worst kinds of junk ads , they got that part of the message across, but you can have it. It doesn't look any better large than it looked small. Lots to do with the message of crummy advertising and practically nothing to do with beauty, as I know it."

The painters were SELECTORS only. They saw in advertising interesting, albeit ugly, visual forms made in the grossest most blatant manner. They copied them, arranged them, made them "extra colossal" large, signed them "Shockingly yours, " and placed them in hallowed museums and gallerys. It might have been interesting to see what would have happened if they had copied a well-done piece of advertising and signed it. The originating ad man might have been irritated enough to have sued for infringement. To extend the point: Did the Pop artist leave the area of self-expression and shift to copying ? Did he copy another media and put it in a wood frame ? Was the reproduced single oil of something meant to be multiple, valid as a means of self expression ? An analogy might be the copying of an oil painting by four color process lithography. The reproduced oil is still a copy of something meant to be single. The copying procedure in either case may give the craftsman money, prestige? , or even help him understand his tools, but it is extremely doubtful that copying will help him grow in the area of self-expression or DOING. If anything, copying tends to stultify development if practiced too much.

If the young advertising designer can realize that the complex tools of his experience can be tremendous sources of original art, as well as copying devices, he will be able to satisfy his yearning for pure self-expression that much sooner. There is an old saying in printing that you can never make the final printed piece better than the original copy. This idea is being outmoded. If your point of view is one of CREATING an uncommon answer, then the processes below become a means of making the final printed piece BETTER than the original art ! Because, in this case, the original art was PREPARED to be shot, stripped, burned, or cast. It was never prepared with the idea of letting the shop make a COPY of it. In other words the "original art" has become a purposely weak gray wash on rough paper, a coarse halftone negative with etch spots and freely painted opaquing fluid spread over its surface by the artist, plus a printing plate with portions of screen images on its surface. The "original art" concept as a mounted unit waiting to be copied by machine disappears. In its place, the artist introduces an IDEA concept. The idea is in his mind, and until it is produced on the paper thru the various processes, it is visible to no one. His hand and mind have been in the total process of making the print from start to finish and that is one of the keys to self expression. Have you as the artist conceived the original idea and CONTROLLED the process up to the final print ? If so, your work may be defined as an original print and not as a copy or reproduction. The difference between an original print and a reproduction then is undoubtedly one of INTENT and has nothing to do with process.

Many museum directors and planners of national, regional or local art exhibits are still not sophisticated enough to see the possibilities in commercial printing machines. They write in bold caps across the entry blank, "No commercial work !" and always followed by an exclamation point, to show that they are above that sort of thing, you know. Give them ten years and they might begin to see that oil painting and sculpture are really not the only forms of self expression. In the meantime then let us go ahead and probably thank Benjamin Franklin that we have not been honored with a carte blanche by the citadels of culture, as it might turn out to be the kiss of death in the long run. The remainder of this section is concerned with specific examples of processes and their possibilities in printmaking.

PHOTOMECHANICAL PROCESSES

ENLARGEMENTS

Reductions used in advertising production are quite common. The resulting clean line and crisp edge are usually desired because the subject matter of advertisements needs extreme readability. In printmaking, readability, in this same sense, is not necessarily a criterion. In many cases the more abstract, ambiguous, nonobjective forms provide the eye of the beholder with the pure beauty of the esthetic elements. The fotografic image becomes secondary to value, texture, line quality, shape, color, or what have you. The eye of the beholder likes to be teased and entertained, and enjoys searching thru these stimulating elements for uncommon sensations.

Enlarging small drawings on the copy camera to four or eight times size negatives provides some extremely interesting shapes that go unnoticed in the small original drawing. Many copy cameras enlarge to only twice size, so this may have to be a step process. Enlarge the drawing as large as possible and develop the neg. Place the neg on the copy board over a white sheet of paper and enlarge the image again. This neg will give you a positive image. Place the positive over a white sheet of paper and enlarge again. This third step will yield a negative again, and so on.

On the first enlargements the rough edges of the drawing will be exaggerated. The added coarseness is often quite pleasing. Details and tiny shapes unseen in the original charcoal, graphite, or brush stroke become significant interesting shapes. What the artist felt intuitively in his small scale drawings has been retained and in many cases, enhanced.

201

202

As the enlargement grows, the edges of the shapes get smoother.
Details become lost. The drawing image takes on a more plastic
organic flowing look. At this stage, portions of the total image may
become more interesting as a point of departure for a print than the original drawing.

The negatives and positives may be shot line, halftone, or with pieces of texture screen taped over the film. Portions may be screened and the rest of the film left in line. Remember that a line shot will tend to eliminate all the subtle light grays and turn the darker grays into solid blacks. A sensitive drawing with many halftones will be changed completely by shooting it in line. The soft quality of the drawing in the small head (see example) was lost and changed into a hard line by processing it as an enlarged line shot. A fine screen halftone enlargement might have enhanced the original by not only retaining the value variations but making some of the tiny significant shapes and spaces more obvious.

Charcoal studies made on toothed paper and shot in line have all the characteristics of a screened shot, because the Ortho film catches and intensifies every black particle of charcoal.

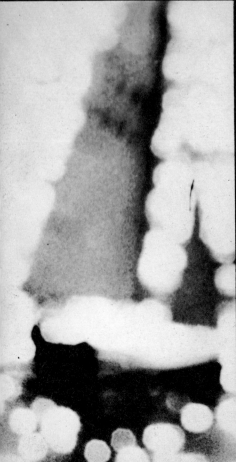

DISTORTION

The artist's work can also be fotografed by using view cameras or 4 x 5 cut-film cameras. The image can then be enlarged on the regular dark-room enlarger and a fotografic print made on a soft paper to the size desired. The fotografic paper will tend to soften the edges. In extreme enlargements the emulsion grain of the paper and the neg give a mottled effect that can be interesting. This image can be shot in line or screen on the process camera, same size, and developed. Then brownline proofs can be made from the neg to give the artist a positive image of the PRINT before he continues to work on the negative , if he so desires.

Tilting the copy board slightly on the process camera while exposing the negative film will cause some unusual shapes and out-of-focus images to appear on the negative.

Laying a crumpled piece of cellophane over the surface being exposed will also cause distortion or softening of the image.

COLLAGES

The fotografic print or brownline can be cut or torn into strips or pieces and put into new relationships by gluing the pieces on cardboard in a different sequence. These COLLAGES can then be processed and made into a negative.

Line and halftone negatives can be cut or torn also and stripped into a flat. Sometimes pieces of percentage or texture screens can be used to gain effects desired by the artist. Moire' patterns can be induced by placing halftone negatives or screens over each other.

LANG

CORSE

TEXTURAL SCREENS

If the textural screens available are too mechanical looking for your purposes, make some film screens of your own. Use a fine pen and scratch or crosshatch freehand a fine irregular pattern of lines over a 10 x 20 inch piece of paper. Shoot this in line on the process camera at 1/2 size. After development the screen neg will be 5 x 10. Make 12 veloxes or brownlines from this neg. Cut the edges of the prints in a random zig-zag manner so no join lines will be visible and glue them down on a 20 x 30 piece of illustration board or chipboard. Go over the whole board now with the fine pen and India ink and add crosshatches wherever needed to fill spaces or strengthen lines that were lost in the reduction process. After you have a well knit overall texture, place the board on the copy board by taping it to the front and shoot it in line to a negative size of approximately 15 x 22. This gives it a slight reduction again, but leaves it large enough to cover a medium size print.

Another interesting possibility for a screen would be to photograph a textural surface like the side of an old wooden shed or a dirty gray, streaked stucco wall. Place the print on the copy board of the process camera and make a negative from the print. Experimenting with reduction, same size, or enlargement on TEST STRIPS would help keep the experiments economical. If the photographic print was too white, the negative (your film screen in this case) may be too opaque. Then when the film screen was laid over the image negative on the flat it would not allow enough light to pass thru to record the image beneath it. Experimentation with contrasty fine textured surfaces can lead to some interesting screen results. Making a positive film screen from a negative screen will change opacity of 60% to a 60% transparency and vice versa, so this can be used as a modifier in some instances.

Using a regular fine ruled screen of 133 or 150 line in background areas can produce some beautiful luminous flat grays. In the detail of the print, "Fog", on the facing page, the background is 133 line screen.

OPAQUING

Opaquing can be used to produce highlights where there were none at all on the negative. In the detail of the print, "Fog", the light reflections in the water are pure white with no trace of dot pattern. They were produced on the negative by stroking the opaquing brush loaded with opaquing fluid over the screened background area much as you would stroke in the color on a watercolor. Do this free type of opaquing on the side of the neg opposite the emulsion. Then if the effect is not what you want, it can be wiped off with a bit of cotton and tried again. There may be some halation when the plate is burned because of the thickness of the film base, but this is often more **desirable than** not when soft edges are your criterion. For crisper edges work on the emulsion side of the negative.

If a process or copy camera is not available, there are ways students can experiment very economically with a few simple materials.

The opaquing method can be expanded by starting with a transparent sheet of film, old exposed film, or plain acetate sheets and painting the image on it with opaquing fluid, or even tempera with a little

ORIGINAL SUMI INK SKETCH
WITH ENLARGED OPAQUED DETAIL.

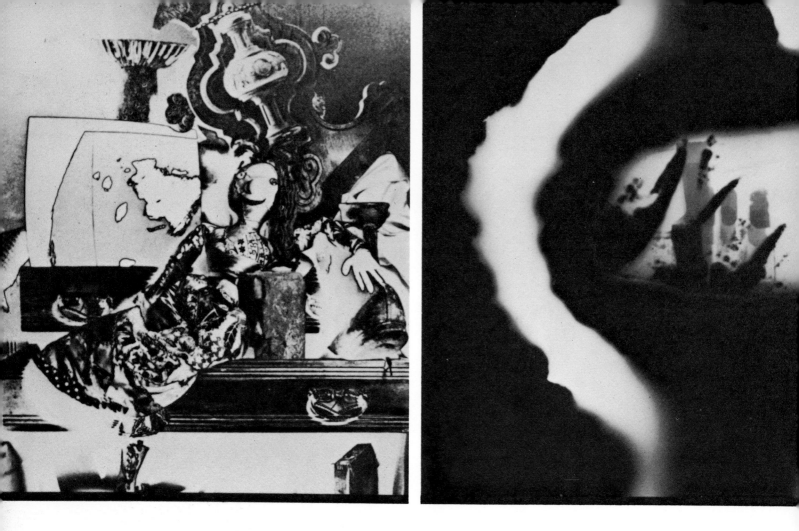

EXPERIMENT

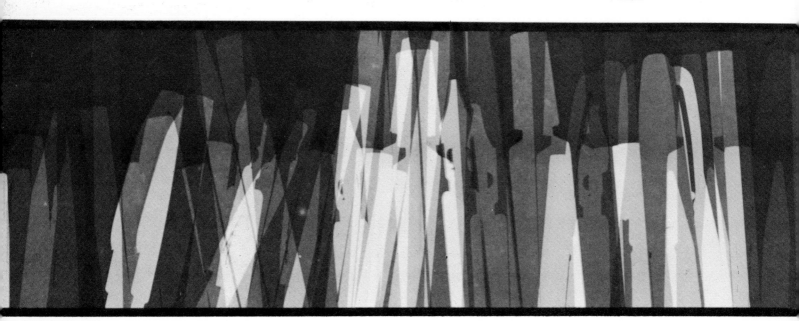

white glue mixed with it. After the image dries draw thru it with needles, sticks, or scrapers. Edges may be softened with cotton dipped in water. To change values, tape bits of percentage screens over transparent or semi-transparent areas. Gauze, gunny sacking, glued down salt, can all act as textural screens.

Keep a MORGUE file of old negatives and occasionally snip out an interesting bit of typography or picture and strip it in just for fun. Again the caution here is not to overdo it. Try to define the objective of the print. If it is to be a potpourri of textures symbolizing traffic signs and hazards, the sky is probably the limit. Go ahead. But if the objective is simplicity, or the quiet of early morning fog, your selection will probably be more restrained.

PHOTOGRAMS

The ortho film can be covered with pieces of porous cloth, texture screens, fragile dried leaves, wire springs, etc., exposed to white light and developed into a negative. This image can be made into a plate and used as a base run in one color over which other images could be run later.

PROOFS

These halftoned and screened flats or acetate collages can be used to make either printing plates or less expensive proofs. In a classroom situation it is not necessary to make litho plates or expensive letterpress engravings to see the results of these experiments. The opaquings or flats can be laid over BROWNLINE paper or VELOX paper and exposed. The brownline paper can then be developed in hot water, fixed in a solution made by mixing two tablespoons of Maduro Salts in two quarts of water, washed again, and dried. These brownline proofs can be exposed for different periods to get variations in value. In some cases a color print, tempera rendering, or color wash can be added to the brownline if color was to be part of the design. Fixing the proofs with several coats of WORKABLE fix makes a good base for the later color work.

The total cost for these supplies in the classroom is very reasonable and provides an interesting approach to the first steps in this type of printmaking.

The brownline paper is not very sensitive to ordinary room light so these brownline proofs can be made without expensive darkroom facilities or equipment.

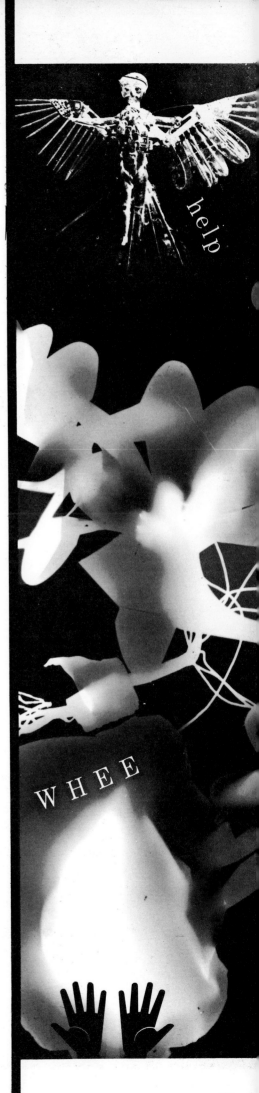

"Romulus Rubbing" 114/200 Bottua

GENERAL INFORMATION

MARGINS

Prints are traditionally centered on the paper with a three or four inch margin left on all sides. This is not mandatory, but the edge of the plate often provides an interesting texture or silhouette. The edge of the plate attracts the ink in a different manner and thus defines the border with varying quality. On prints made from letterpress engravings, woodblocks, or cast metal there is a tendency to emboss along the edge. This slight depression can be very pleasing, as it calls attention to the paper and the printing process impact on it. The kinesthetic sense of leaving an imprint is a pleasurable sensation to most beholders. Whether the child makes his handprint in the mud or pokes' a hole in the frosting on the cake; or whether the sophisticated artist models spaces in his sculpture, or bas-relief in a print... it's interesting.

SIGNATURE

The title of the print usually appears in quotes at the lower left-hand edge. The artist's signature at the lower right, close to the image. Both of these are ordinarily written in (not printed) with a graphite pencil. If the print is one of a limited edition, its number and the total number of prints in that edition is written at the center of the lower edge. For example, 6/20 would mean it was the sixth print off the press of a total run of twenty. 102/200 would mean the one hundred and second print of an edition of two hundred. Etc. Buyers or collectors are often interested in knowing how many prints were made from the original plate. If there is an edition number (like 20 or 200 above) indicated on the prints, the artist is obligated to destroy the plate, scar it, or at least, print no more from it. This protects the buyer, who is interested in rarity or in protecting his purchase as an investment, from finding the market flooded with the same print later on. Occasionally an artist will print other editions, but these should be marked, 2nd edition or 3rd edition, just to the left of the print number.

EDITIONS

Prints were not always limited by edition numbers. More than likely they were limited by the boredom of the artist in making print after print. In the 18th & 19th centuries, however, galleries and other distributors began to see the investment possibilities in limited editions. Holding a few prints as an artist grew in fame increased their value. The edition number helped to stabilize the price of each print also. So eventually it became a tradition to number ALL prints with the exception of 3 or 4 in each edition labelled "Artist Proof" in place of the number. These few prints were kept by the artist for his personal collection or on some occasions sold or given away to friends.

PHILOSOPHY

Times and conditions change, however. The population explosion now is so great it is estimated that 1/6 th of all people ever born are alive today.

In the U.S. millions of people are climbing out of poverty and out of the necessities bracket of income. With extra leisure to appreciate and extra money to buy things beyond minimum food and shelter, these people have created tremendous new markets. The growth in new housing, sporting equipment, and increased interest in all the arts are an indication of the possibility of a new renaissance. Millions of young homeowners on a limited budget have the education, the appreciation and desire to own prints.

With this century and this environment in mind it seems a little ridiculous to produce limited editions of twenty just so they can be labelled "Rare" and especially if the press that produces them can print 100 per minute or 6000 an hour.

"But wait a minute !" says the traditional printmaker. "I'm not interested in quantity. Goodness knows, there's enough of mass production in the world. I want to give people my personal touch." Which is certainly a valid philosophy and the prerogative of any artist. However, there is an implication in this statement that because the press is high speed, the "personal touch" is lost. This is not necessarily so. There is no reason to believe the personal touch has been lost because the tool is more complex. This only has validity as an argument if the artist loses control of his media because he does not understand or CONTROL its complexities.

A caveman might well criticize the traditional printmaker of losing HIS personal touch because he didn't chew up bark to make his own ink; and using a geared steel roller instead of the heel of his hand, ... Tsk Tsk. "But", replies the traditionalist, " I get different effects by using these devices. The handmade papers and machine-made papers together with chemically compounded inks and fabricated zinc plates with asphaltum compounds and high grade acids allow me to say things I can't say on the stone cave wall with berry juice and a stick. " "With my $1500 etching press imported from Germany I can get 1200 pounds per square inch, if I so desire." True. And that is exactly the point the advertising artist can build on.

The advertising artist who turns printmaker can say things in a variety of ways by using a variety of different methods. There is no attempt to compete with a soft-ground etch or try to imitate the grain of stone lithography. He is not interested in reproducing the feathery edged line of a dry point. He gets different effects by using different devices just as surely as the 19th century printmaker.

He can be as vitally interested in his final print as any artist. His 'personal touch' may even be a mite stronger than the average artist, because science has given him automation and improved tools which extend the limits of his control. Ink pistons, paper adjustment, platen pressures can be adjusted to the thousandth of an inch. He uses screen patterns to get soft luminous grays that are just not possible on a ground stone. He uses opaquing inks to blank out highlights on the negatives

PRINCIPLES
CHANGE
SLOWLY——

to achieve pure whites that are extremely hard to get by other means. He prepares artwork with the direct INTENT of enlarging or reducing parts by camera to get certain results that cannot be obtained otherwise. And in the end result he enjoys the dot patterns, regular or irregular; the distortions caused by enlargement; the textures; the off-registry; and split fountains. He happens to like what comes off the high-speed modern presses UNDER HIS CONTROL. Others do too.

Now let us examine the question as to how MANY people receive the "personal touch" of the limited edition ? Rarity may make something cost more, but it doesn't make it better. There is undoubtedly a protective feeling or emotional pleasure in owning something rare that is apart from liking it for many people. But at the same time there should also be room for those who enjoy certain things whether they are rare or not. If I happen to like a simple white porcelain egg cup and keep one on my drawing table, it does not bother me in the least that there are millions of them in the world and more being made every day. They are sheer beauty. Many sculptures fall far short of its form. If my next door neighbor happens to have one and appreciates it also, I think that is wonderful. We have something in common at last.

The twenty prints of the limited edition may sell for $60 to $120 or better per print, and the market for these is as restricted as the edition. The millions of young homeowners just above the necessity income bracket are still not in that market. Is it not possible that modern production methods in the hands of a good artist could bring some interesting prints within the price range of these families ? Original photo-offset or letterpress engraving prints produced in quantity and distributed thru several outlets might sell for as low as $3, $6, and $12.

PRINTING

When the artist finally feels he has something interesting, he can process his negative, collage, or flat and print several hundred as a start. The method of printing will depend to a great extent on what effect is desired by the artist. Any embossing, for example, will have to be accomplished by letterpress or handpresses. The cost of a litho press will probably be somewhere between $30 and $50 for 1/2 hour, depending on the size of the press used and the competition. A print 12 x 16, one color, printed on 17 x 22 eighty pound paper could probably be rolled off at 30 per minute at first, allowing for careful examination of every tenth print or so to hold the ink quality. Allow 10 minutes makeready to get the ink just right, center register and feed conveyer system going smoothly. Allow 5 minutes time to run out ink, gather up proofs and washup. This leaves us about 15 minutes actual running time on the press. At 60 per minute we could run off 900 to a 1000 prints if we wanted that many. But seeing we are not too sure we can sell 1000 of our first print, let us settle for 200 prints. The cost of the paper for 200 sheets of 17 x 22 good stock will be about $15 which allows for some sheets for makeready sampling. The total cost of printing 200 prints in one color then would be roughly $50, which would put the cost of printing each print at 25 cents.

Other costs which may be charged for more complex runs are:

Special ink mixes
Press washups for changing color
Extra makeready for second color
Slip sheets for running porous paper
Running overtime because of production problems
Changes in specifications by the artist at the last minute

BIDS

When running your first print talk with the printer long enough so
that he understands exactly what you want, what he charges to make
the plate from your flat, whether you order the paper thru him or not.
You may wish to make your own plate. If so, make certain you are
using plates that can be used on his presses. He may expect you to
furnish the paper if it is an unusual etching paper that is not ordinarily carried by his paper wholesaler. Mixing ink to a selected color
sample is often a time consuming job. It may be well to make some
arrangement to mix the ink in advance, so you do not use up valuable
press time in mixing. At least get somewhere near the color you desire
Then when the first few color proofs come off the press you can put in
a touch of this and a touch of that to bring it to the right value and
chroma. An ink printing from an offset blanket or steel engraving
often appears different in value than the tapped out ink on your sample
swatches, and this has to be corrected after the press is rolling, so get
as many things done ahead of time as possible.

Printers vary in policy. It is always a good business practice to get
a written firm bid on your job with all details of plate costs, paper,
makeready paper scrap, slip sheets, ink mixes, and press time settled
to the satisfaction of both parties. It is not a question of honesty...
merely that verbal contracts are notorious for **misunderstandings.** Say
you had expected to pay $125 for two print editions, and on the final
bill you discover $18 for platemaking and $9 for special ink mixes,
which the printer thought you realized were NOT included in his
quoted 'printing costs'. This makes for hard feelings and arguments,
especially with people new in the game. Take your time and get the
total, total bid. If it is too high, it is certainly your prerogative not
to accept the bid. But if you do accept, you will, at the very least,
know what your costs are and be in accord with the printer.

MARKETING PRINTS

You now have an inventory of 200 prints which cost you approximately
25 cents apiece. If you can sell 5 of them at $10 apiece, or 10 at $5
apiece, or 17 at $3 apiece, you would have your original cash invest-
ment back, which could be used to print another print. The remaining
prints as sold would represent a GROSS profit for your first venture.
Obviously you have had other expenses such as telephone calls, gasoline and auto expenses, and your own time which must be taken into
consideration. And if you are wise, you will start keeping a written
log of all these items for two reasons. First, you will begin to know
your own costs for making a print. Second, you will have some written evidence to substantiate your income tax deductions.

SHOWALTER

HEIGH HO
AND AWAY_____.

215

ACID
BATH

SCRATCH
THRU

THIN
COAT OF
RESIST

PLATE

PATINA.

2. BUILDUPS

COLLAGE relief

Whereas in a block print the wood was cut away in the negative areas to leave the positive areas in relief, it is possible to achieve a similar printing surface by BUILDING UP the positive printing surface from the base. Masonite or 1/4 - inch plywood can be used as a base and on this can be glued other pieces of material. This type of print is called a Collage print. Cardboard, gunny sacking, cloth, toweling, and other semi-rigid materials may be used, but are usually good for only 10 to 20 impressions on the printing press before they get pressed flat or clogged with ink. However, if you can get one good impression from such materials it could be made into a halftone negative, worked over with opaquing fluid and texture screens, printed and embossed from a photo-mechanical engraving. See the last part of this section under Combinations for more on this subject.

The print on the preceding page is a collage print.

Materials such as flat pieces of wood, metal screen, rope and plastic, of course, stand up much longer under the pressure of the hand cranked press. Again, if the paper is dampened, the embossing effect is emphasized and adds to the richness of the print. Colored block printing inks can be used effectively in certain areas of these prints. The color can be applied to parts of the plate and black on the other portions. The result is a multicolored print which only has to be run thru the press once. Overlapped transparencies are accomplished by inking the second color on a second run and overprinting the first color. There are ink EXTENDERS, a transparent jel substance which can be used occasionally to thin out the ink and make it more transparent. Silk screen supply firms often handle this type of product.

3. PLASTIC METALS

Some background information on traditional INTAGLIO methods is necessary here to understand better the plastic metal plates.

Traditional intaglio

The metal plates used by conventional printmakers for engraving or etching processes make a very fine printing surface. Intaglio is a method of printing from the LOWERED portions of these plates. For example, let us assume the artist has cut grooves into, and etched out (with acid) portions of the metal plate to make his image. He now inks the ENTIRE plate, forcing the ink into the grooves and other rough etched spots left by the acid, as well as the raised surface. The plate is then wiped vigorously with cheesecloth which removes most of the ink from the raised surfaces.

A very thin film of ink still adheres to the raised surfaces, but a much heavier amount remains in the grooves or etched portions of the plate. When the dampened paper is pressed against the plate, it picks the ink out of the grooves and lowered textured etched areas and also receives a very light-gray patina of ink from the smoother wiped surfaces. The result is a subtle variation of grays

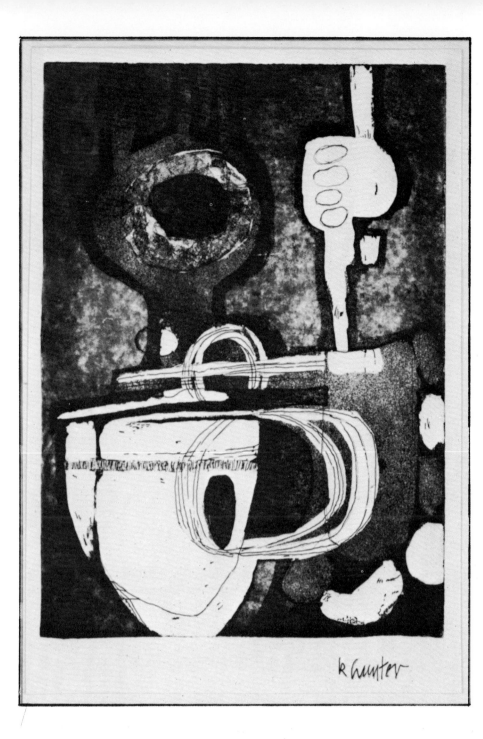

and blacks that is rarely equalled by other materials. The lower portions of these plates are usually very shallow, probably no deeper than 1/16 th of an inch unless the artist makes DEEP ETCH plates or builds up the plate in other ways by welding or soldering or dropping molten metal on the heated plate. So there is very little embossing effect even though most of the printing is done from the lowered portions of the plate.

CAUTION: No student or amateur artist should ever work with acid or molten metal unless under the direct supervision of a trained instructor. Acid fumes are corrosive and sometimes fatal. Tight fitting safety goggles should be worn whenever working with acid or metal. Acid splashes. Molten metal sparks and splatters. Metal splinters fly in all directions from band saws, sabre saws, and grinding wheels. Don't allow others to stand nearby and watch unless properly equipped !

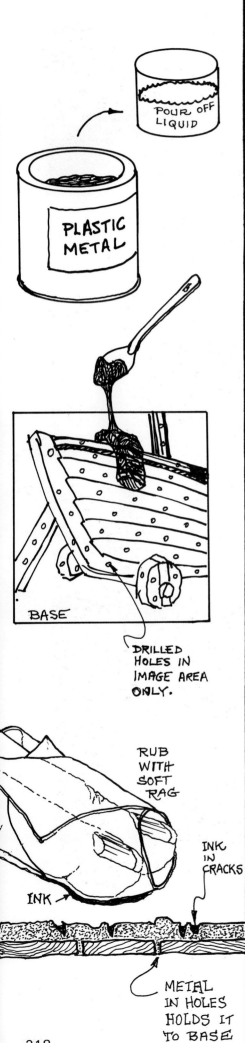

POUR OFF LIQUID

PLASTIC METAL

BASE

DRILLED HOLES IN IMAGE AREA ONLY.

RUB WITH SOFT RAG

INK

INK IN CRACKS

METAL IN HOLES HOLDS IT TO BASE

Plastic metals

There are some interesting ways to produce a similar type of intaglio plate by using quick-set plastic metals on a stiff base or in a mold. The student can thus have the experience of making and printing an intaglio plate without the hazards of acid baths or heating metal plates.

CAUTION: When handling any of the alkyds, plastic resins, or plastic "metals" always work in a well ventilated area and avoid breathing the fumes. Not too much is known yet about the toxic effects these new compounds have on the human body, and it is best to be on the safe side.

Forming on a stiff base

Use a piece of 1/4 inch plywood or masonite and trace or draw your image on it in pencil. Drill 3/16 or 1/4 inch holes in the image area about 3 to 4 inches apart. These give the plastic metal something to hang on to. Open the can of plastic metal and mix it according to instructions. (One tradename on the market is "Sculp-metal") It is best to pour off some of the thinner in the can and add it gradually as you mix. In this way you can control the mixture so it gets no thinner than a soft putty consistency. (If the mixture gets too thin it will run all over the board and be uncontrollable.)

When the material has a workable consistency, ladle out a few teaspoons on to the image area and push it into the form desired. Keep adding metal as desired. The material usually has a stringy consistency that is very interesting if left alone. Too much pressing and pushing for tiny details after the material starts hardening often leaves a spongy, irregular surface that is hard to ink later. Drip and drool the metal on to get the large significant images and keep the pushing and pressing of the metal to a minimum. Don't overwork it. Push the metal into the drilled holes here and there to make certain it adheres to the base. Try to keep the top surfaces of the metal fairly level and no higher than 1/4 inch or there will be difficulty in printing it evenly. Let it dry thoroughly, which may mean as long as two or three days if there are thick spots. The "metal" tends to dry on the surface first, which hinders the deeper drying. If the plate is run thru a roller too soon, the pressure will cause the metal to squish out from beneath the skin and ruin the plate.

The edge of the wood base can be left rectangular or sawed to any shape or size consistent with the print or size of printing paper. The edges should be sanded or rounded off to prevent tearing the paper or puncturing the expensive felts.

A good grade etcher's ink seems to give the best result on metals. It is somewhat finer and more plastic than the block printing ink and defines the minute textures in the metal that make for the subtle variations in a WIPED print. Use a rag wrapped around your fingers or a felt whorl and ink the entire plate by pressing the ink into every crevice very thoroughly. Sepia brown inks and Terre Verte greens mixed with black can provide some interesting variations from straight blacks.

PLASTIC METAL
ON PLYWOOD

Now wipe the plate firmly with a soft rag. Be careful not to snag the edges of the metal image and tear up corners from the base. Because this type of plate is of higher relief than usual, the stiffer cloths, like cheesecloth, tend to skip over the wide valleys. Hence a more cautious wiping is necessary with the softer cloth and fingers to wipe the plate evenly. After wiping, place the plate on the bed of the press and center it.

Soak your printing paper between 3 minutes and 1/2 hour depending on its weight. The thicker and heavier the paper the longer soaking it needs to become permeated with moisture. Lay it on blotters or paper toweling and pat off the excess moisture with paper towels or other blotters. Pick it up carefully by two opposite diagonal corners and lay it carefully over the plate without dragging it. A few small tabs of masking tape on the bed of the press will help you register the paper and keep the margins even. Cover the paper with two felt blankets or several thicknesses of an old army blanket. If the plate is extremely bumpy and varies in relief more than 1/4 inch, put more thicknesses of blanket between the felts and the paper. The added thickness will translate the pressure of the roller into the deeper pockets of the plate and give you a more even print. It will also protect the felt pads from the irregularities of the metal. Crank the plate thru the press. Lift up the print carefully after you remove the blankets. Pin the print on the wall by the four corners to dry or tape it along the edges to a drying board with butchers tape.

The final print will have cracks, wipe marks, white lines and textures combined with a deeply embossed surface quality that is a visual experience quite different than the typical etching or intaglio printed piece.

PRINT ON
DAMP PAPER
FROM METAL
PLATE.

221

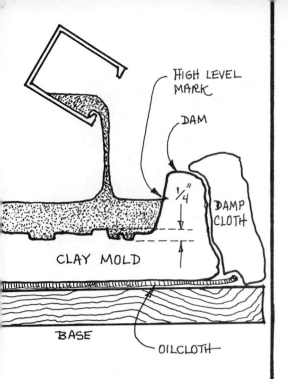

HIGH LEVEL MARK

DAM

1/4"

DAMP CLOTH

CLAY MOLD

BASE

OILCLOTH

FINISHED
METAL
PLATE

Casting in a clay mold

Use a rolling pin and pugged potters clay. Roll the clay out on the back of a piece of oilcloth on a stiff base board (An old drawing board will do.) into a flat slab about 3/4-inch thick, slightly larger in area than the size of your image. A size 7 X 12 is probably large enough for a starter. Press into the surface of the clay slab with your fingers, blocks of wood, clay modeling tools, or any instruments you think will do the job of defining your image. The negative areas can be textured or left smooth. On this first mold keep the relief no greater than 1/4 inch deep. Now push the clay up around the edge of the slab and build a lip or dam about 3/4 inch high all around the edge of the slab. Make this dam at least 3/4 inch thick so the plastic metal cannot flow out thru any cracks.

Mix the plastic metal in the can to the consistency of thick cream. Level the mold by pushing bits of clay under the edges of the base board. Pour the metal carefully and slowly into the mold until it is about 1/4 or 1/8 inch above the surface of the slab. Measured "highwater marks" on the inside of the dam wall would be a good guide. This means the metal may be as thick as 1/2 inch in some high relief areas but will have at least a 1/8 inch thickness in the shallower or negative spaces. To prevent the clay mold from drying too fast and cracking, damp cloths should be laid along the edge of the mold. Be certain not to let any part of the cloth trail in the liquid metal or it will pull out a large gob when removed. Let the metal set up and dry for 3 days or more. When you are certain the metal is rigid, pare the clay dam down even with the metal, lay a stiff board over the whole mold and turn the entire mold upside down. Remove the base board, peel back the oilcloth, and carefully start removing the semi-moist clay from the face of the metal plate.

When the plate is completely freed from the mold it may be glued down on a piece of heavy chipboard or thin plywood to help give it rigidity. It can now be inked and printed like the previous plate.

"Romulus Rubbing" 114/200 Bodkra

223

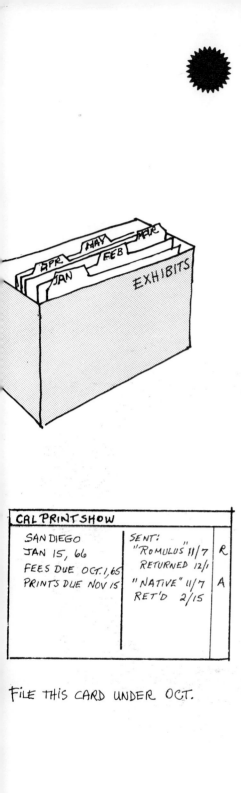

CAL PRINT SHOW

| SAN DIEGO
JAN 15, 66
FEES DUE OCT.1,65
PRINTS DUE NOV 15 | SENT:
"ROMULUS" 11/7
RETURNED 12/1 | R |
| | "NATIVE" 11/7
RET'D 2/15 | A |

FILE THIS CARD UNDER OCT.

Exhibits

The game of entering juried exhibits is a tough one for most beginners. Well known artists are often invited to exhibit, jury exempt, to enhance the prestige of the show. In many cases these artists' works are handled by the artist's agent or gallery with which he is associated. The neophyte, however, if he wants to exhibit in these shows, has to start like everyone else. He must do his own correspondence, pack and ship his entries, keep records of where and when he sent what. Write more letters to track down an entry that was never returned, and so on. It is not easy and is rarely very fruitful unless the artist works at it like any job... HARD.

You must assume at the start that all juries are not going to accept your work. Therefore, as in any other selling job, you have to rely upon statistics and **probability**. Enter shows often and consistently for a period of two or three years over the entire U.S., and overseas if you have the time and money. Prints are cheaper and easier to ship than oils, watercolors or sculpture and thus get you more coverage for your money. Following are a few pointers for the beginning exhibitor.

Card File

Start by compiling a list of exhibits which accept prints and the dates and fees. This info can be gathered by talking to other artists, watching art bulletin boards, browsing thru art magazines many of which have a separate section listing current competitions. Companies which pack and ship art works as a specialty (Bruggers, Los Angeles, for example) often publish a list of coming exhibits and their deadlines for the artist.

As you compile the information start a card index. Use one 3x5 card for each exhibit and put the name of the show at the upper left-hand corner. Under it on the left side of the card put the address, dates when the entry fee is due, date when the entry must arrive, any other eligibility info, and the date of the exhibit. Draw a vertical line down the center of the card. To the right of this line place the name of the print or prints entered, the date they were sent, and allow room for a column for A or R, accepted or rejected, and another column for date returned. (You'd be surprised how easy it is to forget what prints have been returned and which have not when several months fly by.)

File these cards in a box back of dividers labelled for the months of the year in which the exhibit must be ENTERED. Do not file them under the month the exhibit will be held, as the entries are often received and juried weeks before the exhibit opens.

An organized card file like the above helps to remind you of upcoming exhibits and the need for getting application blanks, fees, and entries mailed early. It also gives you a record after the first year of which prints were sent to which show, so you can change entries the next year. My first experience in following a system of this type was that it was much easier. Without an index I always seemed to be wrapping something at the last minute and dashing down to the post office or express office to get it off under the deadline.

PORTFOLIO

The portfolio should represent the student. It should show the student's future design potential with examples such as full color illustrations, package designs, and scale models perhaps. It should also show his ability to produce simple designs such as small black and white SPOTS, a constructed Roman letter, a fluid piece of simple calligraphy, some sharp renderings or perspective drawings, as well as his present technical SKILLS which might be shown in his pasteups, photo masking, retouching, mechanical lettering or what have you.

The DIRECTION a student is taking should be realized first of all by the student himself. No artist can be tops at all jobs. If illustration is the student's forte and choice, then his portfolio should represent his strengths

in this area. Too many portfolios are filled with a hodge-podge of everything, some good, some indifferent, so that the prospective employer and even the student himself cannot possibly know the characteristics of this beginning artist. Yet, on the other hand, many students who have not been able to afford lengthy programs at colleges or private art schools may have to include a broad variety of things in their portfolio in the hopes of landing small or part time jobs in local industry as a beginning. Then as they grow with experience, they can specialize their presentation.

There is no single answer for all students.

It is the rare student who steps into a job doing advanced design work immediately. The first few jobs usually involve directed pasteup and other routine chores. Although at first there is little chance for any creative design work, there IS opportunity to increase one's speed, understand more about production, and gather information about the business.

This section is concerned with four factors:
1. The student's RESUME' (Qualifications)
2. The MODULE size
3. The presentation of 3-dimensional objects
4. The DIRECTION or type of job desired
and Interviews.

DAVID MULLER

I. RESUME'

A resume is a summary of an applicant's qualifications to fill a certain position. It is usually headed with full name, present address, and degrees or latest school attended. Birthdate, birthplace, and high school are included next. Thereafter follows a list of jobs or work experience in chronological, dates order. Some resumes are typed with the latest experience at the top of the list; others are typed with the latest experience at the bottom.

Work Experience

The majority of students tend to forget that employers are interested in ALL types of work experience. Agencies and other firms often have a standing regulation that applicants for art positions must have had some art experience. They do not define the exact experience but leave that to the discretion of the personnel department and interviewer.

When you apply for a job then, you may have a crackerjack of a portfolio, speak excellent English plus necessary qualifications, and the interviewer feels you are a good possibility. But when you state flatly that you have had no experience, his hands are tied immediately. If you had made some effort to recall your past experiences and listed them in your resume, he would have had "past art experience" to support his opinion of your qualifications. He might have hired you. So do not neglect your past work experiences in art, even though they seem trivial to you.

Veteran artists in the field realize that all young artists can not have worked two years with a triple-A agency in New York, and they often are as interested in the variety of your background as you are. After all, it is rather difficult to have lived for 22 years or so and NOT have done a few things in the art line. Following is a list that may help your recall.

On publicity board in high school
Striping auto fenders
Building a hot rod
Sewing your own clothes
Decorating for a banquet
Clerking in a store
Window decorations at school
Built booths for school carnival
Summer work with local newspaper
Modelled dresses
Designed brochure for church
Built 10 ft. high murals for dance
Photographer for school paper
Posters for Little League
Worked on school year book
Made sets for play
Helped with makeup and costumes
Merchandising experience
Built a cabin

TYPICAL RESUME

PERSONAL DATA SHEET

Personal Information

Name: William Hotchkins

Address: 3042 Tanoble Dr.
Pasadena, CA 91002

Phone: (213) 853-1212

Place of Birth: Pasadena, California
Date of Birth: February 21, 1960
Height: 5' 11"
Weight: 160 lbs.
Physical Condition: Excellent
Marital Status: Single
Social Security Number: 471 03 1833

Education

1977   Pasadena High School - Diploma
1979   Pasadena City College - Art Major in Advertising Graphics
1981   University of California at Long Beach - BA
1982   Art Center College of Design, Pasadena - Graduate work in Design

Work Experience

1975   Summer only Mail Clerk Unitek Corp., Pasadena, CA
1976   Summer only Life Guard Huntington Beach, CA
1977   Part time   Apprentice in bindery Janson Printers, Pasadena, CA
1978   Part-time photographer for Altadena "Chronicle" newspaper
1981   Sports reporter for UCLB school paper - 2 years
1982   Worked on floats for Tournament of Roses Assoc., Pasadena
       Also worked part time in library of Art Center College of Design.

Awards and Activities

1977   Received Certificate of Superior Achievement from PCC Art Dept.
1981   Secretary of Student Art Association at UCLB for two years
1981   On dean's list, UCLB, spring semester.

Interests

Photography
Tennis
Antique Autos
Desert Prospecting

Major Curriculum & Military Status Attached

2. THE MODULE

Recommended earlier was a matboard size of 20 x 30, as it was easy to carry under the arm and was exactly half of a standard 30 x 40 matboard. Although experienced artists usually carry smaller portfolios (10 x 14) which contain mainly their latest production pieces, the beginning artist has to carry larger drawings and finished art as "evidence" of his abilities. The next few pages contain a sampling of items that might appear in a portfolio.

Twelve to fifteen boards would be plenty in a portfolio. Some boards may have 3 or 4 items, so approximately 35 to 40 items might be presented at one time.

3. PRESENTATION OF 3-DIMENSIONAL OBJECTS

There are often several structural items, scale models, or packages that an artist would like to include in his portfolio. One of the better ways is to photograph the object in color, have a print made from the transparency, and mat it in the portfolio. Let us use a package as an example:

Place the package on a neutral background. Lay the packaged product next to it. Cellophane wrapped taffy spilling out of the candy box, a fishing reel next to its box, and similar setups make for some interesting compositions. Place the SETUP in direct sunlight. Get as close as you can with a 35 mm camera (Which is usually about 3 feet if you do not have special lenses.) and shoot a color transparency of it. Be aware of cast SHADOWS in your composition.

When the slide is processed, have your local photographer or drug store send it in to have a 5 x 7 color PRINT made. This costs about $1.50 at the present time. If the slide of your setup has too much background around it, cut out a small rectangle in a paper MASK and hinge tape this paper mask to the top of the slide. This shows the processing plant what part of the transparency composition you want printed, and they will enlarge the composition within that rectangle to the 5 x 7 dimension or in proportion. It will cost you a few cents more, but it is often worth it to get a larger picture of the subject with less background area.

When the print comes back from the processor compare it with the transparency before you leave the counter. If it looks washed out or too dark, send it back again with the written criticism, and they will usually be glad to give you another print that has been printed with more care and better FIDELITY. A good print can be made to look almost exactly like the transparency. Of course you should not be too critical, and if the transparent slide is overexposed there is nothing the processing plant can do about that. But they should be able to give you in the print the same value and hues that are apparent in the transparency.

Mount the print of your package and other 3-D problems in your portfolio and you will have the evidence of your training preserved long after the package has been chewed up by the dog or squashed by little brother.

Ken

In some cases an advanced student may have the skill and talent to design a type alphabet. There are already thousands of type faces available, but the practice of making each letter relate to the others for spacing and readability is a real challenge.

Mitchell

Showalter

Showalter

Package comps from Project N, page 92, and a point-of-sale raccoon made from three elliptical-shaped pieces of 3-ply Strathmore. The three pieces are held together at the back with a brass duotang. The nose is held forward by a thread clipped to the base. This unit can be delivered throughout a large department store in a flat package and then easily assembled by the clerks themselves in each section.

The example on the left is from Part 3 of the problem on page 23. It is a very high-key value painting covered with an acetate ink line on a covering acetate flap. An exercise such as this can show a student's ability to work out flat designs from fotos, as well as his ability to draw with ink.

Lord

Steven Cook

Knowledge of basic structural drawing is always helpful.

232

A brownline made from a pasteup or collage of a variety of transparent and opaque materials can produce an interesting variation. (See page 102.)

The block printing process is often very applicable to the illustration of legends. The crudeness of the cut seems to enhance the primitive feeling of the image. Relating a process or materials to the mood of the imagery should be part of the sensitivity of every young artist.

Deusing

233

Kimberly

Quick chalk roughs or comps done with a variety of media, such as markers, ink, color key, or coated paper and cold type can all be important in a student's portfolio.

Rushworth

A drawing was made of an old-fashioned piece of transportation which was then covered with a variety of textures from old magazine scrap. A painted rendering was then made from the pasteup of textures. A good project for learning the color wheel.

Komine

Showalter

Cut paper is a medium that often forces a student to scissor more significant forms than when he uses a pencil or fine pen. (The paper can be color-coated stock or the less expensive chalk fixed on bond.) These "Four Season" storybook covers were done by dividing an 11 x 16 horizontal rectangle into four equal, vertical parts and using celestial objects, the weather elements, and plants to portray the seasons. Several roughs were required before starting on the comp pasteup.

Scale models or miniature toys such as cannon, trolley cars, fire engines, locomotives, etc., make for some inexpensive props and cost cutting. In the example poster below, locating a real cannon would probably have entailed phone calls plus an hour's trip to a park or central city museum. Instead each designer brought in several small toys. A student fotografer was then teamed with several designers to make each a blowup for a poster depicting some imaginary event. In the sample below, the cannon was about one inch high, and the student smeared some mud on the wheels for more realism.

Students often have skills that they never relate to a portfolio. Reworking dragsters or motorcycles into "mint" condition, striping, lettering, (as in the foto), architectural drafting units, engineering product views, boats, dressmaking, flower displays, table arrangements, etc., can all be photographed and placed in the portfolio to show another facet of their skills. Advertising artists have to work with, and have empathy with hundreds of different product manufacturers and distributors. The student's interests and background training are just as an essential part of his portfolio as the ad layouts and spot illustrations. Get it in your portfolio!

Jandegian

Fehring

Again the design students were teamed with several fotografers and sent out to shoot any of the statues around town. The poster here is an enlargement of Michelangelo's "David," 12 x 14, drymounted on cardboard and then covered with a blue acetate flap. The sun and lettering were applied after fixing the acetate with workable fix.

The unusual landscape here is a structural idea taken from Lionel Feininger's unique approach to watercolor landscapes. The entire image must be done with OVERLAPPING straight lines using a sharp B pencil and a ruler on heavy watercolor paper. The student's pigments were limited to Venetian Red, Burnt Sienna, Yellow Ochre, and Payne's Gray. The colors were laid on with a number 6, pointed, red sable very precisely in the various rectangles formed by the lines.

Mangham

Students bring in a fruit or a vegetable and render it realistically in color on the first 6-inch square panel. They then slice the food item and make a design on the second panel using any subdued colors. The third panel must contain an enlargement of any detail. The students should be particularly sensitive to the negative areas in panels two and three. They are not to merely plop each image into the center of the rectangle. Time required is approximately 9 hours for entire unit.

From this basic unit a practical advertising idea may be developed, such as this billboard model.

Caro

When free calligraphy is needed, such as the word, Canada, below, five or six pieces of board or Canson paper are usually necessary for the student artist to achieve a good result. The calligraphic word is tried again and again until a satisfactory image is formed. THEN the constructed lettering and other images are pasted or traced down and painted over that piece.

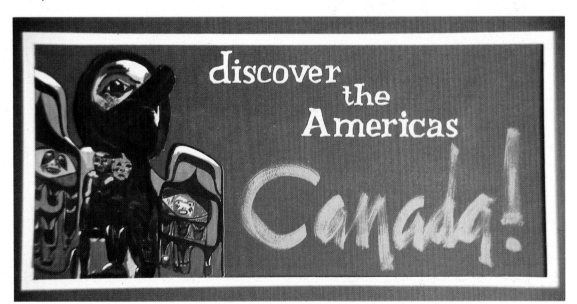

Hardy

4. DIRECTION

The type of job a student wants should be obvious from his portfolio and resume' presentation. Art directors have told me again and again that young artists have portfolios that are so diverse or general in nature that it is hard to know exactly what the student is seeking. Oftentimes the student himself is not even aware of the many different kinds of opportunities in the advertising world. It might be well to look at your own portfolio, do some research on what types of jobs there are, and then see if your presentation is consistent with what you DESIRE in the way of employment.

Are you primarily interested in LAYOUT ? Then your portfolio should have a profusion of roughs and visuals. Perhaps 6 or 7 different visuals presenting a single idea in 6 or 7 different ways could be included. The prospective employer will be very interested in how you THINK and design. What ideas do you have ? Do you use a variety of media ? Can you show several approaches to a single design problem... or do all your roughs look alike ? What is your concept of a well done 1/4 page advertisement in black and white ? Two color ? Half page ? Do you have any sequential pieces like a four-fold travel brochure with indicated photography, or a four-season approach in line only ? Do you have any accompanying pasteups to show ? Can you draw or render fairly convincingly ? With pen, pencil, brush ? Can you present ideas vocally as well as visually ? Or do you talk talk talk too much ? Do you know something about the COST of printing line, halftone, full color ?

Your portfolio should not be loaded with lettering, technical illustrations, and fashion designs, if doing layout work is your present aim. A bit perhaps to show you are acquainted with them, but that would be sufficient. In general, then, if you know what type of work you want, the interviewer is better able to judge whether he has a place for your talents . Much of a company's personnel department's time is spent trying to find a spot for someone who didn't fit the job he was hired for. Most companies do not like to fire people and almost always try to reassign those who did not happen to fit the job for which they were hired. However, this often means loss of training time to the company and loss of seniority time for the employee. So, be prepared, and know where you are going.

The above holds for the fashion designer, letterer, advertising fotografer, the packaging specialist, technical illustrator or story illustrator. Try to put things in your portfolio that will best present your talents in the field of your choice. Keep items from the other areas at a minimum, even though they are related. You can't be tops in all fields.

One final suggestion: Select items carefully. Rather have a few excellent presentations than several more mediocre ones. The WORST item in your portfolio is the standard you'll be judged by !

5. INTERVIEWS

For those of you who have a pretty specific knowledge of where you're heading when you leave school, it might be wise to look over a list of employers who would be able to use an artist with your talents. Do this about 6 months BEFORE you are graduating. Look into their businesses. Find out exactly what they do, who their clients are, the number of employees and the kinds of artists they employ. Who are the owners? Is it a single proprietorship, a partnership, or a corporation? How long have they been in business? Are they contemplating expanding in any certain art area or geographical location? What campaigns are they handling? What do their ads look like?

Some of this information can be gathered by writing a letter directly to one of the owners, tell him you are a student and requesting an interview with an art director or perhaps someone in the personnel department. Let the letter state plainly that the emphasis is NOT on getting a job, but merely to find out something about the advertising field in general. Usually employers are willing to allow this if it doesn't happen too often, and I assure you it happens all too rarely. This takes a little doing and effort but the results are well worth it. After a few months of several interviews of this sort you begin to have a much better picture of the variety of agencies or industrial plants employing artists in your area. Then when you graduate you have a much better background for job hunting than the typical student who has never been outside the classroom.

When you do start job hunting try to find out a few things about the company to which you are applying. While you are in the interviewer's office try to ask him questions as well as answering his. It is usually not good business to discuss salary on your first call unless the interviewer brings it up. As a beginner you cannot be a chooser in most cases. But you can show interest in their firm for example by asking about their products, or types of clients, whether they have branch offices anywhere, do they farm out some of their art work, do they have their own photographer, etc. These questions often start a conversation going that makes it easier for the interviewer to judge your personality and background, and at the same time gives you more and more information about advertising in your area. Memorize the interviewer's name so that you can thank him directly with a letter. Remember that you are going to be turned down in most places with a polite, " Sorry, we don't have an opening at the present. " Nevertheless, thank the secretary on the way out. A month later a telephone call to the same interviewer merely asking about possibilities of an opening would not be inappropriate. Oftentimes he may not have one open in the plant BUT these men communicate with each other in the community and he may well be able to tell you of one or two opportunities he has heard of. Most personnel men are in the game because they like helping people, and to know about a job opening and be able to direct a person to it is their greatest joy, really. You, yourself, probably realize how hard you try to recall any job opening when someone tells you they are looking. So don't slam the door too hard when you are turned away from a firm. An occasional call, a single letter several weeks later may often pay off. A quiet, long term approach to some

(Continued on page 244.)

Illustration from Project E on page 25.   Riley

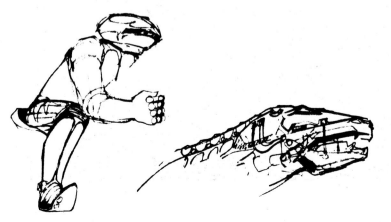

© Roger Dean from the book of his works "Views"
Published by Dragon's Dream Ltd.

Roger Dean is an Englishman. He is also a very creative designer in areas such as architecture, industrial design and illustration. This page shows a portion of a record album cover, "Paladin Charge!", done for Bronze Records plus two of his many 'searching' sketches. Many of his other works also show the interesting relationships between animal and machine.

position in art in your community by reminding people that you are still looking, that you appreciated the time they took to advise you, etc., is ten times as effective as merely walking in an agency, having them glance at your portfolio, and walking out never to see them again. The job for you is somewhere in the community, but you have to have the creative nerve, and quiet persistence to keep your name circulating. Even a simple request for permission to call back in a few weeks is rarely denied, and it gives you a perfect chance to remind the firm that you are still available. One call plus one letter would probably be sufficient and if spaced over a period of several weeks will give you that much more probability that someone will be able to help. In some of the larger agencies a return visit a year later during their peak rush might be a good tactical maneuver.

And for Pete's sake learn to SMILE when job hunting. Most young people have a grand sense of humor but keep it in the deep freeze during the interview. We all know your stomach is tight, your throat is constricted, and your new shoes pinch. Laugh at yourself a little bit, it even makes you feel more at ease. So you don't win this one, win the next.

In most cities there are employment agencies who specialize in placing artists of all types. Standard practice is for the employment agency to notify you of positions open and let you contact the prospective employer. Then if the employer decides to hire you and you accept the job, you pay the employment agency a set sum or a certain percentage of your first months salary. If you don't get the job or decide to refuse an offer there is usually no charge by the agency , and they keep notifying you of openings until you click. This is often a good way to save time and effort in looking for a job. In fact, you may wish to leave your name with several employment agencies and thus make certain you are covering a larger area.

When you do accept a position, notify ALL the employment agencies immediately. And a note of thanks for their effort is certainly in order. Yes, they are somewhat impersonal, but remember , the girl at the desk who sent you the notice of the position to your correct address at the right time, was NOT impersonal. It's people who make the world go around and remembering and thanking people who have helped or tried to help makes living more fun.

The section after this on Agency Organization will give brief descriptions of some of the job opportunities in a typical agency and may help you find a direction. A growing number of students approach the end of their academic education and discover they still haven't settled on a specialty. My advice is don't worry about it. You may be much better off than those who settled on a particular field too soon.

AGENCY

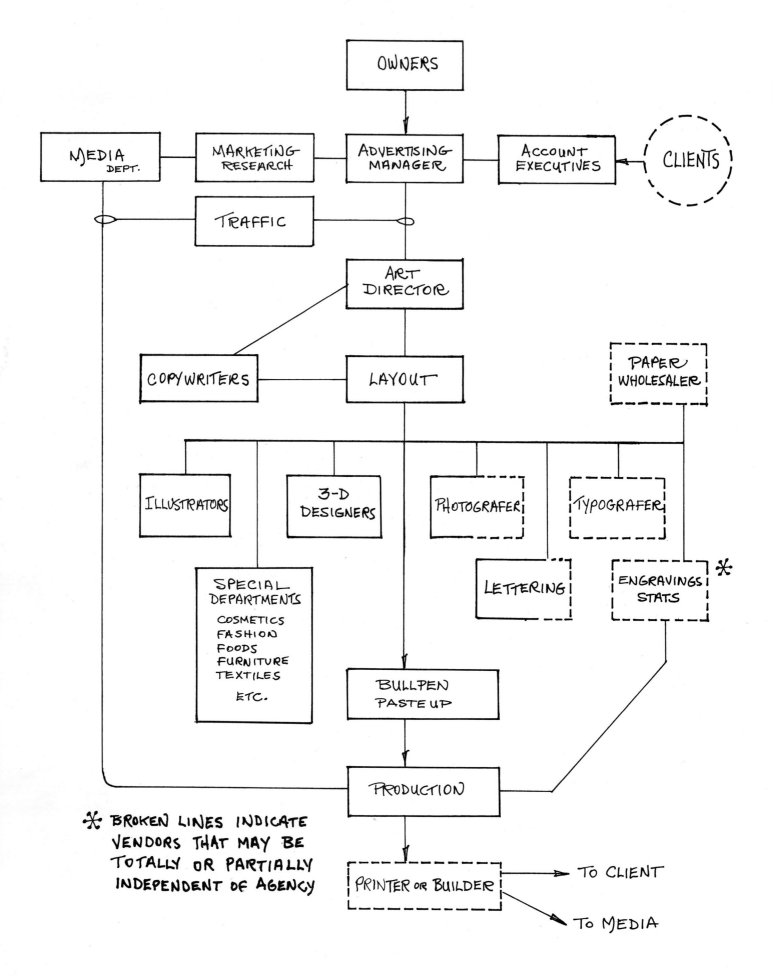

OWNERS

MEDIA DEPT. — MARKETING RESEARCH — ADVERTISING MANAGER — ACCOUNT EXECUTIVES — CLIENTS

TRAFFIC

ART DIRECTOR

COPYWRITERS — LAYOUT

PAPER WHOLESALER

ILLUSTRATORS   3-D DESIGNERS   PHOTOGRAFER   TYPOGRAFER

SPECIAL DEPARTMENTS
COSMETICS
FASHION
FOODS
FURNITURE
TEXTILES

ETC.

LETTERING   ENGRAVINGS STATS   *

BULLPEN PASTE UP

PRODUCTION

* BROKEN LINES INDICATE VENDORS THAT MAY BE TOTALLY OR PARTIALLY INDEPENDENT OF AGENCY

PRINTER OR BUILDER → TO CLIENT
→ TO MEDIA

Section 20   AGENCY ORGANIZATION

An organization chart shows relationships of authority, responsibility, and communication between the various positions in the field. Brief JOB DESCRIPTIONS help the student to understand what abilities might be expected in each work area.

Many artists find niches for themselves in the business world where their talents are particularly useful. The outgoing personality who likes to sell may find many opportunities in selling as an Account Executive. The efficient organizer and expediter may find his forte in Traffic or Art Direction. The mechanical, technical-minded artist may become an excellent Production man. Another artist may prefer to work at the drawing board while other people "front" for him. Some artists have a liking for technical illustration or story illustration. By realizing what positions are available for an artist, the student has a better chance to assess his own capabilities and point for a definite goal. Again, it is not necessary to specialize, and a broad varied education without a specific goal at the present may fit many undecided students. Early specialization, merely for the sake of specialization, can often prove to be a very narrow, disappointing road later in life.

AGENCY POSITIONS

Responsibilities and authority in business obviously overlap and change with each new situation. An account executive may request that a certain copywriter be assigned to a job instead of having the writer selected by the art director. There may be times when the production man gives a layout ok to artwork coming in at the last minute, even tho the art director should have ok'd it first. These are not always situations that are laid out in the Staff and Line Organization Chart, but advertising, being what it is, also has to be flexible.

Advertising has to integrate clients' facts with artists' ideas and sensitivities. It has to equate inflexible deadlines with production possibles. It is very reassuring to an advertising manager to know that ALL his staff can make intelligent decisions outside their own department in an emergency. The following is a very loose, brief breakdown of the more common responsibilities in various positions.

Advertising Manager

Carrying out policies set by management
Coordinating departmental activity

The somewhat timeworn phrase of a "good personality" is as applicable here as anywhere. Creative people can be sensitive and humble as well as sensitive and arrogant. It takes a well-rounded, understanding person to run an agency with a fair, firm hand. Allowing individuals to make decisions concerning their art but retaining the reins in managerial areas requires someone with a broad background of knowledge in the humanities and sciences as well as the arts. Today industry is including employees more and more in decision making in all areas. The democratic approach is always ten times more difficult than dictatorial single-man decisions.

Yet eventually a decision must be made and policy set. The manager who can preside and execute with a minimum of discord and a maximum of continuity in production must be a true artist.

Marketing Research

New product development, or testing uses of the product
Who buys ? Who uses ? What publications do they read ?
What programs do they watch or listen to ?
Interviewing population samples
Campaign objectives

Media Man

Link between the various media and agency
Buys space and time
Knows schedules and rates as well as advantages of:
    Newspapers, magazines, radio, outdoor, transit, TV, etc.
Has contact with men in these media

Account Executive

Link between client and agency
Locates new clients
Salesman and troubleshooter
Must know client's business as well as advertising business

Traffic

Follows all incoming jobs
Numbers and plans schedules for all work
Checks on in-plant and outside vendors work
Keeps art director informed of production steps
Keeps records and folder on each job
Knows vendor's capabilities

Art Director

Problem solver. Responsible for art solution
Assigns work, coordinates, and okays total job
Buys outside art
Spends much of his time in conference with copy writers, artists,
    account executives, suppliers, etc.
For good background he must be EXPOSED. That is, he needs
    experience, first hand if possible, in such areas as:
    Economics, printing production, automation, literature, theatre,
    photography, military, metropolitan New York, various religions,
    education, psychology, etc.
He must know people, possibilities, and methods of getting the job
    done right and on time.
Along with the advertising manager he must have some sense of humor
    and personal values that are not based only on business profits.
    Because in the long run he will have to understand his staff under
    constant pressure and balance their well being and capabilities
    against client's profits or even community needs.

Layout

Responsible for layout visuals and comprehensives for flat,
    3-D exhibits, packaging, etc.
Defines photographs, illustrations, and other art work
Specifies type

248

Copywriter

Creates ideas and headings
Knows people and markets
Writes body copy. Proofreads and edits
Often edits company newspaper
Knowledge of psychology, sociology, literature a must

Illustrator

Creative illustrations
Routine art work of diagrams, renderings, etc.
Art history background very important
Often keeps file as research source for agency

Photographer

Creative photography, 3-D photography
TV tape production
Movie or slide productions for proposals or in-plant training
Routine shots of products, models, charts
Publicity or news shots. Often handles prop department

The Bullpen

A group of artists (new and experienced) who produce the pasteups,
    mechanicals, overlays, retouch work and most camera-ready
    art for production
Receives work from A.D. or Layout. Must satisfy Production
Precise craftsmanship a necessity

Production Man

Has understanding of production methods as well as a feel for
    creative activity.
Buys engravings, silk screen, type, etc.
Knows suppliers, their strengths and deadline capabilities
Works with traffic control to keep jobs on schedule
Liaison between agency and printer or other production unit

Special Departments

Fashion, Food, Textiles, Furniture, Cosmetics, etc.

Depending on organization, responsibilities vary from actual research
    and design concepts to illustration, to consultant, model super-
    vision, TV costume control, or prop and set control.

Lettering

Doing creative original lettering for special accounts
Routine assignments such as callouts, charts, maps.
Assisting on type specification coordination with lettering
Special large trade fair posters or billboards

Designer

Industrial design background
Three dimensional displays or models
Trade fair, exposition, educational in-plant visual aids
Sometimes animation or movies in conjunction with photography dept.
Must know materials and construction or design possibilities

Personnel Service

Handles in-plant education
Trains new employees sometimes
Keeps abreast of new personnel procedures
May direct employee recreation club. Manage athletic groups
Provides lecturers or movies on various art forms
In-plant presentation of competitors' campaigns
Art history background or social history major helpful

POLICY

Merchandising in the early 1900's brought in the adage that " The customer is always right." Agencies later reflected this in their efforts to "Give the client what he wants." and pleasing the client became the not-to-be-disputed objective of many advertising men. This policy may have been natural during the early years of growth, but as agencies became larger , they became more self sufficient economically and have recently begun to look upon themselves as professionals in the marketing area. This means in many cases the client is NOT given the choice between alternatives in a campaign or a variety of art work. The agency examines the client's product and facts, does the research and proposes a solution within the budget allowed. The client then accepts this answer (because that is why he hired the agency in the first place) or he takes his account elsewhere.

And gradually the results are getting better. There are fewer ulcers and there is less kowtowing to mediocre taste "just to hang on to the account". Companies are beginning to realize that agency men are competent professionals and that their judgements in MARKETING have much more basis in experience than people who manufacture or those who are concerned with the mechanicals of distributing. Pleasing the client has a different flavor today. He is pleased BEFORE he selects the agency or he wouldn't have come at all.

STATISTICS

According to statistics and estimates prepared by advertising associations:

The 3500 advertising agencies listed in national directories employ about 70,000 people. Many of these agencies handle national or world wide advertising for a variety of clients and are located mainly in New York, Chicago, Los Angeles, Detroit, St Louis, Cleveland, Minneapolis, Pittsburgh, and Philadelphia. There are thousands of other agencies or art departments within firms that handle the smaller state or local accounts.

There are probably about 100,000 artists working as art specialists of one type or another, plus another 100,000 employed in related clerical or backup activities. It is estimated that this group produces about ten billion dollars of advertising yearly, with the possibility of 15 to 20 billion being spent in 1970. The industry can absorb about 15 to 20,000 new artists per year.

As population rises, advertising is being used more and more in social areas to raise money for schools or depressed areas; to justify organizational policy; or explain politics involved in various programs. This alone will probably expand the industry even if technology improvements did not. As the educational media like TV and movies begin to discover the national economic gain that is possible by using advertising methods to help educate people and thus expand their markets, there will be a greater surge than ever. A poverty-stricken sick man, living in a ghetto, cannot buy and certainly cannot produce creatively.

&...

DESIDERATA

GO PLACIDLY AMID THE NOISE & HASTE, & REMEMBER WHAT PEACE THERE MAY BE IN SILENCE. AS FAR AS POSSIBLE WITHOUT surrender be on good terms with all persons. Speak your truth quietly & clearly; and listen to others, even the dull & ignorant; they too have their story. ᔖ Avoid loud & aggressive persons, they are vexations to the spirit. If you compare yourself with others, you may become vain & bitter; for always there will be greater & lesser persons than yourself. Enjoy your achievements as well as your plans. ᔖ Keep interested in your own career, however humble; it is a real possession in the changing fortunes of time. Exercise caution in your business affairs; for the world is full of trickery. But let this not blind you to what virtue there is; many persons strive for high ideals; and everywhere life is full of heroism. ᔖ Be yourself. Especially, do not feign affection.

PHILOSOPHY ᔖ 21

Neither be cynical about love; for in the face of all aridity & disenchantment it is perennial as the grass. ᔖ Take kindly the counsel of the years, gracefully surrendering the things of youth. Nurture strength of spirit to shield you in sudden misfortune. But do not distress yourself with imaginings. Many fears are born of fatigue & loneliness. Beyond a wholesome discipline, be gentle with yourself. ᔖ You are a child of the universe, no less than the trees & the stars; you have a right to be here. And whether or not it is clear to you, no doubt the universe is unfolding as it should. ᔖ Therefore be at peace with God, whatever you conceive Him to be, and whatever your labors & aspirations, in the noisy confusion of life keep peace with your soul. ᔖ With all its sham, drudgery & broken dreams, it is still a beautiful world. Be careful. Strive to be happy. ᔖ ᔖ

FOUND IN OLD SAINT PAUL'S CHURCH, BALTIMORE; DATED 1692

CREATIVE SELECTION

A creative artist is perhaps less a person of habit in his field than the uncreative person. As the creative person deals in visual images, so must he rely upon continuous RECALL of previous perceptions to help form and reform his present concept. As he paints, or draws, or composes, he seeks a rearrangement or uncommon answer from the myriad perceptions and other concepts in his experience. As he sorts through these images he is confronted constantly with the fact that many of them persist in being stereotype or common answers to his problem.

The untalented person will accept the first stereotypes that occur to him and more or less unconsciously proceed to use them without discretion or selection.[1] Thus he ends up with a hackneyed concept typical of the uncreative. There is a certain soporific security in using the first natural stereotype recall as the answer to any design problem. Matters are further complicated for the untalented if his habits of observation have been concerned mainly with things instead of interrelationships, or if his thought processes have been largely the memorization of rote formulas and stack knowledge. There remains very little fertile soil for research in his mind and no nourishment to develop the seeds.

The talented artist has a knack for discarding the obvious form or image that his million year old heritage insists on molding into easily assimilated stereotypes. He constantly searches for hundreds of answers and then selects what to him is the most unique, uncommon, yet good answer. He is like a good chess player, who is successful because of the hundreds of possibilities he can visualize within a short span of time. The chances of selecting a strong answer from a group are much greater than the chances of selecting a strong answer from two possibilities. You hear instructors say again and again, "Show me some more possibilities. You can't always make a selection from the first two sketches!"[1] They are urging the student to see if maybe there is an oblong, faceted, purple apple somewhere among the spherical, smooth, red ones. In fact, it may be a more interesting design concept than the shiny red ball that represents reality to the uncreative mind.

To the young advertising designer: One of the better approaches to design is to encourage yourself always to select from a group of possibilities. If it is interesting color you are seeking, prepare 10 or 15 color combinations and then make a selection. If it is an interesting composition you are seeking, 3 or 4 layouts may be your limit at first, because this tends to be a more complex problem. But the struggle to create a group of possibilities will eventually force your mind to run out of tired cliches. This does not mean that the first design solution you try is poor. Sometimes this remains the best of the group, but without the group to select from, you will never know whether a better answer existed in your mind. An artist is a selector and an arranger as well as a creator. You cannot select from one lone stereotype solution.

1. See Symbology in Section 8. See thumbnails in Section 8

ECONOMICS and ETHICS

Through sheer exposure, commercial art undoubtedly exerts more influence on American culture and esthetic standards than fine art. From an editorial in the "Journal of Commercial Art" (October, 1959) : "One ad placed in "Life" , "Look", "Post", and "Reader's Digest" is seen by more people than visit all the art museums in the United States in 25 years. More people see the art on one billboard in a month than see all the fine art books in a year."

Today artists are used in almost every business. In addition to the obvious areas such as advertising agencies, TV, and movies, manufacturers, retailers, mills, and even banks employ artists as an essential part of their economic development. Commercial art today is universal.

However, being universal does not necessarily mean that all advertising is a benefit. Let us examine the relationship of ethics and economics in the field of advertising and perhaps come to some personal conclusions regarding our own philosophy as artists.

Advertising is a tremendous force in our system of free enterprise. It is a system of communication between seller and buyer which allows selection by the buyer. He has complete freedom to weigh and choose. Under a competitive system then, the seller who can offer the better product and maintain a margin of profit will remain in business. In theory the efficient producer is rewarded by sales to the well informed buyer with resultant profit. He remains as a producer, and the intelligent, well informed buyer has a better and better standard of li ving. However, if the buyer is incorrectly informed and ignorant of the true facts, the entire free enterprise system is weakened, because inefficient producers remain as marginal producers. And when unethical, or more likely, unthinking advertisers begin to increase by such an amount that congressional investigations are necessary to curb practices of "educated" advertisers, the total effect on consumer judgement in our nation could be disastrous. During the late 1950's, Congress was investigating such areas as TV quiz shows and radio and record programs. One of the disconcerting aspects of these investigations was the defendants' attitudes that deviation from ethical practice is a game everybody plays. Therefore we aren't any worse than any other business. Therefore we've done no wrong. We are the product of our culture, so we can't help ourselves.... These are weak answers from weak citizens. Some of the reassuring aspects of those investigations have been editorials in advertising trade magazines: "Let us stand for truth." "Why didn't we have the foresight to handle poor advertising like this ourselves ?", etc. Agencies started to take a second look at their campaigns. It is becoming important in advertising campaigns to discuss democratic principles, the real values in free enterprise, and ethics. Accounts that do not subscribe to such principles have been rejected by the better agencies. There is hope that action from responsible advertising managers and networks will cut off sloppy thinking and start the pendulum toward a straightforward honest atmosphere. After all, the air waves and channels belong to the whole nation, not just to the advertisers. Responsibility for truth is a must, not an option.

There are some new concepts filtering into the free enterprise system which may help the entire nation educationally and economically.

One is that the TV and radio channels belong essentially to the public, not to the networks. Thus the networks should be responsible to see that there are public service programs to suit the nation's need, as well as the paid commercial programs which supply the enormous budget necessary to run the network. The argument in the past has been that the network must take care of its paying customers first, because, after all, its stockholders demands must be heeded. That may well be until it approaches the ridiculous situation of a large company hiring a network for an entire month and advertising nothing but hairoil 24 hours a day, 5 days a week. The business man who argues that this is free enterprise does not understand that with freedom comes something called responsibility. The people of the nation, who in fact own the airways and have allowed the networks to use them by franchise, must also be served. The best interest of the nation is not being taken into consideration by such a network or company. As interest groups and companies become larger, their horizons of activity become larger also, until they begin to affect the welfare of the entire nation.

Another development is the growing insistence of many people that advertisers tell the whole truth about their product. The government has waged a long battle with manufacturers regarding correct labeling of processed foods and drugs particularly. Yet they have been fought at every step with the idea that the seller has the right to tell the consumer only the best. Caveat Emptor , "Let the buyer beware.", may have been a fine philosophy when one could rely upon his nose and his sight for testing a product, but today's chemical compounds and molecular chains do not lend themselves to everyman's inspection. The philosophy beginning to pervade our production is that the objective truth should be printed or told about the product for the sake of the consumer. Possible side effects of drugs, unusual chemicals in processed foods, as examples, should certainly warrant a notice on a package in larger than 8 point lower case. When the management of a company truly feels empathy with the individual buyer of his product, we will have a true free enterprise system. As long as management continues advertising half truths by hiding the possible "hurt" to that unique individual who might be affected, then advertising will be mere propaganda that spawns ignorance and possible harm instead of producing well informed , intelligent, satisfied customers.

A third awareness in advertising is the dawning realization in model agencies and ad agencies that there are people in the market area besides Caucasians. Faces of other races are beginning to appear on billboards and, although light-skinned and usually timidly hidden in the background, Negro models are finally being used in catalogs, national magazines and an occasional TV promotion. This will grow faster as minority groups gain job opportunities, create greater economic markets, and eventually gain greater acceptance within communities.

A fourth trend which is not new, but is now gaining ground, is the educational approach to a market through a related area of public service. Gasoline companies produce ads stressing highway safety and driving hints for teenagers. Other companies promote cultural programs, with restricted commercials, partly because it creates a good image for the company, but also because the management believes it is good for America. Network executives fight hard to get current news stories or important national events televised in place of the regular soap opera scheduled for that particular hour. They don't win very often yet. But the battle is joined.

A problem faced is a problem half solved. But too many companies, writers, artists, managers, and executives still need to be convinced that culture and children's thought habits are more important to a nation than its bad breath , rough skin, uplift bras, acid stomach, and cigarettes. What do you think ?

Those companies or organizations that do allow unethical or poor taste advertising to continue are contributing directly to the downgrading of the nation's judgement and taste. Too often the unethical or unthinking advertisers forget that their programs are part of a billion dollar program of national education. A program that touches in some way almost every adult and every child, every day, in almost every phase of their lives. For example, there are very obvious problems the beginning artist should be aware of. In the past years, unthinking and uncaring advertisers have implied by one means or another that:

- 'Smoking makes you a good athlete' Professional athletes of all types have been paid to endorse various brands of cigarettes.

- 'The best stories are about sex or violence' Mass-market publishers realize the pocketbook will sell better if the cover has a semi-nude girl on it. This is often done even if the cover illustration has very little to do with the story. Again, this is not to preach that prostitution, sex, and crime should not be shown on the covers of books. This is to say that it is dishonest to have the cover imply that the book is something other than it really is.... just to make a sale.

- 'You can get almost anything by doing almost nothing.' The pitch goes something like this. "Do you want happiness ? It's easy. All you need to do is line up the three dots and the pony is yours ! What you really need though is a mink stole, a trip to Hawaii, and $100 a day for life. Send in this coupon."

  Amusing perhaps now. But multiply this philosophy by 30 million children reading cereal box sides every morning during the most formative years of their life. Thirty million children given a ten minute "educational" program on drivel every day. A cultural philosophy is being developed and driven home with the impact of a battering ram; a cultural philosophy that is in contradiction with every principle a mature American holds.

- 'You can enjoy murder and violence.' Take your pick of books, comic magazines, or TV shows. Murder, torture, beatings become the reason for the play or story. This is not to say that adventure, mystery, and killing are unsuitable subjects for authors. This is to say that when insensitive, unselective executives allow murder and violence to become the dominant theme in plays, movies, and literature, it offers to young people a sop as nauseating as any Roman arena.

A democracy depends on the action of each citizen. Not only upon his awareness of a problem but also action based on firm principle. You happen to be a
responsible citizen particularly sensitive in the visual arts. Do you have the
strength to write a letter of complaint to a company that oversteps truth in an ad ?

Do you, or will you have, the integrity to refuse to work on an advertising program that is unethical, vulgar, or not in the best interests of the people ? You
may not have to make a decision of this nature, but if you do, let us hope it will
be only after you have the strength of character and maturity to help you through.
If, however, you see the educational needs of a nation that bases its existence
on the enlightenment of the individual and the exercise of his free will, you will
be better able to understand your own position better.

What would your answer be to the following ?

1. If you believe there is sufficient evidence that cigarette smoking can cause
cancer, would you work on a cigarette campaign for a tobacco company ?

2. If you had heard that racketeers operated or backed a certain night club or
casino, would you do their advertising brochures and programs or menus ?

3. Will you continue to produce advertising for a pharmaceutical company
that presents only the good effect of its drugs with never a mention of possible
side effects ?

4. Would you work on a radio program that urges students studying for exams
to use tranquilizing pills ?

5. If you feel billboards are a blight on the landscape, will you do the design
for a 24 sheet poster to be erected near a highway that approaches your city
through tree covered hills ?

In other words, do you have the nerve to think beyond the 6 x 9 layout and
your paycheck ?

?

EDUCATION

An Advertising Design Major just finishing high school often discovers, to his surprise, that he may not use the high marks he received in his art courses to offset or balance the marks received in his other subjects for his college entrance "average". Almost all other majors, such as mathematics, history, english , language, and science may use their major subject marks in their average.

The art major is thus often denied entrance to the public universities, because he must make up his 'B' average in subjects outside his major. This illogical curriculum imbalance is being worked on by both state and national art education organizations. In the meantime, private art schools and industry-subsidized art schools have filled this educational vacuum.

Many of these private art schools have seen the need for broadly educated artists and have added academic subjects such as philosophy, economics, psychology , and mathematics to their own curriculum, until they have become colleges , in fact, issuing degrees with state accreditation. They may eventually be supported by public tax money to supplement the already crowded universities.

But at present there is no public parallel in opportunity for the artist unless he happens to have a 'B' average in subjects outside his major, or unless he has the tuition required by the private art schools.

Art talent and creativity are not easily measured on entrance exams. But they should not be ignored or penalized. Educated artists can contribute much to minimizing squalor, smog, ticky-tacky suburbs, and the outrage of waste and pollution in our cities. But we shall have these artists only when public higher education provides the opportunity for their admission and academic survival.

We need to educate for sensitivity to others, sensitivity to environment, and a philosophy of living, just as surely as we educate our scientists to understand matter and space. You can help close this century-old gap if you have faith in your ideas as an artist and realize that you and your type of intelligence, at this moment, are much more important to the world than those who have dealt only with things .

References for Classroom Library

Title	Date	Author & LC No.	New York Publisher
"Advertising Photography" How to Make Money in.	1976	Bill Hammond 74-79950	American Photographic Book Pub., Inc. Garden City, NY
"The Art of Advertising"	1977	George Lois 76-46155	Harry N. Abrams, Inc.
"The Art of Written Forms"	1969	Don Anderson 68-21782	Holt, Rinehart, & Winston
"Drawing"	1967	Mendelowitz 66-13297	Holt, Rinehart, & Winston
"Drawing with Markers"	1974	R. Welling 73-20202	Watson-Guptil, NY Pitman Pub., London
"Early Advertising Art" Pictorial Volume	1956	Hornung 54-9264	Dover Publications 180 Varick St.
"Illustrating Fashion"	1977	E. Sloane 76-26254	Harper & Row 10 E. 53d St.
"Illustrator in America" 1900 to 1960's		Walt Reed 66-24545	Reinhold 450 W. 33d St.
"Illustrators 17"	1976	59-10849	Hastings House, Inc. 10 E. 40th St.
"Ink on Paper 2"	1972	Edmund Arnold 70-156503	Harper & Row
"Lettering for Advertising"		Mortimer Leach 56-10596	Reinhold
"Packaging" An International Survey	1968	Crouwell & Weidemann	Frederick A. Praeger 111 4th Ave.
"Trade Marks & Symbols" Volume 2	1970	Kuwayama	Reinhold
"Trade Marks & Symbols of the World"	1965	Kamekura 62-24055	Reinhold

Magazines

"Art Direction" Advertising Trade Pub., 19 W. 44th St., NY 10036

"Communications Arts" Coyne & Blanchard, Inc., 410 Sherman Ave., Palo Alto, CA

Films

"Partners in Design"	Graphic techniques.	Letraset USA,Inc.
"Adventure in Color"	Color-match systems.	40 Eisenhower Drive
"Type in Society"	Type development.	Paramus, NJ 07654
"The Case for High-Finish Visuals"	Preparation of art using color acetate.	(Free loan for review; $30 rental fee; $160 approx. cost)

Slide Sets

"Half Tones & Other Tones" (Other sets available also) Scholarly Audio-Visuals, Inc. 5 Beekman St., NY 10038

INDEX

GLOSSARY

Album	Binding on narrow edge of book or pamphlet.
Backlighting	Light is transmitted THROUGH the copy on the copyboard. Used to copy or make color separations of color transparencies.
Ben Day	A word which means a screen tint. Use it to avoid confusion with halftone screens.
Blind Emboss	Relief image pressed into paper without ink.
Correction Masks	In color separations a film neg is placed over another film neg to mask out certain areas.
Direct System	Shoot color separations through 3 filters and a split directly through halftone contact screen to litho film for four negs.
Estimate	A bid on a job that may vary plus or minus 10%.
Folio	Page number or a sheet that has been folded once.
Flexographic	A form of letterpress printing that uses rubber plates. Good for printing on plastic film, foil, etc.
Franklin Catalog	Breaks down and standardizes printing costs. Used by professionals for quick estimating.
Ghosting	Putting a sheet of frosted acetate over a halftone to prevent it from copying too contrasty.
Greeking it	Chopping up type so it is recognizable as a block of copy but not readable. Used for comp presentations.
Gutenberg	Invented movable type, 1456.
Indirect System	Method of making color separations and correction masks by using continuous tone film with filters rather than screening on litho film directly through filters.
iph	Impressions per hour. Rate of a printing press. 100 per minute, 6000 per hour is not unusual.
Latent Image	The image in the emulsion on the photographic paper. Cannot be seen by eye.
Orthochromatic	Film insensitive to red end of spectrum. Can be used with red or orange safe lights.
Panchromatic	Film sensitive to entire spectrum. Must be used in total darkness.
Posterization	Separating continuous tone copy into several tones by shooting it at different exposures and using the different density negs to make 3 or more color printing plates. Result looks somewhat like a silkscreened poster.
Quotation	Firm bid on a job. (Unlike estimate.)
Senefelder	Discovered Lithography process, 1796.
Stat	Inexpensive paper proof of art or what have you.
Standard Rate & Data	A set of books with production information and prices of all media.
Type C Print	Typical color print. Not a transparency or dye transfer.
UCR	Under color removal. In high speed 4 color process the ink prints wet on wet and builds up too high without limiting ink deposit on especially the dark areas.
Vignette	Pronounced 'Vin yet'. Edges of halftone are softened until edges fade into background. Similar to old fashioned tintypes.

REPROS

THERE ARE HUNDREDS OF BUCKET-SEAT CHAIRS ON THE MARKET. PERSONALLY I PREFER THE NONBUCKET STYLE. I LIKE TO MOVE ABOUT A BIT WHEN I CARRY ON CONVERSATIONS OR READ, BUT THE BUCKET KEEPS ME OFF THE "EDGE OF MY SEAT". IT ALSO PREVENTS MY COMFORTABLE AFTER-DINNER SLOUCH. A BUCKET SEAT MAY BE GREAT IN A RACING CAR TO HOLD THE DRIVER IN A VISE-LIKE GRIP WHILE HE CAROMS AROUND THE GRAND PRIX. BUT FOR HOME — JUST AN ORDINARY CHAIR, PLEASE. COLORS: WHITE, OLIVE, TOMATO AND SAND. CAN BE NESTED.

THERE ARE HUNDREDS OF BUCKET-SEAT CHAIRS ON THE MARKET. PERSONALLY I PREFER THE NONBUCKET STYLE. I LIKE TO MOVE ABOUT A BIT WHEN I CARRY ON CONVERSATIONS OR READ, BUT THE BUCKET KEEPS ME OFF THE "EDGE OF MY SEAT". IT ALSO PREVENTS MY COMFORTABLE AFTER-DINNER SLOUCH. A BUCKET SEAT MAY BE GREAT IN A RACING CAR TO HOLD THE DRIVER IN A VISE-LIKE GRIP WHILE HE CAROMS AROUND THE GRAND PRIX. BUT FOR HOME — JUST AN ORDINARY CHAIR, PLEASE. COLORS: WHITE, OLIVE, TOMATO AND SAND. CAN BE NESTED.

THERE ARE HUNDREDS OF BUCKET-SEAT CHAIRS ON THE MARKET. PERSONALLY I PREFER THE NONBUCKET STYLE. I LIKE TO MOVE ABOUT A BIT WHEN I CARRY ON CONVERSATIONS OR READ, BUT THE BUCKET KEEPS ME OFF THE "EDGE OF MY SEAT". IT ALSO PREVENTS MY COMFORTABLE AFTER-DINNER SLOUCH. A

BUCKET SEAT MAY BE GREAT IN A RACING CAR TO HOLD THE DRIVER IN A VISE-LIKE GRIP WHILE HE CAROMS AROUND THE GRAND PRIX. BUT FOR THE HOME — JUST AN ORDINARY CHAIR, PLEASE. COLORS: WHITE, OLIVE, TOMATO AND SAND. CAN BE NESTED.

THERE ARE HUNDREDS OF BUCKET-SEAT CHAIRS ON THE MARKET. PERSONALLY I PREFER THE NONBUCKET STYLE. I LIKE TO MOVE ABOUT A BIT WHEN I CARRY ON CONVERSATIONS OR READ, BUT THE BUCKET KEEPS ME OFF THE "EDGE OF MY SEAT". IT ALSO PREVENTS MY COMFORTABLE AFTER-DINNER SLOUCH. A BUCKET SEAT MAY BE GREAT IN A RACING CAR TO HOLD THE DRIVER IN A VISE-LIKE GRIP WHILE HE CAROMS AROUND THE GRAND PRIX. BUT FOR HOME — JUST AN ORDINARY CHAIR, PLEASE. COLORS: WHITE, OLIVE, TOMATO AND SAND. CAN BE NESTED.

THERE ARE HUNDREDS OF BUCKET-SEAT CHAIRS ON THE MARKET. PERSONALLY I PREFER THE NONBUCKET STYLE. I LIKE TO MOVE ABOUT A BIT WHEN I CARRY ON CONVERSATIONS OR READ, BUT THE BUCKET KEEPS ME OFF THE "EDGE OF MY SEAT". IT ALSO PREVENTS MY COMFORTABLE AFTER-DINNER SLOUCH. A BUCKET SEAT MAY BE GREAT IN A RACING CAR TO HOLD THE DRIVER IN A VISE-LIKE GRIP WHILE HE CAROMS AROUND THE GRAND PRIX. BUT FOR HOME — JUST AN ORDINARY CHAIR, PLEASE. COLORS: WHITE, OLIVE, TOMATO AND SAND. CAN BE NESTED.

Distributed by Brian Archer, Incorporated

Distributed by Brian Archer, Incorporated

DISTRIBUTED BY BRIAN ARCHER, INCORPORATED

DISTRIBUTED BY BRIAN ARCHER, INCORPORATED

DISTRIBUTED BY BRIAN ARCHER, INCORPORATED

DISTRIBUTED BY BRIAN ARCHER, INCORPORATED

Distributed by Brian Archer, Incorporated

Distributed by Brian Archer, Incorporated

RIVIERA

CAMEO

STEELSTRUT

EVANS

EVANS

EVANS

EVANS

271

E E E E E EVANS

Є G e e E EVANS

EVANS
E evans

E evans

evans